THE
GARTH
FACTOR

THE GARTH FACTOR

THE CAREER BEHIND COUNTRY'S BIG BOOM

PATSI BALE COX

CENTER
STREET®

New York Boston Nashville

Center Street
Hachette Book Group
237 Park Avenue
New York, NY 10017

Visit our Web site at www.centerstreet.com.

Center Street is a division of Hachette Book Group, Inc.
The Center Street name and logo are trademarks of Hachette Book Group, Inc.

Printed in the United States of America

First Edition: May 2009
10 9 8 7 6 5 4 3 2 1

Library of Congress Cataloging-in-Publication Data
Cox, Patsi Bale.
    The Garth factor : the career behind country's big boom / Patsi Bale Cox.—
1st ed.
       p. cm.
    ISBN 978-1-59995-099-0
    1. Brooks, Garth.   2. Country musicians—United States—Biography.   I. Title.
ML420.B7796C68 2009
782.421642092—dc22
    [B]   2008038469

Contents

Dedication and Acknowledgments ix

CHAPTER ONE
"It's a tough town, son" 1

CHAPTER TWO
Shitkickers & cowboys 16

CHAPTER THREE
"Uncle Joe, you know we owe it to you" 25

CHAPTER FOUR
"I'd have titled it *Randy Travis* if I could have
gotten away with it" 44

CHAPTER FIVE
"Watch your back, pal" 65

CHAPTER SIX
Only in America 79

CHAPTER SEVEN
Good times roll just ahead of the thunder 92

CHAPTER EIGHT
Bustin' in like old John Wayne 99

CHAPTER NINE

"Who in the hell is Garth Brooks?" 116

CHAPTER TEN

Why should rock 'n' roll get all the glory? 124

CHAPTER ELEVEN

Country's Big Boom 132

CHAPTER TWELVE

Damn this rain and damn this wasted day 144

CHAPTER THIRTEEN

"It's a once-in-a-lifetime thing" 156

CHAPTER FOURTEEN

"A white tuxedo and a lot of red paint" 173

CHAPTER FIFTEEN

"I looked like hell and smelled worse, but the
song was finished" 189

CHAPTER SIXTEEN

"I guess we can work with it" 196

CHAPTER SEVENTEEN

"Who the shit is paying for all this?" 205

CHAPTER EIGHTEEN

New York shows up to kick some ass 217

CHAPTER NINETEEN

"Hopefully, we're starting to build a family" 229

CHAPTER TWENTY

"Has Garth lost his freakin' mind?" 248

CHAPTER TWENTY-ONE

"Say it ain't so, Garth" 267

CHAPTER TWENTY-TWO

If you ever wonder what happened to me 283

EPILOGUE

Time is not your enemy 296

Garth Brooks Discography 317

Sources 319

Dedication and Acknowledgments

This book is dedicated to my friend, the great singer/ songwriter Floyd Tillman, who encouraged me to see country music as a big, inclusive family, one that welcomed a myriad of personalities, influences, and styles. Inducted into the Country Music Hall of Fame in 1984, when Floyd died in 2003 country music lost a giant.

Therefore, the first of many hat tips here should go to another industry friend, Kathleen Hayslip, who introduced me to Floyd and his wife, Frances, over three decades ago. Particular thanks go to two of Nashville's finest journalist/historians, John Lomax III and Robert K. Oermann. They took me under their creative wings in 1983, opened Nashville doors, and offered many professional opportunities. I could not have had two better champions. I am indebted to Jim Carlson, who first hired me to write for CBS artists, and Nancy Nicholas, who taught me much about writing.

Many in the press were crucial to the book, including *Billboard* editors and writers then and now, Edward Morris, Ken Tucker, Wade Jesson, Ray Waddell, and Melinda Newman; *LA Times,* Chuck Philips, Richard Cromelin, and Robert Hilburn; AP, Jim Patterson and Joe Edwards; *Chicago Sun Times,* Dave Hoekstra; *Chicago Tribune,* Jack Hurst; *Tennessean,* Robert K. Oermann,

Debbie Holley, Tom Roland, Jay Orr, and Peter Cooper; *The Believer,* Tami Rose; *USA Today,* David Zimmerman.

Garth Brooks, Bob Doyle, and Allen Reynolds gave open access to archives. This book would not have been possible without that availability. The Country Music Foundation has long been the finest resource around. Kudos to Ronnie Pugh and John Rumble. Joel Whitburn's *Billboard* singles and albums series is essential to any music study.

Special thanks go to my Center Street editor, Christina Boys, and to my William Morris agent Mel Berger. And to my family's continuing support: My son, Adam Cox, daughter, Tracy Nath, and son-in-law, Jake Nath, parents of the inimitable Maria Irina. My sister, and sometimes writing partner, Gladys Bale Wellbrock.

THE
GARTH
FACTOR

CHAPTER ONE

"It's a tough town, son"

Nashville was nothing like what Garth Brooks expected on his 1985 trip. Nobody seemed very interested in his music. Well-known songwriters appeared to be unable to earn a living. Men in suits conducted business in office buildings. Where were the guitar pickers? It all seemed out of kilter.

He sat in his truck thinking about what he'd done in making this trip. With little preparation or planning he had come to a major music center and tried to randomly set up appointments with important people. He had no job, no backing, and no connections. He'd left his family behind in Oklahoma, the family he had always depended on for emotional support. And more important, he'd left his girlfriend, Sandy Mahl, with no explanation. But what would people think if he didn't stick it out?

The more he thought, the more he got clear. His family wasn't going to be disappointed that he realized he wasn't yet prepared to make this move. And if his friends found it amusing, well, he'd just have to live with it. And so that night Garth turned around and started back to Oklahoma to rethink and regroup. Driving through Arkansas he remembered that he'd promised to call his mother the minute he checked into a motel. Knowing Colleen Brooks would be beside herself at hearing nothing, he stopped and phoned her.

"It's three in the morning!" She said. "I was about to call the Nashville police!"

"Hold on, Mom," Garth answered. "I'm in Fort Smith. I'm coming home."

There is in Garth Brooks both a great fear of losing and a great confidence that he can ultimately win. Fear is a powerful motivator. Over the years since he became a superstar, Garth heard several other public figures admit that fear was an incentive. "I once asked Magic Johnson what separated the guys who made it to the NBA and the guys who might have the same talent, but didn't make it," Garth said. "He told me that he thought it was fear. He said it drove him to do his best every day."

With Garth, as with Magic Johnson, that fear was coupled with a deep-down belief that he could beat the odds. He just had to never let up, to play the game at 100 percent or better every single time.

That combination of personality traits was nowhere more evident than in 1985, when he left his family and his girlfriend behind to make that first trip. The story has been told many times over. Garth came to Nashville believing getting a recording contract would be relatively easy. He met with ASCAP's Merlin Littlefield, was given little encouragement, then learned that a well-known songwriter was in the lobby needing a five-hundred-dollar loan. Garth was horrified because he made more than that in a week playing clubs in Stillwater, Oklahoma. Dejected, he fled back to Oklahoma.

This scenario is fine as far as it goes, but there's an element missing. Garth may have been somewhat naïve about all things Nashville, but kid that he was, he had sharp antennae. Many Nashville insiders have a set of talking points they pull out for newcomers who come in with no manager or financial backing. It goes something like this:

"It's a tough town, son. There's guys pumping gas that can

sing as good as most of the people on the charts and they can't get arrested. You're gonna need contacts, help, and a lotta luck to get your foot in Music Row. What you got? Are you tough enough to stick it out four or five years, maybe even more? If you don't have a big money backer, pack it up and go back home, kid."

In fairness, these insiders don't want all these young artists to give up. Most of them have seen plenty of hearts broken and dreams crushed and they don't want to suggest that there's a special angel hovering over Sixteenth Avenue waiting to sprinkle magic stardust on every hopeful. But the speeches are canned and Garth Brooks was no dummy. Something else about that encounter bothered him.

He had gotten industry insights from a professional before he ever crossed the city limits. His mother, Colleen Brooks, had been a Capitol recording artist, a professional singer who performed on Arthur Godfrey's show during the 1950s. Colleen's career has sometimes been overlooked, mentioned as a mere footnote to that of her son. But at one time she was traveling throughout the United States, building a following and a professional name. Given the right set of circumstances, there is a very real chance that Colleen Carroll could have been a national star. She had a manager, had recorded in Los Angeles, and was relatively well known from her Arthur Godfrey appearances. In fact, when she first met Raymond Brooks, he confessed that he'd been smitten with her from the first time he saw her on television. The problem was that her career took off after she was divorced with three children, and the constant traveling became impossible.

Colleen was an optimist about everything but the music business, having seen what she called *the ditches* of the industry. Out on the road she'd dealt with dishonest promoters, club owners, and bookers. She'd had to fend off stray musicians and camp followers. Times when she most needed the money owed her, she'd seen it slip through her hands into someone else's. When Garth made his first trip to Nashville she warned him that there were people in town who would beat him up, then pick his pockets. So while he has said that he initially thought there was a recording contract waiting just for him, there was also his mother's cautionary message. *Don't listen to everything people tell you.*

The other element of the legend that has not been factored into Garth's first Nashville experience is his sense of right and wrong. Underlying Garth's shock at learning a famous songwriter needed a measly five hundred dollars was his innate understanding that something was askew. *Why* couldn't successful creative people make a decent living in the business? Maybe it was as simple as a songwriter squandering royalties. But maybe it was something deeper, something in the system.

Garth decided he needed to prepare better the next time he approached this town, and so he headed home.

Home was Yukon, Oklahoma, where Garth had grown up in a split-level house at 408 Yukon Avenue. When they met, Colleen Carroll had three children—Jim, Jerry, and Betsy—and Troyal Raymond Brooks had a son, Michael. Once married, they had one immediate mission, to gain permanent custody of Raymond's son Michael. When Michael's mother finally agreed, Colleen said, "I had him with us and enrolled in school within the hour!" When sons Kelly and Garth were born the family was complete.

"You know, my mother didn't want me to marry Raymond," Colleen once confided to a friend. "She wanted me to marry someone with a lot of money. I guess she thought that with me having three small children I needed extra stability, but she didn't take into consideration that I really loved Raymond. I knew that he loved me and that he was my rock. I've never looked back. In a way, that's how Garth is. When he knows he's doing the right thing, he'll throw caution to the wind and not give up. And it has usually worked out for him."

Except for scattered performances, Colleen gave up her music career to raise the family. Raymond Brooks was a tough ex-marine who worked as an engineer and draftsman for Union 86 oil, and raised his children with a strict code of ethics, fair play, and integrity. Garth once reflected, "Dad's always been one of those *your-word-is-your-bond* men. I took that to heart."

It is to Colleen and Raymond's credit that there was never a division among the children, just one big happy family. "There was never any type of jealousy in this family. You couldn't really tell who belonged to who bloodwise as the years went by," Colleen told *In Country*'s David Huff. "Everyone thought Betsy looked like Raymond. For a long time people thought Michael was my son and Jerry was Raymond's. When you're trying to raise a family like ours that's the kind of thing you want to hear."

In fact, after Garth's career took off Colleen was always quick to point out that all of their children had had their glory days in school and after. Jim was the great athlete, the family hero, especially to his youngest brother, Garth. Kelly, too, was a star athlete. Michael, who was chosen as Most Likely to Succeed, went on to become an educator. Jerry fulfilled his lifelong dream of becoming a law officer. Betsy, voted friendliest at school, became a musician both on her own and as a member of Garth's band, Stillwater. The mother–daughter relation was strong in this house full of males. Colleen called Betsy her best friend. "She's such a free spirit. I worship the ground she walks on," Colleen said.

Like many youngest children of large families, Garth grew up with both adoration and a healthy sense of competition. Colleen often said that Garth shared many of her personality traits. She liked to have fun, enjoyed being the center of attention. "I was only three when I started singing, trying to entertain the family," she reflected. "I loved making people happy. And Garth has always been the same way. As a child he was always making us laugh and clap for some little skit he put together."

Christmas and Halloween were the family's favorite holidays. Colleen, especially, loved Halloween, and she usually dressed as a witch to hand out treats to the neighborhood kids, gathering the children around for ghost stories, including "Galloping

' a takeoff on "The Legend of Sleepy Hollow." The
ιas tree went up right after Thanksgiving, and Colleen
admιϲed it was usually dead by the time they took it down. She
hated to let go of the holiday season, loved sitting in the evening
looking at those twinkling tree lights.

Garth remembers Colleen being the biggest kid in the
family when it came to Christmas, and that tendency escalated
as the years went by. Sometimes when Garth and Sandy drove
home for Christmas, arriving by 7:00 A.M. wasn't early enough.
They'd get to the Brooks home only to find that Colleen had
been up for two hours, and had already started opening some of
her presents.

It wasn't always easy to buy gifts for everyone; the Brooks
family was not well off by any stretch of the imagination. They
ate a lot of macaroni and cheese and hamburger gravy on toast.
Christmas presents were something that Colleen and Raymond
had to think about, plan for, and work into the budget. Garth's
best Christmas memory was of the year he was eight, and he and
his brother Kelly got matching bikes. The fact that Kelly was
eighteen months older and received the same gift impressed the
youngest child.

One member of the family was initially unimpressed with
Garth—big sister Betsy. When Colleen was pregnant with
Garth, Betsy longed for a little sister. When the call came that
the new baby had arrived, one of the brothers played a trick on
Betsy and told her she had that sister she'd wanted. Then, when
Raymond Brooks arrived, Betsy started asking rapid-fire ques-
tions: Did the baby girl look like her? What color were her eyes?
How soon could she hold her?

Raymond Brooks was puzzled. "The baby's a boy," he said.

"Then don't bring him home!" Betsy roared, taking out after
her brothers, who now outnumbered her five to one. She came
around the minute her parents brought the littlest Brooks boy
home, becoming his greatest champion.

Colleen's youngest son says he was an unapologetic mama's

boy. "My mother is the best female singer I ever heard, and the most professional in her attitude about the business, too," Garth says. "I love her love of life and her spirit. I've always been one of those guys who liked women and I don't mean just as someone to date. I've always had a lot of female friends and often they became among the most trusted. I think that tendency comes from having such a good relationship with my mother."

Raymond and Colleen were a classic case of opposites attracting. Raymond could be a tough taskmaster. He believed in discipline and in encouraging his children to strive for perfection. Colleen allowed room for mistakes. Garth picked up both those personality traits. He also learned some lessons from the interaction between his father and older brothers. Years later he would write a song titled "The Night I Called The Old Man Out," about a son wanting independence and willing to fight his father for it. "It's a song I lived indirectly," he said. "Kelly and I were the youngest and we never 'called out' our dad, but we sure saw some of the older boys do it. I got to see two sides of my dad during those times. He could be very strict about things he considered important, but he had an incredible softness, too. I sometimes saw him rush upstairs to hide the tears in his eyes after someone confronted him.

"I think I learned several lessons from having that front-row seat. First, I could understand both sides of the thing. The older boys thought they were right. Dad thought he was. And they were both willing to back up their beliefs with action. I could see that being a father was an awfully big responsibility, and you couldn't ignore moves that you really believe were bad for your kids to make. But most of all, I think I understood that it was somehow good for a child to know that a man can cry and be no less a man. Think how much better off people would be if they knew that."

Colleen said that Garth always had an empathic nature, that from the time he was a child he could always put himself in someone else's shoes. "After school he'd bring special children home with him," she reflected. "These were kids who no one would ever talk to or anything. He would be their friend and they adored him. He would bend over backwards to help anybody because of one thing—he couldn't stand to see anybody mistreated."

Music played a big part in the household. In addition to Colleen's singing and love of everything from the Opry to pop, Raymond played guitar and admired country singers like Haggard and Jones. Again, Garth's status as youngest in the throng played a role in his musical evolution. The older kids all had their favorites and specialties. His big brothers played the guitar, though never as seriously as his sister, Betsy. Brother Jim loved to play the harmonica. Kelly, just a year and a half older than Garth, tended toward kazoos.

The family scheduled weekly talent nights featuring music, skits—anything to amuse the group. Garth especially thrived on not just singing for the family, but putting together shows that included dialogue, jokes, and even plot to an extent. He was starting to understand the basics of entertaining and storytelling.

"Being the youngest of six kids, my influences come from all over the board," he explained. "I particularly liked James Taylor, Dan Fogelberg, Elton John, Journey, Boston, Kansas. But I also loved Townes Van Zandt, George Jones, Janis Joplin, and Rita Coolidge. The '70s rock shows probably influenced my live show the most. My older brothers and sister listened to Styx and Queen, so I did, too."

Perhaps the biggest influence of all was country star George Strait, who Garth first heard in 1981, while he and his father listened to country music on the car radio. The single, "Unwound," was George's first, and it changed Garth's life. Until then, he'd paid more attention to his siblings' favorite rock acts. George Strait changed all that. "I knew in that moment that this was the kind of music I wanted to sing and perform," he later said.

Strait, too, had been an early lover of rock, but it was his time in the military and exposure to Merle Haggard singing Bob

Wills's music that changed his direction. A native of Pearsall, Texas, Strait was also a cowboy, expert in riding and roping. After serving his time in the army, George enrolled at Southwest Texas State in San Marcos, and formed the Ace in the Hole Band. In 1979, his traditional country sound interested MCA Records enough to agree to release one single, "Unwound."

Out of this musical melting pot came Garth's love for arena rock and singer/songwriters. By his teens, he had picked up the guitar and banjo, which led to a love for bluegrass music. In fact, his first "professional" gig was playing banjo at a McDonald's with friends Mark Tate, Roy Farrow, and Steve Clark.

Garth was a quick student who got good grades despite being more drawn to sports than schoolwork. He was well liked, a popular jock who loved to clown around. Just as his love of music came naturally, so did his interest in sports. Raymond coached Little League and encouraged his boys to participate in football, baseball, and track. Garth played for Yukon's football team, the Millers, and threw javelin for the track team.

Garth never got over this early love of sports. In 1992, after he was a star, KNIX in Phoenix held an on-air contest asking the question, "Is there one thing that Garth Brooks would like to do just to be able to say it?" Fans called in with every answer from being president of the United States to being a professional athlete. The winner was a guy named Leroy Kloos, from Casa Grande, who correctly answered "play professional baseball."

Garth's answer: "If I could do one thing just to say I'd done it, that thing would be to play an inning of professional baseball. The only thing that stopped me from being a professional baseball player was that I sucked."

Raymond Brooks's participation in his sons' sports was vital to Garth in immediate and long-term ways.

"One of the greatest things I got from my dad was an appreciation of the importance of teamwork," Garth explained. "And as I started out on my career, I really saw how vital it was to everything in life. Artists have to see themselves as part of the group. I don't mean all decisions need to be made by a committee, but nothing—and I mean *nothing*—is gonna happen without a team."

By the time he followed his brother Kelly to Oklahoma State University in Stillwater, Garth was splitting his extracurricular time between sports and music. In fact, his love of music influenced his choice of majors. It was with the hope of breaking into jingle writing that he chose advertising, a decision that would later be misrepresented in the press as "marketing" and result in the first of many untrue myths regarding his success.

Raymond Brooks once told a story about Kelly and Garth: "Kelly went to Oklahoma State University and two years later Garth followed. Their track coach called us and said, 'Mr. Brooks, there is something I just have to say. Kelly came here and he didn't smoke or drink or party. He wasn't a Goody Two-shoes or anything. He didn't condemn people or judge them and I'm going to admit that some of the track coaches thought he was putting on a front. Then Garth came here and they roomed together, which is unheard of for brothers in college. Garth didn't smoke and he didn't drink and by gosh we realized that these two guys are for real!' "

Sports initially helped pay Garth's room and board at Iba Hall, the campus athletic dorm. He not only had been awarded a track and field scholarship, but also found a part-time job at a sports equipment store, DuPree's. Garth's track future was sidelined when he failed to make the Big Eight Conference finals during his senior year. When a coach told him that he should see it as an opportunity to get on with what was important in his life, Garth wondered just what that might be.

What it was, of course, was his music. Between track and his off-campus job, he participated in college music jams like the "Aunt Molly's Rent-Free Music Emporium" at the OSU student union. He played at any campus party he could find and volunteered time at a local medical center to play music for children.

Garth started several bands, playing in clubs like Shotgun Sam's Pizza in Oklahoma City and Willie's in Stillwater. Like all club singers, Garth relied on cover tunes and took requests. After all, more songs meant more tips from happy fans. His repertoire ranged from James Taylor and Neil Young to George Strait. And he loved to close his shows with Don McLean's "American Pie." Garth would show up anywhere he could find work, and he'd play solo if required. The club experience was crucial, because later, when he started his professional career, the little clubs of America would be where he continued to sharpen his performing skills and widen his audience.

He took an additional job at a night spot called the Tumbleweed Ballroom, where as one of the club's bouncers, he was called on to break up a fight in the women's room. There, famously, he met his wife-to-be, Sandy Mahl, who had thrown a punch at another girl and gotten her fist stuck in the wall.

Two deaths during the days at Stillwater affected Garth tremendously: Jim Kelly and Heidi Miller. Jim was a grad student and hurdler who had coached Garth's brother Kelly, before starting a band with Garth and a friend named Dale Pierce. Like Garth and Kelly, Jim and his brother were extremely close to their parents and often flew home for visits. On one of those trips, with Jim piloting, the plane crashed, killing both brothers.

When Heidi Miller and a girlfriend needed to find a third individual to share their campus apartment rent one summer, Garth moved in. He quickly formed a bond with Heidi. "She was probably one of my greatest friends," Garth reflected. "Heidi had been one of those girls who got stepped on by everybody, and she always wanted a man she could love. The other thing she really wanted to do was graduate. Well, Heidi met this wonderful guy—a football player—and fell in love with him. She was ten days from graduating when she was killed instantly in an accident with a drunk driver."

The death of these two friends influenced two of the most important components of Garth's early stardom. First, these two were heavily on his mind when he wrote his breakthrough single, "If Tomorrow Never Comes," which dealt with the importance of letting people know how much they mean to you. Next, when Garth thought about making the video for Tony Arata's song "The Dance," he decided to relate its meaning to death more than to a lost love. That premise became the theme for the song's award-winning video, and did as much as anything in his first year to establish him as a star.

After Kelly graduated from OSU, Garth roomed with Ty England, who had a long-standing love of country music. The two had met at Aunt Molly's, where both played music. Although Garth appreciated country, his real love was still rock. But the more Garth listened to Ty's tape collection, the more he began to appreciate the sheer power of what a country song could be.

His appreciation for the truths found in traditional country lyrics never lessened. Talking to *Country Fever* in 1992, he explained: "The country lyric is everyday life, the ten o'clock news put to music. I think people are looking for something to learn from. You know, if you're upset after listening to a song—that's good. It's as good as crying after a song, or it's as good as changing your life after a song. As long as it brings an emotion, then you know you're living."

England disputes that Garth learned anything from him; he says it was just the opposite. It was he who learned from Garth, especially when it came to the writing he later did with his old roommate. According to England, story songs come naturally for Garth. "Garth is great with melodies, but it's the lyrics that set him apart as a writer. He's always looking for just the right word or phrase. But what he understands better than most is how to develop a complete story that lasts three minutes."

Unfortunately, Ty and Garth got little accomplished academically that year. As Garth explained: "We couldn't room together anymore after we both got bad grades because we were playing music all the time. But it was my senior year so I could get by with it. It was Ty's sophomore year and he couldn't. So Ty had to go back home and enroll in a school closer to Oklahoma City. We made a deal when he left that if one of us should happen to get a shot at playing music for a major label, he would call the other." And Garth remembered that deal in 1989, when he got ready to set out on the road with a band named Stillwater.

While his appreciation for stone country singers like Hank Williams and Merle Haggard was growing, it wasn't just the male artists who moved him. Loretta Lynn, Patsy Cline, and Tammy Wynette became favorites. In fact, despite his belief that his mother was the best female singer he'd heard, he later would say, "If I'd been a female country singer, I would have wanted to sound like Tammy Wynette."

Garth briefly considered making the move to Tennessee a year prior to his meeting with Merlin Littlefield in Nashville. In 1984 he auditioned for a gig as a staff singer at Opryland U.S.A. Although he was offered the job, after conferring with Raymond and Colleen, he decided to stick it out in Stillwater and finish his senior year in college. It was a wise move. Opryland acts often felt they were carnival sideshow acts and that would have been anathema to Garth. When he did graduate from Oklahoma State, he asked Colleen for her blessings in his quest for a career in music. She wouldn't go so far as to say she blessed the idea, but promised to pray for him.

When he returned from his brief 1985 Music City trip, Garth went back to singing cover songs at Willie's and working at DuPree's Sports Equipment. But this time it was with a map back to Nashville. One person he knew he needed with him was Sandy Mahl, and on May 24, 1986, the two wed.

Garth had often sat in with the Skinner Brothers Band, and when he started putting together his own group, he turned first to Tom Skinner. Together they formed Santa Fe, the band Garth would bring with him on his second Nashville sojourn. The band was a college favorite in part because of the wide repertoire. Garth knew nearly four hundred songs ranging from country to pop to rock and bluegrass.

Garth had come up with a title and an idea he thought had potential, "Much Too Young (To Feel This Damn Old)," about a musician living a hard life on the road. He finished it late one night, and decided to try it out at a club called Bink's.

"That's pretty good," his friend Randy Taylor said during the break. "But I think it could be better."

"What would you do with it?" Garth asked.

"I'd turn the musician into a rodeo cowboy."

"The minute he said it, I knew Randy was onto something," Garth later reflected. "There are a lot of songs about the road and not enough about rodeo. Even though I didn't ride in rodeos, I come from that culture. It's a world I love and the people who ride those broncs and bulls have always been heroes to me. So we sat down and worked on it, putting in a line saluting Chris LeDoux, who was not only a champion bronc rider but also a musician that everybody admired. Chris was a star in so many ways. It never occurred to me that I would later meet him, play shows with him, and make a lifelong friend."

Garth was already developing into the star performer he would become. He was intense and passionate onstage. He didn't just move, he prowled the stage, bringing his audience into the show on an emotional level. But he didn't yet have that rock show element that he would later put to such an effective use. That would come after seeing a Chris LeDoux concert.

But Garth Brooks and Santa Fe were enough of a regional name that they opened for national artists like Dwight Yoakam, Johnny Paycheck, and Steve Earle, and performed on television shows including *A.M. Oklahoma*. In early October 1986 Santa Fe took third in the Marlboro Talent Roundup semifinals, and later that month they were invited to play a show at New Mexico State University. Their reputation was growing rapidly, and with it, Garth's confidence.

In preparing to make the permanent move to Music City, Garth visited Nashville several times to get the lay of the land. He scouted neighborhoods where he and Sandy might find a place to live and attended writers nights to hear Music City's latest songs.

When he made those preliminary trips Garth stayed with an Oklahoma songwriter named Bob Childers, who knew publisher/songwriter Stephanie Brown. A former English teacher, Stephanie loved words, music, and writers. After spending some time with Garth, she suggested he help Childers with the melody of a song he'd been writing. They worked late into the night, then Garth put the song down on tape. That one demo, not more than a crude work tape, was all it took for Stephanie to become a supporter. She invited him to writers nights and small shows.

During a show held at the popular Second Avenue club Windows on the Cumberland, Garth heard Kevin Welch, a smart, poetic writer and fellow Oklahoman who would make some well-received albums a few years hence. Garth listened to Welch's song set and immediately recognized an unusual talent. Welch's lyrics were tight, well thought out, and meaningful, his performance riveting. Garth later admitted that he had a similar reaction to the one he had had in 1985 when he sat in Merlin Littlefield's office and heard a well-known songwriter say he was broke: "If that guy's playing for twenty people I don't have any business being here."

But later, when a group of Oklahoma friends took him to Kevin's house for a guitar pull, where various writers and artists take turns trying out new material, Garth was invited to sing. Afterward, Kevin said, "Man, this town is going to be fine for you."

Prophetic words. And Garth Brooks would prove to be fine for Nashville.

CHAPTER TWO

Shitkickers & cowboys

H arlan Howard, the most revered songwriter in Nashville, composer of "Pick Me Up On Your Way Down," "Busted," and "I Fall To Pieces," sat at the bar in Maude's Courtyard. His hair was a great mane of silver, his eyes sharp with a bit of an impish twinkle. He wore a pair of jeans and a blue denim shirt. He ordered a Black Russian, which he called a milk shake. Aside from penning great songs, Harlan was known for his definitive take on country music: "It's three chords and the truth." That day in 1987, Harlan sat listening as a young writer lamented the current state of country.

"I don't even know what country is anymore," the kid groaned. "The music is getting way too close to rock."

"I don't pay that much attention to the tracks," Harlen mused. "I listen to the lyrics. Two things will tell you if something's 'country'—the words and the audience."

GARTH FINALLY BROUGHT SANDY and the band, Santa Fe, to Nashville in late summer, 1987, this time with his mother's approval. In fact, she gave him her lucky four-leaf clover as a farewell gift. The whole crowd moved into a house in Hendersonville, just east of Nashville. The band didn't last long. As Garth once put it,

"It was five guys with five different opinions of what it took to make it. None of us were right. We were all very scared and the band blew up after about four or five months. Two of them went back home and three stayed in Nashville. They're all happy with what they're doing."

Garth found work at Cowtown Boots while Sandy took a series of part-time positions, including a job at the boot store, where she could cover for her husband if he needed to take a meeting. Driving back and forth from Hendersonville to Music Row, Garth listened hours on end to the tunes played on Nashville radio stations.

In 1987 country music was more diverse than ever and it appeared to be happening with almost a sense of urgency. New faces and styles lived side by side with Old Nashville, and if they circled the other like tail-sniffing dogs, they were hounds chasing the same bone: records that sold.

Traditionalists were well represented by Randy Travis and George Strait, with newcomer Dwight Yoakam's critically acclaimed 1986 debut still making both waves and new converts. Randy Travis's 1987 signature release, "Forever And Ever, Amen," stayed at the top chart spot for three weeks, and snared CMA, ACM, and Grammy awards. George Strait's three '87 hits—"Ocean Front Property," "All My Ex's Live In Texas," and "Am I Blue"—added weight to his own list of career records.

One of the hottest acts in town was ace singer/songwriter/guitarist Steve Wariner, whom Dottie West hired to play in her band when he was still a teenager. A favorite of the legendary Chet Atkins, Steve made a name with RCA releases between 1980 and '84, when he moved to MCA. One of the finest guitarists in any genre, Steve had three number 1 hits in '87, "Small Town Girl," "The Weekend," and "Lynda."

By 1987 country music had expanded to include some high-profile alternative artists like Steve Earle and the O'Kanes. The biggest song of the year was Michael Johnson's "Give Me Wings," followed closely by Reba McEntire's "What Am I Gonna Do

About You" and the Judds' "Cry Myself To Sleep." Established
pop-flavored artists including Crystal Gayle, Gary Morris, Lee
Greenwood, Earl Thomas Conley, and Dan Seals all scored big
hits that year.

Nashville was fertile soil for professional songwriters, and
publishing was growing at an unprecedented pace. Many of the
genre's biggest acts seldom tried their hands at songwriting, and
turned to the well of local talent. Reba McEntire, the Judds,
George Strait, and Randy Travis depended on local publishers
for most of their recordings.

And so, when Garth moved to Nashville he found a city full
of professional songwriters, tunesmiths who had no plans for
stardom but who made their living penning songs for those who
did. Harlan Howard had been the first of this breed when he arrived in the 1960s. But it was not until the '80s that songwriters
outnumbered stars, pickers, and label personnel. Publishers and
the organizations that collected their royalties, BMI, ASCAP,
and SESAC, had a renewed clout.

The American Society of Composers, Authors and Publishers
was born out of outrage after Stephen Foster died in poverty,
having made several fortunes for sheet music publishers. The organization was founded in 1914 and sought to financially protect
composers, primarily those associated with New York's Tin Pan
Alley. Even after radio became popularized in the 1920s, neither
country/hillbilly nor ethnic/race music received much attention.
SESAC, the Society of European Stage Authors & Composers,
was formed in 1930, originally to represent European artists. It
wasn't until 1939 that BMI, Broadcast Music, Inc., was established, partly as a reaction to the ASCAP monopoly and partly
to represent country and ethnic composers.

The 1980s witnessed perhaps the most visible identity crisis
country music ever had, beginning with *Urban Cowboy,* the film
that for many observers came to personify schlock country. Like
most great yarns, the story that juiced up country music's image
in 1980 involved a house divided. The setting was Gilley's club

in Pasadena, Texas, and the players were the Cowboys and the Shitkickers. Within that movie is a conversation snippet that captures the question haunting the decade.

It happened when John Travolta, as *Urban Cowboy*'s blue collar Bud, and co-star Debra Winger, as the tow-truck driving Sissy, uttered their first lines.

Sissy: Are you a real cowboy?

Bud: Depends on what you think a real cowboy is.

That line reflected an age-old quandary in the music industry: what's *real* country and what isn't. When the industry dropped the "and western" part of country's identity, what did that really mean? Is "country" a regional issue, with the hill music of Appalachia more pure than the honky-tonk sounds of West Texas? Where do the cowboy poets fit into the picture? Moreover, is country music defined by a musical style, by lyrics, by message, or possibly, by the audience?

It's certainly worth taking a more reflective look at the 1980 freight train that started rolling with a magazine article, picked up full steam with a movie, and blew into the station with a newly hip redneck culture two-stepping across the nation.

Gilley's was a sprawling honky-tonk in Pasadena, Texas, that captured the interest of *Esquire* publisher Clay Felker when in 1976 he visited Houston and friends took him for a big night out. When Felker returned to New York he asked one of his writers, Texas-born Aaron Lathan, to go there and get a slice of pure Americana for the magazine's readers. And if not for Hollywood, the story of Gilley's, which had been named after singer Mickey Gilley, would have been just another example of a transplanted writer taking a look at redneck America with a wink, a nod, and a check in the mail. Lathan's cover story, titled "Ballad of the Urban Cowboy: America's Search for True Grit," appeared in *Esquire* on September 12, 1978.

There were two crowds at Gilley's. There were the Shitkickers, as owner Sherwood Cryer called them: redneck rockers, refinery workers, hippies, off-duty cops, secretaries, and beauty operators; the guy still living off his parents; the divorcée whose ex had picked up the kids for the weekend; and married couples on a budget who loved good music and cheap beer. It took the *Houston Chronicle*'s venerable pop critic Bob Claypool to bring in the second bunch. When he called Gilley's "the biggest, brawlingest, craziest honky-tonk in Texas," it interested the uptown Houston crowd. They bought new Stetsons and headed to Pasadena, which they'd formerly called "Stinkadena" because of the refineries. Sherwood tagged them the Cowboys. But in the end, they were all Gilleyrats.

Just under the shitkicking and hell-raising at Gilley's lay an important truth long reflected in country music: a lot of bar revelers were, in fact, lookin' for love, as Johnny Lee's hit from the movie soundtrack would say. And that was the story Aaron Lathan found in the short-lived honky-tonk marriage of Dew Westbrook and his ex-wife, Betty. *Esquire* readers loved the article, and Gilley's employees soon started seeing a new out-of-town clientele. If Houston was your destination, a side trip to Pasadena just might prove fun.

Many of the Gilleyrats resented the article's tone, for although Aaron Lathan was originally from Speer, Texas, he treated his subject with no small amount of condescension.

The *Chronicle*'s Claypool weighed in:

"It seemed to irritate [Lathan] that these cowboys lived in the city and didn't really ride the range—he never, for one moment, considered the fact that both groups, old and new, were simple, country-bred men who were doing the best they could at the only jobs they knew, then hoorawin' it up on Saturday night."

It didn't take Hollywood long to see the silver screen sex appeal of *hoorawin' it up on Saturday night*. After all, another magazine article, this one a *New York* magazine piece titled "Tribal Rites of the New Saturday Night" by Nik Cohn, had two years earlier been turned into the blockbuster film *Saturday Night Fever*. And if it worked in disco, why not country?

Urban Cowboy didn't live up to ticket sales expectations, but there was enough excitement to encourage hundreds of bars to go honky-tonk with an almost religious fervor, while in Los Angeles alone, four radio stations jumped on country's fiddle-and-guitar bandwagon. People who saw the movie not only liked the gigantic neighborhood bar concept, but were also reminded that Americans love cowboys more than almost anything else. And they usually don't care if the person behind the image works on a cattle ranch or in a machine shop.

The advertising copy on the movie soundtrack reflected an understanding of the appeal of both film and recording: "It's more than just music. It's a way of life." When the soundtrack sold 3 million copies, Nashville's marketers perked up.

"Nashville didn't learn that you can't consider a soundtrack album indicative of anything other than the buzz on that movie," Chet Atkins explained, referring to the *Urban Cowboy*–inspired country sales spike of the early 1980s. "That's why—as my friend Tom T. Hall might say—the bean counters spent about five years as nervous as long tailed cats in a room full of rocking chairs."

Many in Nashville scorned *Urban Cowboy* and all that it spawned. It was the new Stetsons, carefully pressed Wranglers, and the two-steppin' dance clubs that often switched to disco after midnight that caused the nose holding. Then there were the radio stations changing to country but keeping on ill-prepared pop and rock deejays. Some said the film and what followed did little more than encourage a bunch of pop pap.

Country music had long been sensitive to the idea that it was pop rock's "redheaded stepchild." Very few country artists had ever been able to compete in the pop/rock world, and those were usually iconic figures like Johnny Cash. With few exceptions, their edge, when it held, was more evident in celebrity than tours and per-album sales figures.

Barbara Mandrell took on *Urban Cowboy* by grabbing the mechanical bull by its nonexistent horns. In 1981 she countered the film's influence with "I Was Country When Country Wasn't

Cool," which included a cameo performance by George Jones. The song easily hit number 1, and when Jones stood up in the audience to sing it with her at the Country Music Association Awards, it was something akin to the pope making an appearance at a Catholic League dinner.

But *Urban Cowboy* has taken a bad rap. The biggest influence that the movie had was seen in pop culture, not recorded music. Some of the finest albums of the decade were released the following year: Rosanne Cash's *Seven Year Ache,* Ricky Skaggs's *Waitin' for the Sun to Shine,* George Strait's *Strait Country,* Guy Clark's *The South Coast of Texas.* The positive effect that the movie had on Nashville music was the fact that clubs catering to country opened in droves, venues that booked emerging acts and opened up a far bigger market.

The crossroads where country stood in the '80s had more to do with age and society than with a movie. A new generation started listening to country music, and many had never heard of Ernest Tubb or Floyd Tillman. That generation's idea of classic country was not Webb Pierce's 1953 "There Stands The Glass," it was Waylon and Willie singing "Luckenbach, Texas," which had stayed at number 1 for six straight weeks in 1977.

Some of the decade's biggest acts tried to modernize both image and music. Kenny Rogers, Ronnie Milsap, the Oak Ridge Boys, and Alabama all took some criticism for popish crossover hits like "Islands In The Stream" and "Elvira." Conway Twitty even revamped his look and got a perm. Others, like the decade's biggest chart impact artist, Willie Nelson, made no attempt to do anything other than exactly what he wanted. And it worked, because with Willie image is never an issue. He's always the hippest cat in the room.

Critics chastised '80s country music for being too "slick," but the decade itself fed on glossy imaging. The '80s put on a public face of peace and prosperity with lavish Reagan-era White House galas, television shows like *Dynasty* and *Dallas,* the Donald worship, and yuppies. But just beneath the surface was a world where homelessness grew, the United States built never-before-seen debt, and investors went broke on junk bonds and inevitably faced 1987's Black Monday, when the market saw shares fall half a trillion dollars. So the question about what a cowboy really was could be expanded to what the entire populace really was. One has to wonder, was the real America that of oil executives in Dallas or refinery workers at Gilley's?

In a very important way the shape of the country music business was a reflection of the veneer of success covering some tough economic times in the '80s. Because even with a wealth of consequential music, radio tightened playlists and spun fewer records, especially those from the genre's older artists. Personality radio was on the wane, with more homogenized formats and fewer disc jockeys talking about artists.

One bright spot was The Nashville Network (TNN), which launched in 1983. The network was a joint venture between WSM (of radio and Grand Ole Opry fame) and Group W Satellite Communications. TNN in general, and Ralph Emery's *Nashville Now* in particular, helped connect Nashville's artists and music to mainstream America. Emery gave artists the opportunity to show their personalities—sometimes warts and all. Once, when Johnny Paycheck appeared, he held a note a little too long and spit out his bottom denture. Another time a fiddle player accidentally caught his bow on a singer's toupee and sailed it almost into the laps of those seated in the front row. Audiences loved it, and TNN became the genre's greatest marketing tool since the Grand Ole Opry.

If Nashville attorneys and accountants were hand wringing through much of the decade, America's creative youths still flocked into town. Arguably, because of one song. In 1982, the year that twenty-year-old Garth Brooks won fifty dollars at a college talent show in Stillwater, Oklahoma, one of Columbia Records' most powerful vocalists, Lacy J. Dalton, released a single that quickly became an anthem for singer/songwriters throughout the nation. Garth was just one of the hopefuls who listened and understood that "16th Avenue" contained lines aptly describing the Nashville Dream. The song spoke of lonely songwriters in cheap rented rooms writing some golden words that allowed them to finally "walk in style" on Music Row. No artist ever held those songwriters in awe as much as did Garth Brooks. Nobody wanted the miracle more.

Despite efforts to slick up and cross over, Nashville still had back-door and alley accessibility in 1987—literally. Songwriters, journalists, and floaters of one sort or another could park in an alley and slide in the back door of CBS or RCA to stop by almost anyone's office. And on Friday afternoons at most record labels and publishing companies, more than a few pulled open a drawer and opened up a bottle of Scotch for all comers searching for a TGIF party.

The Outlaw Era, when stoned cowboy singers played pinball down at corner markets, was on the wane but a lot of rowdies still hung at the Third Coast, otherwise known as the Rock 'n' Roll Hotel, where visiting rock bands had holed up while recording in Music City. David Allan Coe still blew into town every so often to upset the Spence Manor management with an entourage of rambunctious chimpanzees. Harlan Howard held court most afternoons at Maude's Courtyard, offering advice to all seeking help from the Dean of Nashville Songwriters.

It is a misconception that Nashville's stars are the ones on the stage. Inside the town's business the real stars are the personalities who run record labels. They control artists and they often control the music. Sometimes that works out, sometimes not. It is a lesson artists would do well to understand, and one that Garth learned early on.

CHAPTER THREE

"Uncle Joe, you know we owe it to you"

W hat's the secret?" Trisha Yearwood asked Garth about his becoming the fastest-selling artist in music history.

It was October 2000, and Garth was preparing for a black-tie blowout at the Nashville Arena hosted by Capitol to celebrate his sales of 100 million albums in one decade. Facing career decisions of her own, Trisha brought up Garth's experience.

Garth hesitated a moment, understanding that she was asking a rhetorical question. But then he said, "I had a tight group of people around me who never blew smoke up my butt."

GARTH TIPPED HIS HAT to one of those people on his 1995 release, *Fresh Horses*. The album kicked off with "The Old Stuff," a nod backward to 1988 and 1989, the days when he and the band were playing clubs like the Kansas City Opry and Tulsa City Limits. When Garth sang the line, "Uncle Joe, you know we owe it to you," it was in tribute to Joe Harris, the agent who took a chance on an unsigned kid from Oklahoma and started booking him prior to anything that resembled success. Harris was only one of the people who recognized in Garth a sense of purpose and a strong will in addition to unmistakable talent.

Garth's first year in town could serve as a primer on how to make it in the music business. He hooked up with smart, savvy people, but more often than not they were not part of the business-as-usual crowd. Most were old-timers, outsiders—or insiders who thought like outsiders.

"I was lucky that the people I found in those first couple of years were on the side of writers, artists, and musicians," Garth said. "I met too many creative people who had been run over by the business and I won't say it made me paranoid, but it did make me watchful. Mom's warnings were always right there in the back of my mind."

Stephanie Brown hit the mother lode for Garth when she played one of his tapes for ASCAP's Bob Doyle. One of the first songs on the tape was "Much Too Young (To Feel This Damn Old)." Though it was a rough demo that inexplicably switched tempo midstream, Doyle was immediately taken with it. "What makes that song great is that it's universal," Doyle says. "You don't have to be a rodeo rider to understand that feeling of get-ting beat up, of being tired of the struggle. No matter what 'road' you're on, it does seem like it just keeps getting longer."

Because ASCAP had once represented primarily pop writers, Nashville writers had been in the BMI camp through the early decades of the industry. But a concentrated effort by ASCAP, along with the smaller SESAC, had changed that trend by the 1980s. By the time Garth came to town, writers debated which company offered the best deal, gave better advances against royalties, and treated writers with the most respect. More im-portant, which one might give you a loan? In many cases, it all boiled down to how various personalities at the organiza-tions were perceived. When it came to public opinion, the guy Stephanie Brown took Garth to meet was one of the favored.

Bob Doyle was one of the most respected song men in Nashville. A trained percussionist, his experience had included rock and symphonic work. An air force pilot, Bob was stationed in Selma, Alabama, when he first started listening to the classic country music of artists such as Jimmie Rodgers and Hank Williams. After his tour, Nashville seemed like the natural place to land. He worked in A&R (artists and repertoire) at Warner Bros., then moved to ASCAP. A&R and publishing are closely intertwined. A&R is the department within the label that looks for songs and artists, and helps develop talent and often career direction. So when Doyle moved to one of the publishing rights organizations, he brought with him a deep understanding of what labels looked for. In both positions the courtesy and respect he showed songwriters made him one of their favorite executives.

Once he heard Garth's demo tape, he asked Stephanie to arrange a meeting. "I guess on a purely personal note, the first thing that impressed me about Garth was that he was a 'West of the Mississippi' guy. He wore the jeans, the boots. And he had a western, rural attitude. I sensed an authenticity in him, honesty and integrity. Combine that with the talent and you just had to be impressed."

Bob had been mulling the idea of striking out on his own for some time, and after he met with Garth a few times, his plans took more solid shape. After trying unsuccessfully to get Garth a publishing deal, he decided to take the plunge. And with an in-for-a-penny-in-for-a-pound attitude, Doyle decided to take an even bigger chance and manage Garth. He believed in the idea so much that he took out a second mortgage on his house to finance it all.

"When you sit on the business side of the desk across from talented people, people with so much potential, you sometimes start wondering if you're really helping them make their dreams come true," Doyle reflected. "I thought a lot about the courage it took to come to town and put everything on the line—it takes a lot of nerve to go for a creative career. Just think about the times these people get turned down. And even after they get going, if they do make it as a 'star,' they get slapped down from time to time. I have a tremendous amount of respect for anyone with the guts to take that path. And in the end, what I decided was that I wanted to be someone who helped people live out their dreams, not one who at some point or other killed their hopes."

Bob now looks back on his decision with a wry smile. "I don't think I really understood the risk I was taking, quitting a safe job to try something completely new. But I had a line of credit and an artist I believed in."

"When I heard that Bob was working with some kid named Garth Brooks, it caught my attention," Silver Line Gold Line publishing's Noel Fox said soon after Garth's debut album was released. "Bob's one of the town's honest brokers."

Virtually all of Nashville's music community concurred. Bob Doyle was a quiet, no-nonsense professional who never played games or pontificated. In a city where the hot-dogging often started at midlevel exec positions, Bob remained a bona fide song man. Cautious in his business dealings, when the Row learned that Doyle had taken out that second mortgage on behalf of a new singer/songwriter, it was almost as if Chet Atkins had tucked an unknown guitar picker under his wing.

Doyle knew he lacked the public relations and marketing chops needed for a management firm to be fully effective, so he turned to a go-getter publicist named Pam Lewis. A veteran of MTV in New York, Pam had worked for RCA in Nashville. The two formed Doyle/Lewis Management and in 1988 signed Garth Brooks. Attorney Rusty Jones and financial advisor Kerry O'Neal were two other important members of the team.

Doyle wanted to keep Garth working on songs and performing them at local writers nights. California writer Larry Bastian was among the first to co-write with Garth. In fact, Bastian was formally signed even before Garth to the publishing company Major Bob, named after Doyle's rank in the air force reserves.

"When Bob Doyle called me about his new company, I was ready to sign with a Nashville publisher to try and open up that market for me," Larry said. "I told Bob I'd be coming to

Nashville soon, and the first thing he said was, 'There's this kid I want you to meet.'"

Bastian was immediately impressed with Garth's writing and singing, but admits that in the beginning he had no clue that Garth would be a big star. "At first he was so quiet, so shy that I didn't see it happening. But over time, as his personality and humor started coming out, I realized I'd been a little hasty in my judgment.

"What I soon realized was that this was a guy who truly loved words, wouldn't give up on a line until it was right. He is incapable of writing a throwaway phrase or of saying, 'Oh, that's good enough.'

"Garth is also fun to write with. I remember one time when we'd been up a long time kicking around some ideas, and I ended up falling asleep. When I woke up, Garth said, 'Man, I got a great track here that I think we can work with.' Then he played me a tape of me snoring."

Bob Doyle tried to set up as many writing appointments and demo sessions for his new client as possible, sometimes to no avail. One song plugger at MCA Music tried unsuccessfully to interest his biggest writers in scheduling a co-write with the new kid from Oklahoma. "I tried to encourage these guys for two reasons," the plugger later said. "First, Garth was writing some good songs. Second, he was after a record deal and I thought he'd get it. In the end, about ten million albums later, one of those writers stormed into my office and raged at me for not pushing him harder to write with Garth Brooks."

The people Garth did collaborate with were arguably a better choice. They were good, strong songwriters but in general not Nashville's elite. Teaming a new artist with a high-powered writer can be daunting, and given Garth's personality, he would have found some of the experiences difficult. Tales of heavy-handed top-shelf writers looking with amusement at hopefuls are numerous. In one case, an award-winning composer walked into an arranged writing appointment, threw down a cassette tape, and, without introducing himself, told the young singer, "Here's our song." Then he left. It doesn't always happen, of course, and the flip side of the story is that some young writers like having a veteran do all the heavy lifting. But by writing with those who weren't resting on the laurels of number 1 hits, Garth forged his own identity quicker than he might have.

Kent Blazy was the first writer who'd had a Top 10 cut who agreed to collaborate with Garth. (Blazy's "Headed For A Heartache" broke world-class vocalist Gary Morris into the upper realms of the charts in 1981.) Bob Doyle first approached Kent regarding demo work, knowing Garth needed both the studio experience and the money. Kent had been using several demo singers who would ultimately end up with recording contracts: Trisha Yearwood, Billy Dean, Rob Crosby. He agreed to give Garth a shot, and Bob threw another suggestion on the table. Would Kent consider writing with Garth?

"A lot of writers don't want to take the chance that they'd waste an afternoon with someone who couldn't write," Kent says. "But Bob Doyle believed in him, and that interested me."

It took several months for the initial collaboration to happen. "Bob first talked to me right after Thanksgiving," Kent says. "Christmas was coming up, and I always take January off to write by myself. So I told Bob I could meet with this new kid in February. When we finally got together, Garth walked in and said, 'I've got this idea for a song, but I've tried to get a bunch of people to work on it with me, and nobody will.'"

That idea was "If Tomorrow Never Comes," a song involving a concept Garth's mother often spoke about. "If you love someone you better tell them so," Colleen said. "Because life is never sure—you might not get the chance again."

"My mother's words inspired me to write 'If Tomorrow Never Comes,' but my dad played a role as well. Dad would snap his fingers and say, 'It can all be over like that. Keep up with what you've got and know what you've got.' That line is never very far out of my head."

The two friends Garth had lost during his college days, Jim Kelly and Heidi Miller, were on his mind, as well as both of his parents' words. "I can only hope both Jim and Heidi knew how much their friendship meant to me," Garth said.

Blazy pitched "If Tomorrow Never Comes" to George Jones. "I would never have had the nerve to pitch a song to George Jones," Garth told a friend. "The idea that a man like Jones would cut *anything* I wrote was unreal, and at the time we wrote it, I just didn't see that the song was that special. I liked it. But it didn't have the effect on me that it did years later. I can still remember the day I finally 'got it.' I was driving in my truck, and the song came on the radio. Maybe it was because I wasn't expecting to hear it, but it was like I was listening for the first time. I actually had to pull over to the side of the road."

Blazy had learned Garth's writing weakness: he often lacked confidence in his own work. "I'm an ideas guy, I'm not a songwriter. They're just nice enough to let me put my name on a few of 'em," Garth said. His collaborators scoff at that depiction.

"It was amazing to me that Garth ever questioned his writing," Kent says. "He spoiled me for writing with newcomers. I loved his understanding of rhyme and metaphor, and how he could visualize each song and add extra depth to it. He impressed me right on that first day, while we wrote 'If Tomorrow Never Comes.' I thought, 'This guy is twenty-five going on fifty.' He seemed like he must have lived a lot longer than his age—so good at seeing the microcosm/macrocosm of what a song can be."

Blazy was impressed with Garth's vocals and began hiring him as a demo singer. And it was through this connection that Garth met a young Belmont College student, Georgia native Trisha Yearwood. To help get her foot in the music door, Trisha had taken an internship at MTM Records, owned by film and television star Mary Tyler Moore. There Trisha worked with MTM's singer/songwriter Judy Rodman, whose "Until I Met You" and "She Thinks That She'll Marry" had met with considerable success, and Honky-Tonk Piano Queen Becky Hobbs ("Jones On The Jukebox"). As soon as Trisha graduated with a degree in music business at Belmont, the label hired her as a full-time receptionist.

When Garth and Trisha first met she had recently married Christian / heavy metal rock guitarist Chris Latham and was singing demos to help family finances and get in studio time. Kent Blazy believed that Garth's and Trisha's voices were perfect for each other, and that they would be excellent on duet demos, as well as switching out harmonies. Garth was immediately struck by her voice, as would be the entire industry within a few years.

"Listening to Trisha sing those first few times was a blessing and a curse," Garth said, laughing. "It was a blessing because I thought, 'Man! If I ever get anything going I'm gonna beg her to sing on my record!' It was a curse because every time she opened her mouth I wondered why I *ever* thought I was a singer."

One of the first things he did was take her tapes to Bob Doyle. "You need to sign her," Garth advised. "She's going to be the hottest singer in the business." Doyle/Lewis began working with her on an unofficial level.

Garth and Trisha had much in common. They were ambitious, knew that the road ahead would be rough, and had the ability to laugh at the ups and downs they encountered along the way. They combined sophisticated savvy with small-town sensibility. The two made a pact that if either one "made it" that one would help out the other.

Nashville's writing community soon recognized Garth's talent. He became known for his intensity during collaboration, pacing back and forth across the room, staring out the window searching for the right word, the sweet chords. He often took on the personality of the song being written, sometimes somber, melancholy, at other times laughing and boisterous. "He really digs down deep into the meaning of a song," Kent Blazy says. "He puts himself right there, and that's why he's so effective."

But as active as Bob Doyle and writers like Kent Blazy were in promoting Garth, much of the groundwork laid and contacts came through Garth's own efforts. One of the first pieces of advice Doyle gave Garth was to always be on the lookout for songs, no matter who wrote them or who had the publishing. "Don't ever start to think you can outwrite this town on a day-to-day basis," Bob said. "Because if you do, you're gonna have a short career."

Garth took the advice to heart. He met many of his early contacts in bars. But unlike many new writers and artists who come to Music City, Garth wasn't in those bars to party. He wasn't a teetotaler, but he was there for the music, not the beer.

"That's where you hear the songs," he says. "A lot of big publishers aren't that interested in talking to a new guy in town. And they sure aren't going to play him their best stuff. But writers are a different ball game. If you go out to those clubs, you'll hear their best songs. You'll hear their newest songs. And if you get to know them, they might even let you sing 'em."

There was another, more personal side to Garth's lack of interest in the party aspect of the bar scene. "Sandy and I were working our butts off at a boot store and I was still afraid that it would end up having been for nothing."

By 1988 Nashville's hottest writers showcase club was the Bluebird Cafe on Hillsboro Road. Small and cramped, its employees often shushed the audience with something less than elegance. Some industry types avoided the Bluebird when they could. Trouble was, that's where they heard the hits. It wasn't easy to get a spot on a Bluebird show. Singers and writers had to give an audition tape to owner Amy Kurland, a tough but open-minded critic who listened and pronounced judgment. In Garth's case, she gave the thumbs-up. Garth sang there any chance he got, and spent countless nights listening to other writers, looking for the songs he would need should a record deal materialize.

Bryan Kennedy was scouting for songs at the Bluebird one

night when he heard a voice that he said knocked him on his rear. "I've heard it said that unless you've been to one of Garth's concerts, you can't completely 'get' how he connects with huge crowds," Bryan says. "But I'd also say that if people haven't heard him in a small, intimate setting, they may not quite understand what an impact he had on people before they had any idea who he was. I'd been around the music business all my life, and let me tell you, I almost fell off my chair the first time I heard him sing."

Kennedy grew up in the music business, the son of prominent guitar player, record producer, and former Mercury/PolyGram Records label head Jerry Kennedy. Bryan had two things in common with Garth Brooks: a love of music and a love of sports. An All State football player in high school, Kennedy went on to play defensive end at the University of Mississippi. And like Garth, he went to college on an athletic scholarship.

After college, Bryan started working for his father's newly formed JK Productions, and later for MCA Music Publishing, where he produced the first sides on Terri Clark. He made a name for himself as part of the Nashville-based trio Chuck Wagon and the Wheels, a group known for wearing outsized cowboy hats and using tongue-in-cheek comedy between songs. When he first heard Garth sing, Bryan knew this was something big.

The Nashville Entertainment Association held regular show-cases for writers to present new material to producers and A&R personnel. And it was on one night in 1988, while working for JK Productions, that Bryan stopped by the Bluebird Cafe. This was a time when few of Nashville's working artists wore cowboy hats and boots. It was the era of Steve Earle and David Lynn Jones. Even Randy Travis went hatless. The exceptions were George Strait and Dwight Yoakam, but they were seldom in Nashville. When Bryan walked into the Bluebird wearing his cowboy hat, he saw Garth Brooks wearing Wranglers and Ropers and pegged him as an Oklahoman or Texan. A fellow spirit.

"Here's a guy who can sing a pretty good country song," the show's host said.

Then Garth sang "If Tomorrow Never Comes."

"I turned to a record company friend of mine who was there, and said, 'You ought to sign that guy,'" Bryan says. "When Garth came offstage, I introduced myself and fell all over him with praise—I gotta admit, I embarrassed myself. Then I went home and called my dad."

A native of Shreveport, Louisiana, Jerry Kennedy started out playing the Louisiana Hayride and touring with artists including Johnny Horton. He wound up doing session work in Nashville, playing on records with Bob Dylan, Elvis Presley, and Roy Orbison to name a few. He headed Mercury Records for twenty years, worked with Roger Miller, Reba McEntire, the Statler Brothers, and Tom T. Hall, and remains one of the industry's most respected executives.

As it turned out, Kennedy had already heard about Garth from Bob Doyle. So after hearing his son's endorsement, he was anxious to meet the singer. And when he did, he called his son and said that Garth was the greatest artist he'd ever heard. "That stunned me," Bryan says. "Given all the artists Dad had worked with, and the fact that he doesn't usually heap praise on people, it was just astonishing."

Kennedy called up his friend Joe Harris at Buddy Lee Attractions and asked him to meet with Garth. Joe hesitated, because Buddy Lee didn't book acts without record contracts. But again, he had also heard about Garth from his friend Bob Doyle. Getting a second pitch from Jerry Kennedy told him that he ought to give the kid a listen.

Harris had a long history of booking acts. He'd started out while stationed in Vietnam in the late 1960s, bringing package shows to entertain the troops. After an injury and exposure to Agent Orange, Joe returned to the United States to try and find his way back into society. He worked a series of unfulfilling jobs including punching time cards at a milk company, a tire company, and the post office, before starting to ease back into the band-booking business.

One of the people Harris met during that time was power booker Buddy Lee, who in 1979 convinced him to move to Nashville. Despite Lee's implied sponsorship, Harris had to start out at the bottom of the company, the mail room. Once he worked his way up in the pecking order, he started booking some of the top acts in the business: Willie Nelson, Waylon Jennings, George Strait. He'd been at the company just under a decade when Garth Brooks walked into his office and handed him a tape.

Garth didn't stop at giving him the tape, though, as Harris later explained. "He asked if it would be all right if he played a couple of songs on his guitar. Before he got through his first line I knew what I'd been told about this Oklahoman was true. Corporate policy stated that no artist could be signed without a record deal. Normally, an artist is showcased then discussed at a weekly meeting among all agents as to whether to sign or pass on booking that act. But I heard something in Garth and I was afraid of taking the chance of losing him to another agency."

"I figured Joe Harris would throw me out on my butt," Garth said. "But he shook my hand and offered to work with me."

In fact, Harris had some fancy footwork ahead of him, and for the next few days he felt he was on pins. "I kind of overruled everybody and because of my standing in the company they took my word and signed Garth without going through all the formalities. But then, I couldn't track down Bob Doyle right away so it was a week before I actually got a signed contract."

Joe Harris had to tap-dance as fast as he could to get an unsigned act bookings, and slid Garth into gigs every chance he had. One that brought a chill to Garth's bones involved a show at his old college town, Stillwater, Oklahoma, and the True Value Country Showdown. The opportunity came up after Tulsa promoter/agent Ray Bingham had booked his client

Pake McEntire. When the show date changed from September to October, Pake was already booked and Bingham turned to Joe Harris at Buddy Lee Attractions. Harris immediately said, "Hell, Garth Brooks would be perfect for that, being as how it's in Stillwater, where he went to school." Bingham got Randy Schell and the Shot Glass Band to back him up. Right after the show, Bingham told the *Tulsa World*'s John Wooley how much he appreciated the newcomer's professionalism: "Garth sent me a letter, thanking me for booking him on his first big job."

"Ray called and told me that Garth put on an amazing show," Joe Harris recalled. "I told him that Garth always came through. I never knew him to have a bad night. But I also knew that it was important for Garth to go back and make his college town proud."

Years later, Garth nearly teared up remembering that show. "The whole time I was working on my first record, all I could think about was making the people back in Yukon proud, the people in Stillwater. You feel like you are representing them out there in public, and if you fail, you fail them."

Bob Doyle says that Joe Harris was one of the most important people in Garth's early career. "I give credit to Joe for breaking Garth as an act," Doyle now says. "In the beginning Garth didn't even have a label. But Joe used his contacts and his powers of persuasion to get him booked into clubs all over the country. These promoters and club owners had no idea what they were getting. They just took Joe Harris's word. And then, of course, Garth delivered."

Two more who played a central role in Garth's early career were Capitol chief Jim Foglesong and his A&R man, Lynn Shults. Known around town as "Gentleman," Jim Foglesong at Capitol was the elder statesman of Nashville's record executives. He began producing for Columbia in 1953, working with a wide variety of artists: Roy Hamilton, Robert Goulet, Lester Lanin, Al Hirt, and Miriam Makeba. He later was hired by RCA, then moved to Nashville in 1970 with Dot Records, where he handled a roster that included Donna Fargo, Hank Thompson, and Roy Clark.

After ABC bought Dot, Foglesong signed Barbara Mandrell, the Oak Ridge Boys, Don Williams, and John Conlee. Yet another merger made Foglesong the president of MCA, where he signed George Strait and Reba McEntire to the label, which already had Loretta Lynn, Merle Haggard, and Conway Twitty. After an L.A. transplant named Jimmy Bowen took over MCA, Foglesong was named president of Capitol.

Lynn Shults had a background in radio and record companies, and was known as an affable lover of unique stylists, like Capitol's Tanya Tucker. He was often out and about, scouting the clubs for new songs and new singers. That would prove vital in Garth's ultimate signing.

One day in late March 1988, Foglesong stopped by Lynn's office and told him that he'd scheduled an audition with a new artist Bob Doyle was working with. On April 4 Garth sang several songs, including "If Tomorrow Never Comes." When he finished, Foglesong was convinced the label should sign him. But in a meeting later that day, Lynn was less than enthusiastic. Foglesong decided to hold off, and told Bob Doyle to keep sending him tapes.

Doyle had been pitching Garth all over Nashville. "I went to everybody," Bob said. "Besides Jim Foglesong, the one person who really 'got' Garth's potential was Renee Bell at MCA. She took a tape to her boss, Tony Brown, who set up a meeting with Jimmy Bowen. But Bowen also turned us down."

On May 11, Lynn Shults happened by the Bluebird Cafe for a writers night, and heard Garth sing "If Tomorrow Never Comes" for a second time. "Everything changed for me," Lynn later said. "It was like I saw Garth for the first time and he blew me away. That night at the Bluebird, in an intimate setting, with a real audience, Garth was as good an artist as I'd ever seen."

Lynn immediately walked over to Bob Doyle. "Where did Jim leave this?" He asked.

"We're supposed to stay in touch," Bob answered. Lynn was relieved that Garth was still unsigned.

Shults said he was convinced that Foglesong would guarantee an album contract, as opposed to a singles only, and the two shook hands. Label offers vary in scope. A development deal means the artist gets a producer and the opportunity to work on his or her sound. It works for some, but many languish in endless demo sessions with no end in sight. A singles agreement means that songs will be chosen for hit potential, and if the hits don't come, neither does the album. A guaranteed album at least means a real shot to prove oneself.

A little over a month later, on June 17, Garth signed with Capitol. That presented a problem for Jerry Kennedy. After disagreements with Capitol during the time he produced Mel McDaniel, Kennedy didn't feel that he had good relations with the label. So he bowed out and told Garth he should ask Capitol for a slate of potential producers.

Lynn hoped Garth would choose Allen Reynolds as his producer. He had worked with Reynolds in connection with Jack Clement's JMI (Jack Music Incorporated) in the 1970s and knew him to be a producer who stretched out, was willing to experiment, and who treated his artists with great respect.

"I thought Garth needed that kind of guy at the helm," Lynn noted. "Allen knew how to keep country honest but he was always open to newer or alternative musical influences. I also liked the Cowboy Jack connection. Jack had a way of looking at music that influenced us all. Maybe it was his Sun Records connection, but for Cowboy an album was never just a bunch of songs. It was something bigger. Garth saw things that way, too—your music is a reflection of something inside you."

"Cowboy" Jack Clement first made his name as an engineer/ producer at Sam Phillips's Sun Records working with Elvis

Presley, Jerry Lee Lewis, Johnny Cash, Carl Perkins, and Roy Orbison, among others. When Clement moved to Nashville he worked with Cash and Charley Pride, building several studios throughout town in the process. One of those he sold to a songwriter/producer in his coterie, Allen Reynolds. The two shared this: a love of good music and a suspicion that it was just possible that industry executives could be something less than trustworthy. Out of respect for Clement, Reynolds kept the name: Jack's Tracks.

Allen Reynolds had given up a safe banking job to work with Clement in Memphis, then moved with him to Beaumont, Texas, to open a recording studio. In 1970 Clement came to Nashville with Reynolds and Dickey Lee, a writer ("She Thinks I Still Care"/George Jones) and artist (1962's pop hit "Patches"). Reynolds wound up writing some big songs including "Ready For The Times To Get Better," "I Saw Linda Yesterday" (with Lee, who had a pop hit with the song), and "Five O'Clock World" (a 1966 pop hit for the Vogues). Reynolds's grasp of well-crafted lyrics that tapped into far-reaching topics would play into his production of Don Williams, Crystal Gayle, Kathy Mattea, Emmylou Harris, and Garth Brooks.

On first look, Reynolds is an unlikely comrade for the flamboyant, oft-outrageous Cowboy Jack. Quiet, thoughtful, and thorough, Reynolds preferred to be behind the board in deep thought while musicians and artists took the spotlight. The Cowboy was more often waltzing through the studio strumming on a ukulele. But the two had one thing in common: neither played politics.

Like Lynn Shults, Bob Doyle believed Allen Reynolds was the perfect producer for Garth. "The genius of Allen Reynolds is that his records have a timeless quality to them," Bob said. "If you listen to Crystal Gayle's 'Don't It Make My Brown Eyes Blue,' you'll find that the music is there as a setting for the song," Bob notes. "A Reynolds record isn't about the latest technology—it's about the song."

Since her debut in 1970, Crystal had suffered from a series of records on Decca that showed little of her own vocal character, but were vaguely imitative of her sister Loretta Lynn's style. Crystal moved to United Artists in 1974 with Allen Reynolds as her producer. With the studio freedom Reynolds encouraged, she found her voice and began a hit-making streak that included "Wrong Road Again," "I'll Get Over You," "You Never Miss A Real Good Thing," and "I'll Do It All Over Again."

Then, in 1977, Reynolds put a jazz-flavored touch on her recording of "Don't It Make My Brown Eyes Blue," and it made Loretta Lynn's little sister an international superstar. The song spent four weeks at number 1 on the country chart, and hit number 2 in pop and number 4 in adult contemporary. Crystal took home two Grammy awards: Best Female Country Vocal Performance and Song of the Year. For the next two years she reigned as CMA Female Vocalist, and for three as ACM Female Vocalist.

When his studio business slowed down in the early 1980s, Reynolds briefly considered putting Jack's Tracks on the block and returning to songwriting full-time. Then, he said, he realized that he stood at an important career crossroads. "I finally said to myself, 'I'm gonna stay right here on this corner and make the best music I can, whether anybody wants it or not.' But I also decided to stay as far away from record labels as possible. I wanted to make music away from label interference. My ideal situation was to find an artist I could work with where the label stayed out of my business—the music—and I stayed out of theirs—selling records."

He found just that arrangement working with the eclectic Kathy Mattea, who ran up a string of hits at Steve Popovich's Mercury/PolyGram, including 1987's "Goin' Gone" and '88's signature "Eighteen Wheels And A Dozen Roses." She was the CMA Female Vocalist of the Year in 1989 and 1990.

Reynolds knew the first time he heard Garth sing that he was listening to an important talent. But it went deeper than that.

Reynolds saw Garth as a solidly grounded individual who loved music and took it seriously, someone who wanted to be an artist more than he wanted to be a star. Reynolds thought Garth's value system would hold him steady when stardom arrived. For his part, Garth knew he'd found his producer fifteen minutes into that first meeting. And he came to rely on his producer for sanity in a crazy business.

"There's an angel missing in heaven and his name is Allen Reynolds," Garth confided early in his career. "He knows how important it is to separate the career and the music, but, and this is a big one, he also believes that artists have to pay attention to the business side, and stand their ground when things get crossways. I can always go to his studio and get away from it all. But the best thing about recording with Allen at Jack's Tracks is that he's got this motto: *check your ego at the door.*"

Right away, Garth and Allen started putting together a team of musicians. One of the first people Garth mentioned was bassist Mike Chapman. Reynolds says he was thrilled with the suggestion: "Mike Chapman and drummer Milton Sledge had been friends since childhood. I was a great fan of Milton Sledge, so we brought him on board as well. To have that kind of musical history on the bass and drums was tremendous."

Next, they added Mark Casstevens on acoustic guitar and Chris Leuzinger on electric. Bobby Wood on keyboards rounded out the rhythm section. They then called in Rob Hajacos on fiddle and Bruce Bouton on steel. "That's the core band we had from that day one," Allen Reynolds says. "I thought that we'd make changes from time to time, but Garth was very loyal to these guys, and over the years I came to understand that his instincts were right on."

A few years later Garth talked about working with his customary crew, explaining that he never liked drum loops, metronomes, or any sleight-of-hand studio techniques, and neither did they. "I don't mind making a mistake," he said. "I can come up with some incredibly stupid idea and they'll run with it. And, of course, they feel free to come up with dumb ideas, too. If it works, fine. If not, nobody is keeping score."

One of his primary considerations was that he wanted the group to sometimes sound like a band and not a collection of studio musicians. "Garth likes his music to kick and kick hard, sometimes to the point of suggesting that we put in the kind of musical punches and stops that a bar band would do," Chris Leuzinger explained. "We get away with a lot of things on Garth's records that we wouldn't normally be able to do on a typical Nashville album."

The next step in putting together the debut album was to establish perimeters. Allen Reynolds believed in making music in what was considered by some to be an antiquated method. Even though Jimmy Bowen had ushered in the age of digital technology, where out-of-tune vocals are pitch shifted, or shrugged off with a "fix it in the mix" attitude, Allen preferred analog. He didn't like the idea of dressing up bad songs with studio tricks, either.

"You know the old Jack Clement saying," Allen laughed. "If a song's not good enough to be recorded two-track it's not good enough to be recorded."

Of course, recording at Jack's Tracks was not a two-track experience, but more than any major studio in town, what you heard was what you got. Garth loved the idea of keeping his records real and agreed on the no-nonsense analog approach. Reynolds and Brooks were of like minds when it came to songs, too.

"We determined right away what an album should and should not be," Reynolds says. "It should not be a selection of radio-friendly songs to release as singles, surrounded by filler. An album should be able to stand alone as an actual show. You should be able to get on a stage and sing every song in the sequence that it appears on the album and hold an audience's attention."

CHAPTER FOUR

"I'd have titled it *Randy Travis* if I could have gotten away with it"

I think every song on an album should be a song of conse-quence," Allen Reynolds said.

"Songs of consequence?" Garth repeated, then smiled. "I think I've got 'em."

The next time the two met, Garth put an overflowing box of cassette tapes on Reynolds's desk. "I've been collecting songs ever since I got to Nashville," Garth said. "I've been hitting all the little clubs, the writers nights, the showcases—and these are the best of what I heard. Most of them knocked me to my knees."

"Those are just the kind we're looking for," Reynolds replied.

"I'D BEEN WRITING AS much as possible, but didn't want to overload the album with my own material. No more than five songs, for sure," Garth explained. "I think it works for some writer/artists to record an entire album of their own compositions—but I didn't see myself as a writer of that caliber. I'd been out in the clubs and heard the wealth of material Nashville writers had to offer. Plus, I was afraid of sending the wrong message. I didn't want writers saying, 'Oh, he'll just cut his own stuff' and send their good songs to somebody else."

Reynolds was relieved to hear that Garth's writing ego wasn't going to get in the way of his selections, but he soon learned that the attitude could be a double-edged sword. Garth often hesitated to cut his own songs that Reynolds believed in. "I loved quite a few of Garth's songs and couldn't believe it when he balked at recording some of them," Reynolds says.

"I had to be pushed into cutting 'Not Counting You' because it didn't seem right for me," Garth adds. "I wrote the song for a friend who was trying to get a record deal and wanted exactly that kind of light tune. But I didn't see it as being right for me."

In fact, both Reynolds and Bob Doyle saw the song as classic midtempo country fare, perfect for anyone from Faron Young to George Strait. Reynolds believed in the song so much that, in looking at the album selection as a performance set, he believed it should come first, the show opener. Indeed, Garth opened shows with the song for the next four years.

Although George Jones had considered cutting "If Tomorrow Never Comes," and even had it on hold for a few months, when Garth signed with Capitol Records the song was once again available. At Reynolds's insistence it was included on the debut album. It would have been a serious omission had it not been. The song is what won Garth his record contract and it went on to be one of the most awarded of the time. In 1991 "If Tomorrow Never Comes" was named Favorite Country Single at the American Music Awards. London-based *Country Music People* magazine named it the International Single of the Year, and at the *Music City News* Songwriter Awards the song took home honors as one of the Top 10 songs of the year.

Guitarist Mark Casstevens talked about the importance of being sensitive to the story during the recording of "If Tomorrow Never Comes."

"It's critical that what I play follows the emotion of the story line. That usually means starting with simple parts and voicings and then building them as the story develops." That technique was critical on the intro to "If Tomorrow Never Comes."

"I wanted to play a simple, yet recognizable, part, so I suggested this intro. We ended up making it a turnaround lick that the whole band played." And because Casstevens started out as a banjo player, and plays his guitar with both a thumb pick and his index and middle fingers, a close listen to "Tomorrow" will show the banjo technique where the thumb hits two notes at once.

"If Tomorrow Never Comes" wasn't the only song Reynolds had to sell Garth on. "The Dance" almost didn't make the cut.

"If I was at a writer showcase and heard something, I made sure I either got a tape that night or knew where I could pick one up the next day," Garth said. "And I brought them all to Allen when we started working on my first album. When I came back in a couple of days, he asked me about 'The Dance.' I told him it was one of the best songs I'd ever heard, but that I didn't think it was country. Allen said, 'Country or not, you've got to cut it.'"

There was another initial concern. The song dealt with what must have been an obviously devastating breakup, a hurt Garth hadn't experienced. Later he would see "The Dance" on a deeper level, but at first he wasn't sure if he was the person to convey the meaning. After reflection, he decided that there was no way he could ever personally experience every sentiment in every song he wrote or recorded.

"I don't think a writer *can* live everything he writes about. Of course, sometimes it helps, even if it's something you've heard or learned from a friend or acquaintance," Garth says.

Reynolds advised against trying to *country the record up.* "Allen told me he wanted Bobby Wood, a writer and keyboard player, to be heavily featured on the song," Garth recalled. "I'd never imagined putting keys on the record, and got nervous about it.

But once I heard that haunting track I knew it was right. I'm always in awe of Bobby's playing. He is without a doubt one of the best, most original and innovative I've ever heard."

"Much Too Young (To Feel This Damn Old)" was one of the three songs Garth brought with him when he moved to Nashville. Garth's earlier decision, to change the song twist from musician to rodeo rider, not only made for a more interesting lyric, it established a practice that would continue throughout Garth's recording career. Each album would contain at least one song that dealt with cowboy and rodeo culture, the world Garth had loved growing up in Oklahoma.

Garth knew exactly how he wanted the music played on this song, and it went back to his idea that sometimes the studio band should go for a bar band sound. Mark Casstevens explained that when they recorded "Much Too Young" Garth sometimes borrowed his guitar and played the licks he heard in his mind: "I watched his hands to catch anything that struck me as essential to the song. Then I turn that motif, lick, or melody into a signature part of the song. As a rule you take the best of what is on the demo and you make it better."

Story songs were in abundance on this debut album. "Alabama Clay," written by Larry Cordle and Ronnie Scaife, was one of the fifty or so songs Garth brought to the studio. Here, as in so many great country songs, a small-town boy learns how lonely the city can be and yearns for the feel of dirt between his toes.

"Everytime That It Rains" was another three-minute movie, one Garth penned with his old college roommate, Ty England, and Charley Stefl. Ty reflects that the co-write was an important learning experience. What Garth insisted on, according to Ty, was that they not just tell a story, but they follow it up. Never leave the listener dangling. In this instance, a man reflects on a one-night stand between a traveler and a truck stop waitress. But while Ty believed that told the story, Garth insisted on bringing the song full circle, to another encounter years later, when the two realized that rekindling the flame was futile.

One of the story songs on Garth's debut that continued to resonate over the years was "Cowboy Bill." It's about an old man who tells young neighbors tales of being a Texas Ranger. The kids love him, and the adults snicker at the codger's imagination. Only after he dies does the town learn that the stories were all true.

"Larry Bastian and I were over at Major Bob when he played me that song," Garth says. "He was sitting on a window ledge, with the setting sun shining in. He started singing that story, and I sat there in a trance. Then I literally begged him for the song, even though I didn't have a record deal yet."

Although the song was never a single, it became something of a signature in Garth's career. "Anybody who thinks they should be looking just for songs that might have that radio-hit thing going should take a listen to 'Cowboy Bill,'" Garth said in 1998. "I can't tell you how many times I've heard fans at concerts shouting out, *Play 'Cowboy Bill.'* And I mean *years* after that album came out."

Bastian also contributed "Nobody Gets Off In This Town," written with DeWayne Blackwell. It's classic Bastian/Blackwell wry humor about looking for a drink in a dry county, a good time in a whistle-stop that's lost its steam. Like "Cowboy Bill," this song has remained a fan favorite through the years.

"I worried a little about that song," Garth later said, laughing. "I come from small town America, and I didn't want it to sound like we were making any jokes about it. But as time went by I realized that people got it, that the song wasn't meant to put the experience down. It was just having fun with it."

Since they still needed another song, Allen Reynolds suggested several that Garth had written. "I had a handful of tapes that I really liked," Allen says. "But Garth wasn't buying any of them. He worried that he was getting too much of his material on the album, and he also knew Bob Doyle didn't want it to look like we were too heavy on Major Bob songs. So he asked me if I had any other ideas." Reynolds turned to his old boss,

Jack Clement, and played Garth a tape of a Clement-penned song titled "I Know One." What Allen didn't tell his artist was that the song had been a hit for Jim Reeves in 1960, two years before Garth was born. On the day that Garth was set to record "I Know One," the BBC's Bob Powell was at the studio, and dropped the news. Allen laughs now remembering how Garth felt the pressure, but in the end, everyone, including Cowboy Jack, loved the cut.

"Garth was going up to the studio when Bob mentioned Jim Reeves's hit," Reynolds said. "He almost fell down the stairs."

It was conventional wisdom at the time that newcomers should simply name their first albums after themselves, and feature a good close-up cover shot—all the better to remember them by. So that decision was preordained at Capitol. And when asked why he opted for a self-titled album, Garth replied, "I'd have titled it *Randy Travis* if I could have gotten away with it."

Garth Brooks was well received when it hit the streets on April 12, 1989, but there was no universal ovation. It would take years before critics examined what had really happened with this newcomer's album.

In 1995, *Billboard* editor Edward Morris wrote, "History lesson: Six years ago this month, the most momentous event in modern country music occurred and nobody knew it. On April 12, 1989, Capitol released the self-titled debut album by Garth Brooks. It got good but not ecstatic reviews at the time. The label sensed it had a promising act on its hands, and to demonstrate that point it rented a rehearsal hall near Music Row and invited a few dozen industryites to watch the new kid perform. The audience liked what it saw and heard. Brooks was not flamboyant, but he worked the stage with exquisite confidence and ease. When it came time for introductions, producer Allen Reynolds expressed his pleasure with the album and cracked a joke about how strong-minded Brooks had been in the studio. Then everybody applauded and went home.

"The thing that kept Brooks afloat until he caught fire beyond

his own determination was the across-the-board strength of
that first album. It simply had no throwaway songs or lackluster
performances. The lyrics were vivid, the stories intriguing, the
melodies memorable, the wit restrained and the emotions be-
lievably woven in. If Brooks is ever to be equaled or matched in
artistic and commercial impact, it will take another such powerful collection, one free of vanity, filler and publishing politics."

"Much Too Young (To Feel This Damn Old)" made it to the
Billboard Top 10, and would have gone higher if some radio stations had not refused to play a song containing the word "damn."
It almost didn't make it out of the Top 40. Capitol Records was
a minor Nashville player and lacked the clout to promote several
singles at once when *Garth Brooks* was released in 1989. When
the promotion team traded out "Much Too Young (To Feel
This Damn Old)" to concentrate on a more established artist's
release, it was a watershed moment in Garth's outlook. "I'm
laying there in a fetal position saying, 'This can't be,'" he said
later. "But you come out of it stronger. 'Much Too Young' was
one of the three songs I'd brought to town in '87," he reflected.
"And I think that the first song you get on radio is like a first-
born child. You're very protective of it."

Flying in the face of the label decision to drop the single midchart, Bob Doyle and Pam Lewis hired a team of independent
radio promotion men who pushed it up to Top 10. One Wyoming
radio listener was especially glad the song stuck around.

"I was driving my truck from Kaycee to Casper," recalled
Chris LeDoux. "This song came on by a guy I'd never heard of
before. Garth Brooks. Since the song was about rodeos, I was
really paying attention to it, and thinking, 'Now there's a pretty
good song.' Then I heard a line that went '. . . a worn out tape
of Chris LeDoux,' and I nearly drove my truck off the road. All
kinds of people started asking me about my music!"

Chris LeDoux could have answered a simple "yes" to the
Urban Cowboy question, "Are you a real cowboy?" Chris discov-

ered rodeo at age twelve while his family was living in Austin, Texas, rode his first bareback bronc the following year, and won the Little Britches Rodeo Bareback World Championship in 1964, when he was fourteen.

At the same time he was discovering a love for music, and by the time he started high school he was composing songs on harmonica and guitar. His first: "Participial Phrases—I Wonder What They Is." Talk about a writer who loved words. He wrote and sang so much during his rodeo career that people started asking to purchase tapes, and he was soon selling his music from the back of his truck out on the rodeo circuit. Eventually he became not just an underground but a galactic hero, when NASA used Chris's version of the Marty Robbins classic "Cowboy In A Continental Suit" to awaken Colonel James Anderson during a space shuttle *Atlantic* flight.

But the part of Chris LeDoux's story that Garth Brooks most loved involved his 1976 world championship bronc ride. Chris was in sorry shape in 1975, having injured his collarbone and torn ligaments already damaged by high school football. Chris, who had often joked about the idea of people riding mechanical bulls, decided to rig up a backyard bucking bronc machine. "I figured out a new way to tape my leg and shoulder, modified a garbage can, then got people to pull the ropes and help me ride out the pain. By the time I got to Oklahoma City for the 1976 finals, I was feeling pretty good, but way down in the rankings.

"There's a 'bidding' that goes on at big rodeos. People put up money as bets, and they win or lose as does the contestant. They bought me for peanuts," Chris laughed.

For his final ride Chris drew Stormy Weather, considered by far the toughest bronc in the competition. Taped together and gritting his teeth against the pain, Chris climbed on and hung on. When the bell rang out Chris LeDoux was the world champion bareback bronc rider.

In part, Garth's insistence on using a rodeo song reflected a western attitude that is different from simply a "country" outlook. Chris LeDoux once put it best:

"It's a lot like the West itself. It's wide-open spaces and big skies. It's a love of freedom and a dislike of boundaries. It's a willingness to take a chance on a game or a piece of land or eight-second ride: having the grit and the guts to go for it."

Chris once spoke privately about his belief that Garth's music embodied his definition of a western attitude.

"From the first time I heard 'Much Too Young (To Feel This Damn Old)' I paid attention to Garth's music—the songs and the performances. If you listen to his albums over the years, he's that poet and dreamer I believe lives within a cowboy's heart. But he's also got the grit to go for broke. He takes chances on his records and in his shows. Nothing is safe with this guy. I've seen him take some hard body blows, take the knocks with no regret, then tape himself together and make the ride."

Just a year after Chris heard himself lauded in song on country radio, in April 1990, Garth and Chris played their first show together at the Cocky Bull in Victorville, California. Chris spoke to the *Dallas Morning News*' Michael Corcoran: "The first time I met Garth, I wanted to thank him for the recognition, for everything he's done for me. But before I could say anything, Garth thanked me. He told me that his career has really taken off since my name was on one of his songs!"

What Garth really got from Chris was tacit approval for the way his live show was evolving. There was no doubt that Chris LeDoux was singing cowboy songs backed up with a rock 'n' roll performance. The energy level transcending most country shows was conspicuous. Garth's own show was full-tilt boogie, but after exposure to Chris, he kicked it up a notch. Garth called it "country with muscle" and laughed that he stole all his moves from Chris LeDoux. He paid tribute to the rodeo star by saying at each show, "God bless Chris LeDoux."

When one examines the reasons that '90s country music broke so many album and ticket records that it ruled rock,

Garth's record sales are one part, but the road show he says he stole from Chris LeDoux is of equal if not greater importance.

Garth's road band, Stillwater, was a solid group, but unlike the musicians he used in the studio, there were few Nashville insiders. A couple of Oklahoma boys were included. Dave Gant, from Ada, played keyboards, fiddle, and added harmonies. He was classically trained in the viola, and had played for Reba McEntire when she was still an unknown Oklahoma girl dreaming of coming to Nashville.

Garth kept the promise to call his old Oklahoma State roommate Ty England when he had something to offer. In fact, on the very day he signed with Capitol, he phoned Ty.

"I called him up and asked him if he wanted to come out," Garth said.

Ty was hesitant at first, because he finally had a good job with benefits, a car, and a secure future. "I had cold feet. I had faith in Garth, but I never had faith in myself. I asked him if I could think about it." The next day Ty called to tell Garth he was on his way to Nashville. He gave his notice at work and was on the road in his 1954 Chevy two weeks later.

"Ty quit a thirty-five-thousand-dollar-a-year job with a company car and came out and worked for a hundred dollars a week," Garth said. It was a leap of faith of Music City proportions. And it worked out.

Garth had met electric guitar and fiddle player James Garver, a Kansas transplant, at Cowtown Boots, and after asking him to come on board, James brought up fellow Kansan Steve McClure's name. "He's the greatest steel player I ever worked with," James said. Then, through Steve, Garth found his drummer. "I told Steve I was looking for a high-energy drummer who can cut a new path," Garth said. Steve replied, "I've got your guy, a Plant City, Florida, boy named Mike Palmer." Tim Bowers rounded out the band on bass guitar and background vocals. A singer/ songwriter from High Point, North Carolina, he'd played with Billy "Crash" Craddock for eleven years.

From the beginning, Garth and the band held quick post-show meetings to talk about what went right and what went wrong. "We do that within the first five minutes when we come off," Garth told the *Atlanta Journal-Constitution* at the time. "It's almost like a confessional with us saying we're sorry we did this or that—or that something ain't working. We are a band—not just an artist. It's important to have people around you who don't fear you. You need people who'll walk up to you and tell you when you're wrong and not worry about getting fired."

In 1990 Garth talked about Stillwater to the *Gavin Report:* "They're not just a bunch of guys that are looking for a job that pays more money than the next one. They work for the dream. They still remember the basement. They still remember what we all joined out here to do, and that was to take music to the people."

That same year he joked to *Music City News,* "The band's contract is that if they leave, I have to kill them."

IT DIDN'T TAKE LONG for Garth to tell Joe Harris that he wanted Stillwater to accompany him to shows. Even though he had a single on the charts, he was virtually unknown.

"The guys need to work, they need to eat," Garth said.

This presented a problem. Record labels generally agreed to pay a certain amount of tour support for artists but not for their bands. Joe Harris had already broken with company policy by agreeing to represent an artist without a record label; now he was faced with another dilemma: either get enough money from promoters or risk offending Capitol Records by asking for tour support.

But Harris also knew that Garth would be a much more valuable act with Stillwater. "The normal procedure was for a club owner or promoter to provide an artist with a local band," Joe explained. "Sometimes this caused the artist to look bad, if the band's timing was off or if the musicians weren't familiar with the material. I even saw George Strait backed by a rock and roll band one night. It was really hard on the artist not knowing what they had to work with at each new gig. Garth and his management had a plan, a strategy, and it worked. When he and Stillwater went out on the road they were tight. Garth and his band were well rehearsed, and their performance proved that."

Harris approached fair producer Variety Attractions and convinced the company to work with his newcomer. But Garth's insistence on taking Stillwater with him on early road trips set a precedent. As Harris noted: "Some people blamed Garth for this. It was the beginning of people claiming he 'changed the business.' If so, that was a change for the better."

Garth's live show started to draw crowds simply by word of mouth, a "hard ticket" act. "My job became a lot easier every time a promoter saw Garth perform," Joe Harris said. "That guy would talk to the next guy and so it would go. I started hearing back from people that the fans were also passing along the word. That's a booker's dream." Not content to stand and sing, Garth moved all over the stage, horsed around with band members, interacted with the audience, and in general, turned the performance into a party where fans felt like welcome guests and joined in the revelry.

On August 10, 1989, Garth headlined a show at Tulsa City Limits. John Wooley, music critic at the *Tulsa World,* wrote, "After seeing what he can do in concert, I'll go out on a limb and predict that Brooks, showman and talent that he is, is going to be country music's next big thing." As it turned out, the limb was pretty solid.

The following month Garth would start to transform into the next big thing with his second single release, his deal-maker, "If Tomorrow Never Comes." For this one, Capitol decided to spring for a video. Recording the song had come naturally for Garth, but making a video was another story. "When I see myself on TV I throw things at the television," he laughed. "When you see yourself on TV you realize that it's not how you see yourself. I swear to you that I do not have double chins! And I know I've got more hair than shows up on television!"

Garth also instinctively understood some of the pitfalls of the video medium. "Onstage every singer is a three-minute actor," he said. "You live it every time you sing it. But the flip side of this is that you make certain faces while you are singing, that are heartfelt but still don't look good on camera."

Despite his own misgivings and the short period of time and a small budget allotted to shoot the video for "If Tomorrow Never Comes," it was a top-flight piece of film work. Sandy Brooks is featured in the video, and Steve Gatlin's daughter Aubrie plays the child. And playing the dual role of singer and husband/father turned out to be easier than Garth had thought. "It felt comfortable to be on camera with Sandy and Aubrie," he said. "They put me at ease."

"If Tomorrow Never Comes" opened with a shot of a small girl playing in front of a farmhouse and fades to Garth singing. As it turned out, using that particular house was serendipitous. "When Sandy and I first moved to Nashville, we'd drive around town looking at houses we particularly liked," Garth explained. "One of them was a wonderful 'mail order' house that had been brought to Tennessee in pieces and built in the 1920s. We used to park the truck and just sit and stare at that place. Then, when the video director, John Lloyd Miller, brought in a picture of the house he'd found for 'If Tomorrow Never Comes,' it was *that* house!"

Like the single, this video was an award winner, one of three included on a compilation winning Best Selling Music Video at the NARM (National Academy of Recorded Music) Best Seller Awards in 1991.

GARTH BROOKS ULTIMATELY BECAME the biggest-selling country album of the '80s, and established Garth as a serious contender in Nashville's star struggle. But it was not 1989's big news. Clint Black's *Killin' Time* was the headline grabber. Black's first five releases topped the singles charts, helping *Killin' Time* stay ensconced at number 1 on *Billboard*'s country album chart for thirty-one weeks. Clint had everything Garth did not: high-powered management, extensive financial backing, and movie star looks. Moreover, he was signed with the mighty RCA, which Chet Atkins had built into a superpower while Capitol's country division was still being run out of Ken Nelson's back pocket in L.A.

There were other artists who made an impact that same year, who became known as "the Class of '89." Travis Tritt's debut single, "Country Club," installed the young Georgia native as a fixture on the charts. Tritt was an unlikely success story. He had no real contacts, no money backers (no new artist did when compared to the $1 million ZZ Top manager Bill Hamm allegedly put behind Clint Black), and no established producer. But working with upstart Gregg Brown, Tritt put together a stellar project and Warner Bros. snapped him up. "Country Club" skated right around the edges of Waylon's country and Hank Jr.'s Southern rock, so both two-steppers and rockers lapped it up.

A late starter by mere months, Tritt's fellow Georgian Alan Jackson also scored big with his debut album, *Here In The Real World*. Unlike Tritt, Jackson had some heavy-duty help awaiting him in Nashville. Glen Campbell, who'd been handed a demo tape in an airport by Jackson's flight attendant spouse, sent him to his own publishing company, headed by longtime Nashville figure Marty Gamblin. The Jacksons moved to Nashville, where Alan took a job in the Nashville Network mail room, spending every spare moment writing and trying to get his music heard. Many of the people Alan worked with at TNN wouldn't have bet a nickel on his chances for success. He seemed shy, lacking in the drive and charisma usually associated with stardom. Later, one prominent TNN executive privately confessed that every tape Alan had given him had ended up in the trash can, unheard.

Finally, after signing a management deal with publisher Barry Coburn, Jackson became the first artist signed to the newly formed Arista Records headed by Tim DuBois. The two, Jackson and DuBois, were destined to become two of Nashville's most important figures. Oklahoma-born DuBois was a highly regarded songwriter ("Love In The First Degree" and "When I Call Your Name") and producer when, in 1989, music executive Clive Davis asked him to open a Nashville branch of Arista. The label had attempted to promote country artist Tanya Tucker from New York some years earlier, and it hadn't worked. Tanya only charted two singles before leaving Arista, signing with Capitol three years later.

Making Alan Jackson his first choice was a first-class move on DuBois's part. He ignored the sometimes almost self-demeaning manner and spotted a star. Jackson donned a cowboy hat, opened up enough to show the public his amicable and often witty persona, and won over any doubters. His classic country writing and traditional styling took radio by storm with career-making hits in 1990, particularly "Here In The Real World" and "Chasin' That Neon Rainbow."

Although not technically considered part of the Class of '89, several others deserve mention. Columbia Records' Mary Chapin Carpenter had been quietly making inroads since *Hometown Girl,* her folk-oriented debut in 1987. "Quittin' Time," from 1989's *State Of The Heart* made it to number 7, then "Down At The Twist And Shout," from *Shooting Straight from the Heart* climbed to number 2 in 1991. As a writer/artist, she stood in the ranks of Rosanne Cash and Pam Tillis.

Joe Diffie released his first single in 1990, the number 1 "Home," followed by chart-toppers including "If You Want Me To," "If The Devil Danced In Empty Pockets," and "New Way (To Light Up An Old Flame)." Diffie had been one of Nashville's most-sought-after demo singers when he signed with Epic Records. One of the finest traditionalists in the honky-tonk vein, Diffie's album debut, *A Thousand Winding Roads,* was a country music history lesson, with styling often reminiscent of Haggard, Jones, and Frizzell.

Lionel Cartwright started playing music at age ten, became proficient on ten instruments, and as a high school student was already a regular on live country radio shows in his native West Virginia. After working his way through college, Lionel started playing on the WWVA Wheeling Jamboree before making the move to Nashville. Signed by Tony Brown to MCA, his 1989 debut album made no waves, but the following year *I Watched It All on My Radio* yielded two Top 10 hits, followed by *Chasin' the Sun* in 1991 and a number 1, "Leap Of Faith."

Lionel is an accomplished writer and vocalist. But in many ways, he suffered the same fate that Capitol's Billy Dean would a couple of years later. He was too pretty. One veteran media figure said he lacked "the sweat factor." But in the end, it wasn't his lack of a sweat factor that sunk Lionel Cartwright's chart hopes. It was that he tried to take charge of his own career— a no-no in some Nashville circles. It had worked during the Outlaw Movement of the 1970s, when Willie and Waylon had the clout to effect change. Less so through the 1980s.

Artists in Nashville tended to learn hard lessons about trying to exert any real control over their careers. Promotion and marketing departments wield tremendous power within most record labels. Label heads and A&R departments sign artists and usually play a role, along with artists and managers, in picking material. But other divisions can make or break an artist and an album. If, for example, the promotion department dislikes the song an artist wants sent out as a single, the artist should beware. A preliminary warning from promotion gives perfect cover if a song stalls out on the chart. And if marketing is disinterested in an artist or unsure of a strategic approach, sales reflect it. If a label head is particularly behind an artist, he may step in. But not always.

A good example of how the relationship between divisions ought to work involves Nashville executive Randy Goodman, who was Joe Galante's second in command at RCA. Goodman, who now runs Disney's Lyric Street Records in Nashville, went with his boss in 1990 when Galante returned to New York to run RCA's pop division for four years. During his time in New York, Goodman was approached by one of the company's marketing men about the Dave Matthews Band. Goodman went out to hear their show and was impressed. "Sign them," he said.

"Well, we love them too," the marketer said. "But we just don't have any idea what to do with them."

"But that's your job, isn't it?" Goodman answered, making the line of demarcation very clear.

Goodman kept watch over the label's handling of Dave Matthews, and of course, in the end RCA had another major act on their roster.

Image is another area where an artist often faces challenges. Public relations departments can make dangerous changes when it comes to the way an artist is presented to the public. One young female singer was the subject of countless glamour photo sessions as her label readied her debut album. Her press kit showed her to be ultrafeminine and sexualized. To the public, she looked very *Cosmopolitan*. In reality, she was closer to *Outdoor Life*. She preferred carefree hairstyles and little makeup, and often dressed in military-style shorts and T-shirts. None of this, of course, had anything to do with the fact that she was a singular musical talent. When she began playing the clubs where country singers get their start, promoters began to call Nashville with complaints.

"Who the hell is this little hippie chick singer? The photo you sent me showed her in some contraption that looked like a bra."

The image problem reared its head early in Garth's career, but this time it concerned the press, not the record label. With the emergence of three presumably viable artists in cowboy hats, the press seized on a term to replace "Class of '89": *hat acts*. Garth Brooks, for one, hated the term, thinking it stereotyped them and demeaned the western traditions found within their music.

"I don't like labeling things," he said. "Sticking people or music into little boxes just so it's easier to talk or write about makes no sense. Everything has layers, textures, and that's where the beauty of it comes in."

It was one of the "hat acts," Clint Black, whose debut album captured the most attention when it was released, and it was he who was named the Country Music Association Male Vocalist of the Year in 1990, when Garth took home the Horizon Award, for newcomers.

Everybody loves a horse race, and that's what the media attempted to set up between Brooks and Black once Garth proved to be an able adversary. The two were often compared, with Black usually winning by a nose. Several magazines even approached the artists to pose together, almost in combative mode.

"This is messed up," Garth confided. "There's no conflict between Clint and me—why act like there is? I love Clint Black music and I hope he likes mine. The whole thing sounds like some kind of a setup or a game, and I am not going to play." Garth wisely turned down the photo ops, continuing to build his fan base on the road.

There was an initial bump in Garth's relationship with the press when the story of Sandy Brooks's fist-through-the-bathroom-wall spun out of control. Always candid to a fault, Garth mentioned it to a newsperson, and once that horse was out of the stall, it ran. Garth's family, of course, had long known about it. It was an amusing incident that showed the new family member was a woman to be reckoned with. And in the end, that's how America looked at it. When it first grabbed headlines, Garth was aghast to see a funny family story become tabloid fodder, and feared it would in some way tar his wife. Sandy, of course, was made of strong stuff and couldn't be brought down by the flurry of stories.

★   ★   ★

GARTH PLAYED A SERIES of important shows in 1989 when he opened for superstar Kenny Rogers: the Philadelphia Civic Center; the Northfork Theatre at Westbury, New York; and the Fox Theatre in Detroit. Although Rogers hadn't had a chart-topper in two years, he remained one of the genre's biggest stars. What Garth saw impressed him. "Kenny treated his opening acts with great respect," reflects Bob Doyle. "They didn't have to worry that they wouldn't get a decent sound check, or that they would be ignored on the tour. Kenny made it a point to get to know his opening acts, to appreciate their music and to let them know about it. He also treated his band and crew very well. Through all the tours of the 1990s, no matter how big Garth's career got, I never saw him do anything less."

Unfortunately, out there on the road Garth ran into the oldest problem in the world: another woman. Garth counted on the "code of the road" to protect him. Bands and crews usually keep indiscretions to themselves—what happens on the road stays on the road. But too many within his circle were very loyal to Sandy. And when word got back to her, suffice it to say she was not amused. On November 4, 1989, she called her touring husband and laid down the law. The next night on tour in Missouri, Garth broke down onstage, explaining his emotions to his fans by saying that his marriage was in trouble and he was to blame. When he finished that concert run, Garth headed home where Sandy again explained that it was "my way or the highway." Garth said, "Your way."

In 1993 Garth talked to Rolling Stone's Anthony DeCurtis about what had gone wrong. He explained that when he had left Sandy to come to Nashville in 1985, he'd envisioned himself as becoming a hot guy around town, surrounded by girls. When he went home to Oklahoma and got married, he believed he'd matured. Once he got a record deal, he learned otherwise. In the end he regretted his actions not only because of Sandy, but because of friends he'd expected to cover up his deception.

"I was playing in a ballpark that I had no license to play in. But another thing was, I had some great friendships that I ruined because I pushed them over the line of friendship, and now I don't get to talk with those people anymore. And I learned a lot from those people because as human beings they were cool. So apologies to both need to be made. I was fortunate enough to be given a second chance."

Did he see the infidelity as a natural part of being a musician on the road?

"I don't see it as a necessity. Anybody starting out saying, 'Man, it has to happen'—bullshit. It doesn't. I'll put it this way: If I was a lawyer, it would probably have happened the same way. I think it had more to do with a guy growing up and accepting the responsibilities of marriage than it had to do with somebody playing music."

If Garth thought his mother would stay out of this fray, he was wrong. Colleen was always willing to tell her son the unvarnished truth. Colleen's main worry was that Garth didn't understand why it had happened and how to guard against temptations in the future.

So she sat him down and asked him if he knew the difference between an isolated incident and an actual *affair.* Garth's face reddened. "Well, I guess an affair keeps on going."

"That's right," Colleen continued. "And you didn't have an affair. What you had was an infatuation with an older woman who treated you like no one has before, made you feel like a man of the world and very exciting. Son, you could be the ugliest man in the world, but in that spotlight you're going to find hundreds of women who'll make you think you are the handsomest man on the face of this earth. It's the spotlight. Don't fall for it."

From then on Garth made Sandy an integral part of his career. When possible, she traveled with him. He not only brought her to industry events and awards shows, he took her with him on the stage when he won. Sandy, in fact, started to become nearly as much a public figure as her husband.

With his marriage starting to mend, Garth thought his troubles were behind him. He always believed that no matter what Nashville said, his audiences would tell him the truth. And audiences told him that "The Dance" was a hit.

"I think 'The Dance' is definitely right for a single," he told Allen Reynolds. "The audiences are really responding to it." He was so excited at the prospect of taking the song out to country radio that he started thinking about some ideas for a video.

On December 9 "If Tomorrow Never Comes" hit number 1.

But trouble was brewing on another front, and Capitol Records was just about to be thrown into a tailspin.

CHAPTER FIVE

"Watch your back, pal"

L ynn Shults pulled into a parking space, slunk out of his car, and trudged into the bar. He planned on getting drunk. Not just any old garden-variety drunk, either. He planned on getting blitzed, hammered beyond recognition, bust-up-the-bar drunk, bust-your-ass-and-still-lose-your-job drunk.

He found his fellow pink-slipped Capitol staffers still in shock and contemplating their bleak futures in an industry that wasn't hiring. One of them had placed his Capitol Records corporate credit card on the table, offering to put every drink on the card as an adios to corporate duplicity.

"Hell yes," Lynn said. "Let's drink the best damned booze they've got and charge it to Jimmy Bowen."

ON DECEMBER 11, JIMMY Bowen took over Capitol Records and fired all employees but two, who were left to sit alone in the empty building once Jim Foglesong, Lynn Shults, and the rest of the staff had been ousted. It was the second time Bowen had told Foglesong to hit the bricks, the first being in 1984 during an MCA takeover.

Bowen had moved from L.A. to Nashville in the late 1970s, learning the country end of the business from Outlaw Tompall

Glaser. He soon convinced an old friend, MCA Records' Mike Maitland, to name him vice president and general manager of the label's Nashville branch, replacing Jim Foglesong. One of his first tasks as a power broker was to begin the upgrading of Nashville's analog studios to state-of-the-art digital. As Bowen often laughed, "I taught the hillbillies how to make a forty-thousand-dollar record for two hundred thousand."

Bowen hadn't stayed long at MCA the first time around, accepting a job at Elektra/Asylum after only a few months at MCA. Over the years Bowen would head MCA, Elektra/Asylum, Warner Bros., Universal, and Capitol. And while his first stay at MCA was short, he usually stayed about five years at a company before moving on. He almost always brought his own team to the labels he took over. The word that Bowen was sniffing around a company prompted night sweats among staff.

Despite some grudging admiration for Bowen's making many of Nashville studios state-of-the-art, a sizable contingent feared him, considered him as tough an executive as the town had ever seen. And while he had been accused of publishing conflicts, as a label head, Bowen once famously said, "If you get the music right, you don't have to steal a penny."

In fact, Bowen appeared to wage a battle against producers using songs they owned on their artists' albums, decrying the practice loudly and repeatedly. For many, the real issue involved just how and why Bowen always ended up producing the big-money acts at every label he ran.

This latest takeover had started during Bowen's second run at MCA Nashville. Like most of Bowen's deals, the Capitol deal had roots in L.A.'s pop world, where Bowen had old friends and old enemies. Al Teller fell into the latter category, and when he was named president of MCA Records, Bowen knew his reign as head of the label's country division was in jeopardy. Bowen didn't like Teller. He believed him to have both a lack of respect for the music and an ego problem. And as Bowen wrote in his 1997 memoir, "I wasn't going to kiss his ring—or his butt."

Bowen went higher up and started a joint venture with the head of MCA Music Entertainment Group, Irving Azoff. MCA funded the new label, Universal Records, and as part of Bowen's deal he was allowed to start a publishing company, Great Cumberland Music. Of course, that set tongues wagging about label/publishing collusion, but Bowen never minded gossip. Universal signings favored established artists including Lacy J. Dalton, Eddie Rabbitt, Eddie Raven, Gary Morris, Larry Gatlin and the Gatlin Brothers, and the Nitty Gritty Dirt Band.

Although Universal had sales and critical success with the Dirt Band's *Will The Circle Be Unbroken II,* the label had trouble with radio. Lacy J. Dalton's "The Heart" hit number 13 in 1989 and that was about it. Once rumors started flying that the label hadn't received the amount of funding it had anticipated, Music Row observers figured that Universal was a wash.

With Universal apparently under a deathwatch Bowen approached EMI and suggested he could fix Capitol Nashville. Jim Foglesong had long been perceived as a less than aggressive marketer, something Bowen could never be accused of. So Bowen promised to have Capitol viewed as a major label within six months, vowing that Capitol would be making $50 million to $60 million with a 10 to 15 percent profit a year in seven years.

Capitol had potential as far as Bowen could see. He had passed on Garth Brooks when Bob Doyle made his pitch a year earlier. But when he heard "If Tomorrow Never Comes" on the radio, he thought it sounded familiar. Then he remembered the intense kid from Oklahoma, whose second single was catching fire. Bowen approached Allen Reynolds at a party Waylon Jennings threw for some friends. "I really screwed up," Bowen told him. "I didn't get what a talent Garth Brooks is."

In one of the most astonishing cases of a secret well kept, Bowen actually started promoting Garth Brooks while he was still negotiating with EMI. He called his Universal promotion team together a couple of months before the takeover, and gave them their instructions:

"Every time you talk to a radio station, after you give them the Universal pitch, tell them that when all is said and done, Garth Brooks is what's making news in Nashville."

Some of the Universal team said they felt guilty when talking to Capitol promo pals. "They'd say radio was telling them that other labels were singing Garth's praises," one said. "I knew what was coming and it made me feel like hell." But nobody talked out of school, and nobody connected the Bowen dots.

Bowen believed that a marketing push and expanded roster would right the Capitol ship, not to mention new employees. "I needed a staff with a proud, kick-butt attitude. There's a negativity that comes off being a perennial loser," he later wrote.

Label head Jim Foglesong would be an obvious casualty. But Bowen knew that firing Lynn Shults, the likeable around-town guy who was credited with Brooks's signing, would make him enemies. But as Bowen often said, he'd rather be successful than popular on Music Row, and besides, he planned on bringing his Universal A&R guy, James Stroud, with him, along with the label's roster.

Capitol employees felt as if they'd been body slammed, and left their building in shock. There had been no warning that a tsunami was headed straight at them. The label wasn't making money, but sales were flat all over town.

Despite the fact that country music was in an exciting time creatively, the hit singles and innovative records were not bringing out a record-buying public in droves. Most labels on the Row were nervous, and not in the mood to hire. The group of people who'd been let go perceived their prospects as slim to none.

Lynn Shults, in particular, was devastated. Every A&R person in the business wants a legacy, that one great successful discovery he or she can point to with pride. The day he was fired, Lynn knew two things: Garth Brooks was on the verge of a career that would put Capitol Records on the map and Jimmy Bowen was going to grab the credit. Shults went on to work at *Billboard* and Atlantic Records, but he never really got over walking out the door at Capitol Records that day in December 1989.

When word reached Garth, he was shaken. "I'd never heard of a wipeout like that—so many people losing their jobs at once," he said. "I had no clue what to expect from Jimmy Bowen. When I talked to Allen Reynolds, he said, 'Watch your back, pal.'"

Two days after the takeover Bowen phoned Reynolds and asked for a meeting. Bowen had a history of doing business from his Franklin Road mansion. Or, once in a while he had his driver stop by offices and pick people up for a rolling meeting through Music Row. He didn't like offices, and, some said, if he was actually in the office people took note of the amount of time he spent on the golf course. In Bowen's defense, a lot of business got done on Nashville's golf courses. Bowen offered to pick up Reynolds in his chauffeured Town Car.

"I don't hear anything else on this album," Bowen said. "I'd like you to get me a new one ready by February. Can you do that?"

"No," Reynolds answered. "We can't do that and measure up to our standards."

"Then how soon can you get one ready? Can you do it by June?"

"Yes," Reynolds said. "But before you leave this album, you really should listen again. There's some more great music there, and one song in particular, called 'The Dance.' Garth is doing it live and the audience loves it. I know he wants it as a single."

Reynolds talked at length about "The Dance" and its ability to reach a range of emotions. "It's a song that will help distinguish Garth from the competition," he concluded.

Bowen dropped off Reynolds at the studio, promising to give the album another listen.

He called back a few hours later and said, "Two more singles."

THE CAPITOL BUILDING STOOD empty for some time, producing a deathlike atmosphere on Music Row. Bowen waited for

the air to clear, then started putting together a staff. One of
the first aboard was Cathy Gurley, president of Gurley & Co.
Public Relations, who had handled Bowen's media through the
Universal days. She would play a critical role in much of Garth's
early career, but especially during his first major controversy,
the "Thunder Rolls" video.

After Bowen went out to one of Garth's shows he again called
Reynolds and asked for another of those Town Car meetings.

"Allen, I just got back from seeing Garth play live at Tennessee
Tech in Cookeville. The kid's a natural—a true natural. We
don't have many of those. You're lucky if you know one in a
lifetime. What I want you to do as you make this album is to get
as much as you possibly can of that guy I saw onstage onto that
recording. Get as much of that energy as you can capture!"

Reynolds says it was the best mandate he could have hoped
for. "Nashville was a pretty conservative town then," Reynolds
reflects. "I don't know of another recording CEO who would
have said what Bowen did. What it meant was that we could
make the music we wanted to make without worrying about
label and radio filters. It meant we could have all the fun we
wanted to—and we did."

Bowen knew that he had a superstar in the pipeline, and began
to fuel the career in earnest. He hired the L.A. firm owned by
Sandy and David Brokaw to help boost Capitol's image in general, and Garth's in particular. The Brokaws, one of the most
effective teams in the business, got Garth exposure on telethons,
at fairs, and even a choice spot on *Night of 1,000 Stars* at Radio
City in New York. The *1,000 Stars* show was one of Garth's first
experiences in rubbing elbows with nonmusic celebrities. On one
elevator ride, he stood next to Muhammad Ali and confessed that
he could barely catch his breath. Later, while the show's taping
went on, Garth sneaked off to a pay phone where he could call his
parents out of earshot from the other participants.

"You won't believe all the stars here!" he whispered, hastily
hanging up when a group of people ambled by.

Doyle and Lewis were busily setting up press opportunities and radio station meet-and-greets as well. The Doyle/Lewis team's importance during these early years cannot be overstated; Pam, in particular, was a street fighter when it came to her artist. "Pam and I did everything we could to get Garth known," Bob Doyle laughs. "Sometimes I felt like we were Mickey Rooney and Judy Garland, saying, 'Let's put on a show!'"

Bowen then brought in a high-powered marketer. Because he loved to make noise in Nashville's executive suites, he went outside the country end of the business and hired Joe Mansfield, who had started out with CBS Records working with Barbra Streisand, Pink Floyd, the Pointer Sisters, Hall & Oates, and Jefferson Starship. He left CBS to develop CEMA, EMI's distribution arm in Los Angeles, where, as VP of marketing, he was instrumental in breaking Bonnie Raitt, Heart, Hammer, Poison, and Tina Turner.

Mansfield was named Capitol/Nashville's VP of sales and marketing, and the way he saw it, his first charge was to get *Garth Brooks* in as many stores as possible. Under Foglesong, the label had shipped a mere thirty-thousand units. Both Bowen and Mansfield were aghast at the lack of a serious sales push. "I give Jimmy Bowen a lot of credit for the free hand he gave me when it came to marketing Garth," Mansfield said. "I believed in keeping his debut album, *Garth Brooks,* alive even as we started marketing the follow-up album. It took a leap of faith on Bowen's part to okay that budget."

A lot of insiders thought Mansfield was crazy to start heavy promotion on Garth's debut while a new album was coming within months. But Mansfield refused to dump *Garth Brooks.* He believed the buyers were out there, and he planned on getting them on board. In Texas especially, where live music ruled, he found fertile ground. He shipped more records, and once "The Dance" kicked in, sales soared.

Mansfield believed two marketing strategies could play well for Garth's career: maximizing the catalog and event marketing.

After all, a good part of Capitol's wealth had been built on catalog items from acts such as the Beatles, Frank Sinatra, Nat King
Cole, Pink Floyd, and Steve Miller. While many labels tended
to ignore catalog, an artist's entire body of previously released
work, it was at their peril. Further, lessons could be learned from
the role television exposure had played in breaking out Capitol's
biggest-selling act, the Beatles. Anything and everything having
to do with the Fab Four became an event. And years later, when
the label looked to the band's catalog, they understood that without radio airplay, new marketing strategies had to be considered.

"There's no reason—especially for an artist like Garth—to
turn your back on the previous album just because a new one is
coming out," Mansfield said. "That's one reason I don't buy into
that album-every-year concept. I think you end up leaving both
singles and sales on the table. Every new release can generate
renewed interest in the previous one. And as the catalog grows,
I see it as a whole artistic package, not just a series of records."

That was music to Garth's ears. When Bowen had briefly
considered ceasing to promote the debut album, *Garth Brooks,*
he'd been horrified. "So much great music has been forgotten
because labels either didn't give them the attention they needed
or shelved them for the *next thing,*" Garth explained. "Through
my life I've run across wonderful albums that nobody ever heard
of because they either got overshadowed or ignored. What I
hoped to do—what I set out to try and do—was record a body
of work that fit together, could be heard from the perspective of
the times of an artist's life."

For that reason, Mansfield was no fan of greatest-hits packages, especially those released after just a few years of hit making.
"Think about the *songs* that get lost because of greatest-hits
albums," he said. "Some of the finest songs on an album are
never released as singles for one reason or another. They might
not quite fit into the radio niche, or they might run too long.
When you issue a hits package and discourage people from hearing the original collection, I think it diminishes the craft."

For Garth, it meant something else: protection for songwriters. When a writer has a song on an album and it's not released as a single, they are paid "mechanical" royalties, based on the number of albums sold. Singles royalties are paid per times played on the radio, plus for sold copies. There are in Nashville, as with the entire industry, many writers who have hundreds of album cuts, but not many singles for the reasons Mansfield noted. Garth felt close ties to the writing community and many of the songs he most loved from his own releases were not the singles, but the album cuts. By keeping the albums in play, the continued sales benefited him, certainly, but the writing and publishing community as well.

Mansfield also understood that Garth was a natural for event marketing, television specials, widely promoted concerts, and appearances. "He had the personality to pull that off," Mansfield said. "He was a real guy, smart, honest—sometimes to a fault— and people loved him for that. Some artists start to lose their luster as people are around them. Familiarity often breeds contempt. But I noticed that for the people Garth interacted with it was exactly the opposite. The more people got to know him the more they liked him as both an artist and a person. We couldn't get him out to meet every fan personally, but we could bring him into their homes through television, and bring his shows to their venues."

Nobody was happier about Bowen hiring Mansfield than Bob Doyle. "I've always thought that the genius of a great record executive was when they understood that an artist knew *who* and *what* he was, and said, 'Okay, let's give him the resources to make this work.' That's how Joe Mansfield looked at Garth's career."

The longer Garth spent working with Mansfield, the more he trusted him. The two only had one real disagreement in those first months. "I believed that the price of each CD should be raised by one dollar," Mansfield recalled. "When we did it, Garth told me that he saw it as a hardship on the consumer. So I said, 'I'll give you back a dollar for every fan who complains.'

"Garth immediately told me that he'd already had one fan question the decision. I handed him a dollar and told him to send it to the fan. In the end, I don't believe his fans paid much attention to the price change. But it was a concern for him."

Although Garth had never been the marketing major so many reporters were determined to claim, he was a quick study and loved being an integral part of both planning and execution. It never occurred to Garth that his "key man" at the label could be jerked from the equation as quickly as his original Capitol team had been.

Allen and Garth were convinced that "The Dance" should be the fourth single, so that left number three to pick. Since Garth hadn't even been sure that "Not Counting You" belonged on the album, he was surprised that it was chosen. But it was probably the wise choice. It was midtempo, with an infectious melody and strong lyrics with a humorous twist—a perfect interlude between two serious ballads. It was released on February 3, 1990, and shot up the chart to number 1 so fast that "The Dance" had to be released just four months later.

"The Dance" stayed at the top of *Billboard*'s chart for three weeks, nourished in part by a clip that changed the standard for music videos. Garth knew that his vision for the video would take the song to a different level.

"I decided very early that I wanted to make videos with a third dimension," Garth said. "I wanted to expand the vision instead of funneling it. That way they would reach more people and more emotions. To a lot of people 'The Dance' is a song about love gone wrong. But to me, it was also about life and death."

He wanted to spotlight people he believed lived life to the fullest, and with few regrets: Martin Luther King Jr., John Wayne, Keith Whitley, John Fitzgerald Kennedy, the crew of the *Challenger,* and rodeo star Lane Frost. They were all dreamers and risk takers.

"I'd never compare myself to these people," Garth said. "But if somehow I leave this world unexpectedly, play 'The Dance.'

I don't think I would trade one yesterday for one more tomorrow. I'm gonna have a ball with the time that the Good Lord has given me. And if anybody's crazy enough to shed a tear for me, don't do it. I had the time of my life.

"This piece means the world to me. And while I'm proud of the awards it has received, I'm even more proud of the letters I've received. People have written to say that the video helped them deal with the death of a loved one. People played it at funerals. That's real life. And the Good Lord willing, that means the video is doing what it's supposed to do."

As with "If Tomorrow Never Comes," when Garth recorded "The Dance," the deaths of friends Jim Kelly and Heidi Miller weighed heavily on his mind: "Until Heidi and Jim died, death hadn't been a part of my life. But the deaths of those two friends happening fairly close to each other really hit me. In fact, when Jim died in 1982, there was a period of about six months that I don't even recall happening. It just seems black to me. But during that time I realized what death is. Death is a cheat. It's a cheat because you don't get to do the things you want to do. Then and there I decided that I was going to try to do everything I wanted to do. But then the video for 'The Dance' freed me from death, from worrying about when it happened. I have myself right there in film and audio saying that if I die, play this for me. It's okay."

Making this video made Garth think a lot about dreamers: "When I first started doing music, maybe my dreams seem small to some. But they were big to me at the time. My first goal was to hear my debut single, 'Much Too Young (To Feel This Damn Old),' on the radio. I still remember where I was when I first heard it. I was driving home from a writing appointment, coming up on the 440/65 split. The song came on and I was all over the highway! Then I flipped to the other Nashville country station, and there it was! If I had wrecked that truck and that was it, it would have been enough. That's the lesson I hear in 'The Dance.'"

The Complete Guide to Country Music Videos described the video as "simply one of the most moving and eloquent videos ever made. It was probably the single biggest boost to Brooks's career, other than his own remarkable talent."

In June, when Garth performed at Capitol's Fan Fair show, he was presented with his first gold record. One of Garth's first reactions on hearing about the sales award was to request that Lynn Shults and Jim Foglesong be among those receiving plaques. As of 2008, *Garth Brooks* has sold 10 million albums.

GARTH'S SCENE-STEALER ALBUM, however, was standing right there in the wings, waiting for the curtain to go up. *No Fences,* his second album, was complete and scheduled for an August release. Garth knew it was good, but he also knew expectations had risen since "The Dance." His days of being an underdog newcomer who just wanted to make his hometown proud were over. Sophomore releases have long been a peril of the music business; time and again an artist busts through with a home run debut, then strikes out on his second time at the plate.

Even when a follow-up outsold its predecessor it often caused critics to raise eyebrows. Randy Travis's brilliant 1986 debut, *Storms of Life,* sold fewer copies than 1987's *Always & Forever,* yet *Always & Forever* was criticized for being a somewhat formulaic pitch to the female fans. If so, it proved to be an effective strategy.

Sometimes the second-album problem comes from a feeling of invincibility that comes with instant stardom. And there are those artists who unwisely decide to record an entirely self-penned album so as to collect the royalties outside writers were pocketing. Sometimes it is the result of distractions on the road.

Case in point: The O'Kanes—Jamie O'Hara and Kieran Kane—were singer/songwriters who got together in 1985 with the goal of writing some hit songs. It didn't take long before the two became a duo. Their 1986 self-titled Columbia album was a start-to-finish class-act fusion of country and bluegrass, with harmonies sometimes reminiscent of the Everly Brothers. Their Top 10 debut single, "Oh, Darlin'," set up the biggest hit they scored, 1987's "Can't Stop My Heart From Loving You." But extensive touring cut short this excellent duo's career. "The road affected us as writers," Kane lamented. "Some people find touring gets their creative juices flowing. We didn't."

If Jimmy Bowen had continued to operate in the spirit of his initial conversations with Allen Reynolds, the Garth Brooks story would have been far different. In the early weeks of the new relationship, despite all the Music Row stories about Bowen's heavy-handedness, Garth was cautiously enthusiastic about their potential working relationship. At first Bowen appeared to be solidly behind the kind of music Garth wanted to make, and willing to give him the freedom to work unfettered by the usual restraints. But those who knew Bowen best said it simply was not in his personality to stay out of the recording process of his biggest star.

Before Garth even began cutting *No Fences,* Bowen warned him that his recordings sounded dated, laying the fault squarely at Allen Reynolds's door. Bowen described the meeting where, he explains, he gave Garth some straight advice. "I've listened to your album, and I frankly don't feel it's up to standards, technically, of your competition. Allen is a good man and when it works for him, he is a terrific producer. But he owns his own studio and cuts a certain old-fashioned way, which worked for Crystal Gayle and others. But it's not gonna work with you."

Garth rejected the advice, telling Bowen he didn't like studio tricks and preferred to keep on recording analog and later transferring the entire recording to digital. "Allen and I are a team," he said. "This is how we record. We like to keep it real." It was a clear rejection of any suggestion that he'd dump Reynolds in favor of the label head. When Bowen told Garth that he had to trust him, Garth told him that as far as the road to trust went, consider him just boarding the bus in Oklahoma.

Bowen didn't let the implied pressure drop for long, and at a later meeting asked with a smile, "Hey, pal, when am I gonna be producing your records?"

Garth smiled and shook his head. "It's not gonna happen."

Bowen's irritation at being ignored started bubbling up over seemingly insignificant things. When Garth asked that song lyrics be included in the *No Fences* CD package, Bowen was furious. At a meeting with a financial officer Bowen went over the cost of adding pages of song lyrics. "Does he know this expense is recoupable?" Bowen asked. The man shrugged. "Then do it and charge it back to the SOB," Bowen responded sharply. Another Capitol employee, waiting to see Bowen, said the hair stood up on the back of his neck. People at the label already had a sense that *No Fences* was going to be a monster release. Why would Bowen take such a petty—and angry—attitude? The employee speculated that it could only be because Bowen wanted to produce the star himself.

Word leaked out onto Music Row that Bowen had made his move and Garth stood his ground. One country artist, who believed Bowen had destroyed his career when the two crossed swords at Elektra Records, expressed concerns to a music journalist at one of Nashville's watering holes. "I don't think this kid has any idea who he's dealing with," the singer said. "Bowen's gonna bury that kid."

The journalist, who had come to know Garth well, disagreed. "If I was betting, I'd put my money on the kid."

In Garth's world, fair play was vital. It was a character trait he'd learned from his marine veteran father, and one he took seriously. People who betrayed that sense of fair play were usually stunned at how quickly he could take on Raymond Brooks's tough personality and dig his heels in.

CHAPTER SIX

Only in America

I n the summer of 1990, the *Winston Cup Illustrated*'s Tom Higgins was covering the races at Michigan International Speedway. One of Higgins's favorite side trips during the NASCAR weekend was a stop at the nearby Lenawee County Fair in Adrian. That year's fair headliner, Tanya Tucker, was ill and had been replaced by a relative newcomer. Here's what Higgins had to say about the experience some years later:

> We bought tickets and found seats about six rows back from the temporary stage, situated on sand where trotters had raced a day or so before. It took Garth Brooks only two or three songs to make a crowd of 750 or so forget that he wasn't supposed to be the star.
>
> He came out into the crowd and touchingly told of visiting a children's hospital and having a little girl entice him into singing "The Dance" a cappella. With that introduction, Brooks and his band performed the song that was soon to be a hit. The audience seemed mesmerized until after the final note, then rose for a standing ovation.
>
> A soft rain began to fall. The entertainer ignored it and sang on . . . a variety of numbers ensued: "Cowboy Bill," "Two Of A Kind, Workin' On A Full House," "New Way To Fly," and "If

Tomorrow Never Comes." Finally, Brooks related an anecdote about giving his mother a tape of a new song that held promise of becoming a mega-hit. A local radio station somehow obtained the copy and played the number on air prematurely. Since it was already out, Brooks reasoned he'd go ahead and let the Adrian audience hear the feature from a forthcoming album. "Friends In Low Places" brought the crowd to its feet again, clapping, dancing, shouting, and dancing in delight. That song, along with "The Dance," was to take Brooks to higher places than he ever dared dream, selling out shows faster than any country music entertainer before him.

Who would have imagined during that drizzly Friday night during Michigan race weekend at the Lenawee County Fair that the guy on that stage was destined to become an international show business icon? Only in America.

And for country music in America, it was the day of the newcomer. Five of the top acts during the first half of 1990 were new to the charts: Garth Brooks, Alan Jackson, Travis Tritt, Clint Black, and the Kentucky Headhunters.

Fans had Harold Shedd, the man behind Alabama and K.T. Oslin, to thank for the Headhunters. While Shedd-produced acts had generally resided at RCA, he was running Mercury when he heard the guitar-driven band from Edmonton, Kentucky. The band's chart positions belie the real level of their success during that first year in the public eye. The debut album, *Pickin' on Nashville,* was a wild ride through Hank Jr., Charlie Daniels, and Lynyrd Skynyrd Land. Looking like they stepped out of a Willie Nelson Fourth of July concert video, the band had signature songs, "Walk Softly On This Heart Of Mine" and "Dumas Walker." Their only Top 10 was the boogied-up "Oh Lonesome Me." Though they didn't chart again after 1991, the band remained a force on the concert trail and, along with Travis Tritt, proudly carried the banner for Southern country rock.

The album that lifted Garth out of the country up-and-comer crowd was *No Fences*. Part of the secret of the album's creative juice was that Garth still had the cardboard box of songs he'd spent a year collecting. One of those songs had a long history.

Stephanie Davis was already sick of hearing about Garth Brooks when she first met him. Stephanie had been working a series of low-paying jobs and trying to plug her songs when she began meeting with Bob Doyle, who she'd heard was one of the most writer-friendly Music City insiders. She was happy that Bob seemed to like her material, but soon annoyed that he kept bringing up a third party, a kid he believed was going to be the next big thing, Garth Brooks.

At one Bluebird Cafe writers night Stephanie sang her song "Wolves," about economic hard times, turning the plight of the American farm family into an allegory about natural selection. Standing in the back of the room, Garth was transfixed.

The song hit him on several levels. First, he was taken with Stephanie's mastery of words woven into lyrics. Next, he loved her brooding delivery of the song. The message also struck a deep populist chord involving Garth's Oklahoma roots, not that far removed from dust bowl days. But finally, he related to the concept of being one of those people the wolves pull down. "In the end, I thought the song was about death," he said.

He was listening so intently, Garth forgot what he was doing. "I walked right up to the edge of the stage and stood there, invading her space, in reality," Garth ruefully recalled. "All of a sudden I realized how close to her I was standing and how crazy I must have appeared staring at her. I thought, 'This woman probably thinks I'm some kind of a stalker.' But that didn't stop me from telling her that I wanted to record the song."

"Sorry," Stephanie answered. "It's on hold for Willie Nelson."

Garth got a copy of "Wolves" anyway. Even if he didn't get to put it on an album, he loved listening to the song.

By the time he started recording *No Fences,* Willie Nelson had moved on to other songs and "Wolves" was available.

To accentuate Garth's plaintive vocal on the cut, Allen Reynolds brought in classical upright bassist Edgar Meyer. "Edgar is a world-class talent," Allen said. "What we wanted was a powerful low end, one that the listener might not even be aware of, but would feel. And Garth loves that low-register underlining of the mood."

Garth placed "Wolves" at the very end of the album to indicate that it was his favorite, as he had done on his debut with "The Dance."

What Garth didn't know was that this song would earn him the ire of a music legend. When Willie didn't cut "Wolves," fellow outlaw Waylon Jennings decided he wanted to record it, only to learn about Garth's cut. It seemed to Waylon that an upstart had jerked a song out from under him, and he did not forget it.

"Friends In Low Places" was another song on *No Fences* that a fellow artist had wanted to release. Mark Chesnutt also recorded what became the monster single from *No Fences.* Chesnutt's version was closer to a classic country honky-tonk tune, but lacking that over-the-top party atmosphere that permeated Garth's cut: hit material but probably not the presentation that would have caused college students to line up singing the song's chorus outside America's bars. What made the difference in Garth's cut was its attitude, one that came from the crowd of rowdy pals who came to the studio to sing on the chorus. They had so much fun that the company that mastered the record tried to send the album back.

"The mastering people called and said, 'You've got a real bad glitch on 'Friends In Low Places,'" Garth laughs. "We almost died, because we were on such a tight schedule it would have been almost impossible to go back in the studio. It would have set us back weeks. Then, when we listened, we realized that what they were hearing was either Rob Hajacos or Steve Morley popping a beer can right by the microphone. And if you listen closely, you'll hear someone yell out, 'Push, Marie!' That's because [road guitarist] James Garver was with his wife, Marie, at the hospital, where she was having a baby. We figured all of it was good luck and should be left in."

In concert "Friends" gets thunderous applause from the minute the intro begins. Originally the song didn't have a real intro, so Mark Casstevens decided to create one utilizing the first four chords of the song. Ty England laughs when he recalls Garth telling him that they needed to follow Casstevens's lead and emphasize the intro. "It's true," Ty says. "Garth anticipated what was going to happen. In concert the minute I start to play those first notes, the crowd goes nuts."

The history of "Friends In Low Places" contains a music business tale made to order for *Nashville* film director Robert Altman. One afternoon DeWayne Blackwell was drinking at the LongHorn restaurant with a writer named Bud Lee. Neither was known for his fiscal responsibility. In fact, writer Larry Bastian, Blackwell's close friend, credits his own deal with Major Bob to DeWayne's finances. The two were writing for Snuff Garrett's L.A. publishing company in the late '80s, and according to Larry, Bob approached Blackwell first.

"DeWayne always needed money," Larry laughed. "One time I remember he was trying to get to Nashville from L.A., and ran out of money somewhere in Kansas. He had to call me to wire him some, which I was able to do since I was working at the time. DeWayne was all set to sign a deal with Major Bob, but before the papers could be signed, Bob got called up for two weeks of air force duty. DeWayne got an offer with cash up front and had to take it. When Bob got back, DeWayne said, 'It's too late for me. You ought to talk to Larry.' So I ended up getting the gig!"

Bud Lee was a well-liked, immensely talented character around the Row, but prone to drinking too much and running up his tab. One afternoon following a wealth of alcoholic riches, Blackwell asked Lee how he planned on paying his share of the tab.

"Don't worry about it," Lee laughed. "I've got friends in low places."

It was a hook made in hillbilly heaven, and even before they wrote it the two knew they had a hit on their hands. The problem was, Bud usually had a drink in his, and he could count on only a few of those lowly pals to spot him for more. Others who hung out at the LongHorn knew that it was only a matter of time before "Friends" started making money. By the time it was over, Bud Lee had traded a considerable percentage of his song royalties to pay a LongHorn bar bill.

"Friends In Low Places" became an overnight college anthem, and was named the 1991 Single of the Year at both the CMA and ACM awards shows. It also made "Garth Brooks" a household name. On the day that "Friends In Low Places" hit number 1, October 6, 1990, Garth was the sixty-fifth artist inducted into the Grand Ole Opry.

The *Orlando Sentinel* explained why Garth's cut hit all the right chords: " 'Friends In Low Places' starts out wistfully, almost like a folk song, and grows increasingly countrified and rowdy. The chorus is as catchy as they come, with Brooks's bravura dip into the very bottom of his vocal range and the whooping crowd sing-along on the last chorus. The lyrics are a masterpiece of irony: A man crashes his old flame's wedding in a misguided attempt to show how little he needs her. Writers DeWayne Blackwell and Bud Lee ought to get some special Country Music Association award for rhyming 'social graces,' 'low places,' and 'oasis.' "

"Unanswered Prayers" followed "Friends" to the number 1 chart spot. Larry Bastian calls it his "phantom song."

"Garth had the idea for this song and talked to me about some of the lines he'd already written. He just couldn't come up with a title. So I suggested 'Unanswered Prayers.' The next thing I knew Garth and Pat Alger had finished it and my name was included as a writer. I said, 'Well, *that* was easy!'"

Then Bastian laughs and adds, "But I ain't giving the money back."

The song's intro features one of Garth's favorite sounds: two acoustic guitars playing in harmony. Chris Leuzinger played the second part, although it wasn't credited on the album, Mark Casstevens said. The sound they created resulted from Casstevens's thumb-pick-and-fingers technique and Leuzinger's flat-picking.

"Unanswered Prayers" became one of Garth's signature songs, but not quite in the way Garth thought might happen. "It was the second single from the album," Garth reflects. "I thought, 'I'll get 'em laughing with 'Friends In Low Places,' then hit 'em in the gut with an emotional song.' But it backfired. The fans didn't want to let go of 'Friends' and it took a while for them to pay attention to 'Unanswered Prayers.' Since I loved the song so much, I was really worried for a while there, thinking I'd really messed up."

Garth had met "Unanswered Prayers" co-writer Pat Alger through Allen Reynolds a few months before his debut album was set for release. A New York native, Alger had been a member of the Woodstock Mountain Review, and written songs for both Nanci Griffith and Kathy Mattea. Alger had his own album out in 1991, *True Love and Other Short Stories,* on Sugar Hill. Reynolds was a fan of Alger and thought his acoustic folk background would fit well with Garth. There was an immediate creative bonding and the two went on to collaborate on a string of hits.

As with "Friends," another artist had staked a claim on "Two Of A Kind, Workin' On A Full House." The first time Garth heard the song he knew he wanted to record it. Unfortunately, a friend of his was working on a deal of his own and the song was a part of it. "I wish I'd heard it first," Garth laughed.

Then, while he was recording *No Fences,* Garth got a call
from his friend. "Do you remember that song I cut that you
loved? Well, my deal didn't work out and I wanted to let you
know that the song's available." Garth didn't think twice. "Two
Of A Kind, Workin' On A Full House" was the third single and
third number 1 radio hit from *No Fences.*

Warren Haynes, who was one of the writers on "Two Of
A Kind, Workin' On A Full House," is a perfect example of
the diverse musicians who developed in Nashville through the
late '80s and early '90s. Named by *Rolling Stone* as one of rock's
greatest guitarists, Haynes has had one of those careers that successfully bridged rock and country. An exemplary guitarist at
a young age, Haynes joined David Allan Coe's band when he
was barely out of his teens. He was capable of switching from
mournful country ballads to hard-core honky-tonk to wailing
rock 'n' roll on a dime. He played with many high-profile rock
stars, including Dickie Betts, who in 1989 asked Haynes to take
the Duane Allman guitar part in the Allman Brothers Show.
Haynes went on to found the band Gov't Mule, and release a
string of critically acclaimed albums. But he never lost his respect and affection for country: "One of the things I'm most
proud of in my writing career is Garth's cut of 'Two Of A
Kind,'" he told a Nashville journalist. "I love the fact that he
can step from one musical style to another with ease and never
lose the authenticity of any of it."

Again, Garth sequenced the album like a live show and placed
"The Thunder Rolls" first. This was another song Garth wrote
with Pat Alger. "I brought the idea of thunder rolling inside of
a marriage and outside at the same time to Pat," Garth says.
"The first thing he did was pick up his guitar and start with this
D-minor rolling thing. He was picking and coming up with
lines and ideas so fast that I could barely keep up with him."

Because Garth loved Pat Alger's original guitar work on
"Thunder," he asked the singer/songwriter to play on the session.
"I was in the studio that day and had my 1979 Martin M-36,"

Alger explained. "They said, 'Hey, you wrote it, you want to play on it?' And I said, 'Sure!' We recorded it live, with no click and no overdubs," Alger recalls. "It was a magic take—we tried to reproduce it later but couldn't do it."

Garth and Pat had originally pitched the song to Tanya Tucker, adding an extra verse at the suggestion of Tucker's producer, Jerry Crutchfield. When Allen Reynolds learned that Tanya was recording the song, he almost fainted. "That's one of the most powerful songs I've ever heard! Why are you giving it away?" he asked.

Tanya's version didn't make it on her album, and when Garth began recording *No Fences,* "The Thunder Rolls" was at the top of their list. Allen Reynolds suggested leaving out the final verse to add some mystery. When they got the cut they wanted, Reynolds recalls Garth sitting in the studio looking thoughtful.

"Garth asked what we'd think of adding the sound of thunder to the recording, and I thought it was a great idea," Reynolds says. "What made it possible to experiment with this technique was Bowen's having already approved of us taking chances to help create excitement.

"As it turned out we had actual thunder on tape from a song called 'Delta Rain' that Mark Miller and I had produced on the Memphis Boys. When we rolled the multitrack to dub in the thunder, Garth was in charge of turning the sound on. It had to be a 'feel' thing, and he nailed it perfectly."

Critics agreed. As Parry Gettelman wrote in the *Orlando Sentinel,* "It's punctuated with thunderclaps—a device that actually works, believe it or not!"

Garth's video for "The Thunder Rolls" was a dark minimovie with a spousal abuse theme concluding with the woman striking back. Although the video would ultimately win a CMA award in 1991, it became the object of controversy, banned at first for implied violence. "If I could change anything in my career, it would be the contention over this video," Garth says.

"It's a good song that got overshadowed by a controversy. It was unfair to the song, and that hurts. I never wanted something like that to draw attention to a song of mine."

"The Thunder Rolls" was the fourth number 1 single from *No Fences,* and took home honors as the Favorite Country Single at the 1992 American Music Awards.

When word drifted back to Capitol that Garth was using fiddles on "Mr. Blue," the old Fleetwoods swing hit, more than a few eyebrows were raised. Even the song's writer, DeWayne Blackwell, questioned the approach. But when he heard the final mix, Blackwell got tears in his eyes. "I feel like it's 1959 again," he said.

Despite concerns, "Mr. Blue" was a favorite among critics. The *Orlando Sentinel* called it "an absolute winner. There's just the right amount of fiddle and piano in the arrangement, allowing Brooks's lovely voice plenty of room to stretch out." The *St. Petersburg Times* called Garth's vocal "inspired." And the *Los Angeles Times* added, "[Brooks] reveals a canny sense of style in a witty swing treatment."

No Fences was stylistically sweeping. In addition to the down-and-dirty "Friends," the menacing "Thunder," reflective "Unanswered Prayers," and spine-tingling "Wolves," there was swing ("Mr. Blue"), acoustic ("Same Old Story"), and rodeo ("Wild Horses").

A deliberative listen makes Warren Haynes's point about authenticity. The songs flow seamlessly, but each one takes on its own musical style and mood—a tribute to the studio musicians, artist, and producer. There is another individual whose influence is felt on all of Garth's albums, yet is seldom mentioned: engineer Mark Miller. "No one can make great records without a great engineer," Reynolds once reflected. "Especially when you record without all the studio tricks. People sometimes think of engineering as a technical skill. But when it's done right, it's an art form. The engineer has to understand the music, artist, the producer, the players, and have the best ear in the building—Mark does."

The album was one of the most critically acclaimed of the year. *Time* magazine said, "Brooks makes a direct assault on the heartstrings." *USA Today* said that *No Fences* showed that there was "no limit for Brooks." The Syracuse *Post-Standard* called it "a work of art." Journalists compared *No Fences* to defining albums like *Thriller* and *Rumours*. One critic said that Garth's debut "was so powerful that even his champions feared his follow-up couldn't match it. It has."

No Fences was released on August 27, 1990, and sold 700,000 copies in the first ten days. Keeping Garth's first album visible while *No Fences* was in the spotlight paid off. That October, *Garth Brooks* reached a million copies sold five days before *No Fences* was also certified platinum. When the sales were tabulated in December the two albums had sold five and a half million records.

Writing in *Request,* Rick Mitchell pointed to the effect of a new generation of artists: "The numbers don't lie. In 1984, at the depths of the country-pop era, there were only seven country albums certified gold (indicating sales of 500,000 or more). *Billboard*'s end-of-the-year chart for 1990 showed thirty-three gold albums. By reminding listeners of what made country music great, these young artists have attracted a whole new generation of country fans."

Despite Jimmy Bowen's dire warnings that Garth and Allen needed to slick up production or else, the label head loved *No Fences,* calling the album "fabulous" and "Friends In Low Places" a "killer." In one staff meeting he praised Garth for his appreciation of Nashville's songwriters and understanding that songs were what made the industry tick.

Bowen described a scene of Joe Mansfield analyzing the sales trends, and momentum, then predicting the album's full potential:

"We're at four million on *Fences*. It's unbelievable. It's gonna hit ten million," Mansfield told his boss.

"From your lips to God's ears, now, what was that you said—and why?"

"That's right. Ten million."

"Well, we'll just ride this baby as long and as hard as we can," Bowen answered. "We got us a gusher here."

To another trusted executive, Bowen said he thought he was going to be able to relive his glory days, when he worked with Frank Sinatra at the superstar's label, Reprise. But the executive was concerned, because Sinatra had been at a completely different stage of his professional life. There was no reason for Sinatra to try to protect his already legendary career from label machinations.

The spring of 1991 started out like it had been scripted for prime time. On March 16, Garth returned home to Yukon, Oklahoma, for the dedication of a new sign on the town's water tower: "Home of Garth Brooks." On April 6, "Two Of A Kind, Workin' On A Full House" hit number 1. The following day, Garth performed a free "Yellow Ribbon" concert in Norfolk, Virginia, to salute Operation Desert Storm families.

On April 24, 1991, Garth dominated the Academy of Country Music (ACM) Awards by taking home a record-breaking six top honors: Entertainer, Male Vocalist, Best Song and Best Video ("The Dance"), Best Single ("Friends In Low Places"), and Top Album for *No Fences*. He might have won all nominations but for the fact that "The Dance" and "Friends In Low Places" were competing against each other for Best Song. When Alan Jackson took the stage to collect his Top New Male Vocalist trophy, he quipped, "First off, I'd like to thank Garth Brooks for not being nominated in this category." Garth told the press, "I'm happy, scared, and embarrassed all at the same time."

Garth's video for "The Thunder Rolls" had been released to The Nashville Network (TNN) and Country Music Television (CMT). Although the lines were not performed, the video utilized the concept of the third verse Garth and Pat Alger had written for the song. In that verse, the "thunder" is domestic violence.

"Allen Reynolds was uncomfortable with the third verse, so we didn't include it on the recording," Garth said. "When we

made the video, we'd been playing 'The Thunder Rolls' in concert for about a year. One night on a whim, I included that third
verse, with the line 'tonight will be the last time she'll wonder
where he'd been.' The audience response was immediate. It was
just amazing. So when we started talking about a video, I wanted
to include the concept, even though we wouldn't be singing that
verse. It was a way to tie the two performances together—the recorded version and the one we were doing in concert. I decided
to play the role of the husband because I wanted to make sure
he was *so* despicable that the whole viewing audience wanted to
shoot him!"

By April 30 Garth's single for "The Thunder Rolls" was
making big news at radio. One hundred and eighty-three stations immediately added the song, the most in *Radio & Records*
country chart history, and the number 25 chart debut was the
highest in *R&R* rotational reporting era. His video had been
added to CMT as a Pick Hit.

The real storm hit the following day.

CHAPTER SEVEN

Good times roll just ahead of the thunder

It was May 1, and Capitol's head of public relations, Cathy Gurley, was thrilled with the media cards she'd been dealt. Garth Brooks was fresh off six big wins at the Academy of Country Music Awards, *No Fences* was the hottest album in the nation, and that success was helping piggyback other artists to national television spots and magazine coverage.

Despite some early concerns about Garth's video for "The Thunder Rolls," it appeared to have great acceptance. Because of the implied spousal abuse, Cathy had called together a group of industry women and professionals to view the film clip prior to its release. The response was unanimous. It was a ground-breaking piece that could not only stand as a work of video art, but could have a beneficial effect on society as well. One of the women in the panel had lost a sister to domestic violence. She said it was one of the most powerful statements she'd ever seen. When Country Music Television made it a Pick Hit, Cathy knew it was on its way to taking video into new territory.

She was sitting at her desk going over a stack of press requests when her assistant buzzed in.

"Garth's on the phone."

"Congratulations," she said, picking up the phone. "I guess you know 'Thunder' made *R&R* history!"

"Cathy, I need your help on something," Garth said. "Could you come with me out to The Nashville Network?"

"Of course," she said. "What's going on?"

"They want me to add a message to the end of the video, and I'm uncomfortable with it. I don't want it to look like I'm trying to use abuse as some marketing ploy."

"But why?" She asked. "I don't understand."

Garth paused. "Well, the video has been pulled. They've banned it."

LATER THAT DAY TNN issued a statement in which the network's Paul Corbin said he was left with a "horrible, helpless feeling" that he'd just witnessed a beating and a murder. CMT also pulled "Thunder" off the air. CMT's Bob Baker said the channel was "in business to entertain, not to promote or condone gratuitous violence or social issues."

"I was told that the ban was initiated by two executives at TNN," recalls Cathy Gurley. "There was no company-wide consensus—just the opinions of two people. And I also heard that a number of female employees disagreed vehemently with the network's decision. Right away they offered a 'compromise.' If Garth would tape a disclaimer to be added as a tag, they'd play the video."

Garth and Cathy went to TNN, where Garth attempted to comply, reading from a script the network provided.

"Hi, I'm Garth Brooks. What you've just seen, though very sad, is very real. Unfortunately, domestic violence is very much alive in our society." The script went on to ask men, women, and children involved in domestic violence situations to seek professional help.

As Cathy Gurley watched Garth try to comply, she could see him becoming increasingly tense. Before he even told her, she knew he would refuse to film the disclaimer. "They completely underestimated Garth's feelings about the whole thing," Cathy said. "He felt the script they gave him was, in effect, pandering. And I guess they didn't realize he couldn't be pushed into something he didn't believe in."

"It felt wrong," Garth said. "I thought it looked like I was trying to use a controversy to promote a video. And while I anticipated the video making an impact, I certainly didn't foresee this."

Manager Pam Lewis agreed, saying, "If there's a problem with the video and if TNN feels there's something they want to say about it, that's fine. If they want to run an 800 number, or have someone from a women's group do it, feel free. But we don't feel it's Garth's place to do it."

Garth also talked about his thought process when it came to making videos: "I refuse to do a video that is ordinary. It wastes the viewer's time and mine, and my label's money. My videos are real life, and they're meant to add another dimension to the song."

Most of America had no idea just what was being banned, because "The Thunder Rolls" had only aired briefly. That quickly changed. Radio stations, country dance clubs, television, and print outlets across the country requested copies in an effort to make up their own minds—and to let their listeners make up *theirs*.

For example, on Friday, May 3, WCOS in Columbia, South Carolina, set up a video player at a local shopping center. According to WCOS disc jockeys Gary Dixon and Rob Mason, the viewing public saw the clip as a snapshot of real life, and likely to help raise awareness of a social problem. WCOS used the viewing event to raise money for Sistercare, an organization that aids battered women.

In San Angelo, Texas, one country venue premiered the video for club patrons and raised money for Assault Victim Services and the ICD Family Shelter. According to the *San Angelo Times,* response was so strong that KGKL radio decided to replay the video continuously at its studio the following night, where more money was raised for battered women's shelters.

WSIX in Nashville ran the video at the Wrangler and the city's locally produced television show *Down Home, Down Under* began airing the clip on WXMT-Channel 30 as part of a focus on domestic violence. And Nashville's Tower Records played the video nonstop from 4:00 P.M. to 8:00 P.M. from May 6 to May 11.

Women's shelters began to contact Capitol detailing ways the video had helped them raise awareness. For example, the Genesis Shelter in Dallas wrote to a Capitol representative: "The Genesis Shelter phone number was tagged each time 'The Thunder Rolls' was aired on Channel 27 resulting in many hot line calls, as well as many calls in support of the video itself. We feel public education is a critical step in combating domestic violence. Each of us has the opportunity and the obligation to help break the cycle of violence. Please extend to Mr. Brooks our appreciation as he joins us, and shelters all over the nation, in impacting the cycle of violence."

Colleen Brooks had this to say: "Wife abuse has been pushed aside by a predominantly male society for too long. Maybe this will give some woman the courage to get out. Or, if this helps one man stop what he is doing, it's worth it."

TNN's and CMT's actions perplexed virtually all those who reviewed the video.

"The themes in that song are not new to country," said Tom Rivers, program director of Tampa Bay area country station WQYK-FM. "The video simply shows nuts-and-bolts reality."

Most agreed with Loretta Macias of the *San Angelo Times,* who wrote, "Country music has a real shot to delve into some social commentary, maybe cast a realistic light on a tragic societal condition and perhaps even help a few folks."

David Medzerian, writing in the *Orange County Register,* put it this way: "What's the big deal? I've seen the controversial video for Garth Brooks' hit 'The Thunder Rolls,' and it's a dramatic, mesmerizing piece of work. By banning it, the only thing two cable channels have accomplished is to deprive their audiences of this riveting interpretation of a haunting song.

"The video hardly advocates spouse abuse. Critics will note that the words to 'The Thunder Rolls' don't mention wife-beating, but videos have never been limited to strict interpretations of lyrics."

The *Arkansas Gazette*'s television critic, Paul Johnson, wrote in his "Small Screen" column,

> Even a cursory examination of Brooks' phenomenal output of monster songs reveals that many deal with thoughtful topics of greater than average relevance. For every "Friends In Low Places" type of song Brooks has recorded, there's a sober-minded and contemplative song such as "Wolves" or "Unanswered Prayers" or "If Tomorrow Never Comes." So, TNN executives obviously were aware that Brooks occasionally deals with topics other than drinking till you can't see straight, moaning over a two-timing lover or driving an 18-wheeler faster than the law allows.
>
> Which brings us to the point: TNN has found nothing objectionable in literally hundreds of country music videos that deal with adultery, alcoholic lovers, two-timing drunk adulterers, drunk two-timing truck-driving adulterers and other topics of a less-than-savory nature.

By Thursday, May 7, when VH-1 announced that the pop channel would begin airing the video, "The Thunder Rolls" had taken on a life of its own.

Capitol was turned into a clearinghouse of information. Employees took calls from hundreds of shelters, women's groups, and individual women wanting information, assistance, or help raising visibility for the domestic violence issue. Within weeks the label had compiled a nationwide bank of contact numbers. Radio and retail outlets undertook huge fund-raising efforts.

Women within the Nashville music community reported that many began sharing personal experiences previously kept secret even from their closest friends. One woman talked about her experience in a very frank letter to the Nashville *Tennessean:*

> The video supports those victims of abuse who live in destructive relationships. I am a survivor of such a situation. I knew changes had to be made in my home when I, like the woman in the video, saw what my child went through having to live with this abuse. However, instead of getting a gun, I got a lawyer and subsequently divorced. The resulting hardships for what was left of my family included total financial collapse, bankruptcy, loss of my business, home, autos and then major depression.
>
> Rebuilding our lives has been accomplished through hard work and desire, with assistance from support systems. For those caught up in the same video re-runs as those pictured in "The Thunder Rolls," I say: "There is help available for you and your family. You are worth it."

"The Thunder Rolls" had a lasting impact, giving other artists the freedom to make higher-impact videos relating to family violence. They would range from Martina McBride's powerfully charged "Independence Day" to the tongue-in-cheek "Goodbye Earl" from the Dixie Chicks and Big & Rich's potent "Holy Water."

By early summer, when the initial Country Music Association award nominations were being considered, Jimmy Bowen sent out a mass mailing of "The Thunder Rolls" in case members still had not seen the video. For his part, Bowen loved the controversy. "It sells records," he laughed. "You can't buy this kind of publicity."

On October 2 Garth was named CMA Entertainer of the Year. "Friends In Low Places" won Single of the Year and *No Fences* Album of the Year. And when "The Thunder Rolls" was announced as Video of the Year, the applause at Nashville's

Opry house, with President George H.W. Bush in attendance, was deafening.

The win was bittersweet for Garth. His video had massively raised awareness for a very serious social problem and his vision was vindicated. But the controversy had overshadowed the song. It was not the result he'd wanted. As he explained, the video controversy "didn't hurt my career. It hurt my feelings."

CHAPTER EIGHT

Bustin' in like old John Wayne

The 1991 tour schedule was grueling. Between the coliseum and amphitheater dates was a long string of one-night gigs at clubs, jamborees, fairs, festivals, and rodeos. As the holidays approached, Garth realized that just getting home for Thanksgiving was going to be a problem. He had shows booked through December, with only a brief break between a November 23 date with the Judds in Lexington, Kentucky, and a December 6 show at the Mississippi Coliseum in Jackson. On Thanksgiving Day, Garth and Sandy made a quick trip home to Yukon, Oklahoma.

Colleen Brooks was horrified when her son walked through the door.

"I looked like hell," Garth said. "My voice was gone, my hair was gray on the sides. So when I left early the next morning I wrote her a note that read, 'Mom, if this kills me, I'll die happy.' "

IN JUST ONE YEAR Garth's life and career changed with frightening speed. Instead of his management trying to capture interviews with prominent reporters, Pam Lewis was having to field requests. Garth's time was no longer his own. Joe Harris was flooded with concert requests. "Friends In Low Places" certainly started the gusher, but Garth's tour kept it pumping, and it was starting to garner a lot of high-profile press. On December 30, 1990, the *Los Angeles Times*' Robert Hilburn wrote, "Advisory to rival country music singers: Think twice before agreeing to follow Garth Brooks on stage."

As his career had heated up in 1990, Garth was still signing autographs until late in the night. By 1991 he would find it impossible, and the decision to cut signing sessions short was excruciating. As he explained to the *L.A. Times,* "I stayed up nights, wondering what I was going to do. I finally had to look at the reality of the situation, that things had changed, and hope they understood. This business has a way of changing you, picking away at you until you are a different person. I want to give people the best show we can, but more than anything I want the people who came to see us a long time ago to go away from the show now thinking: 'That guy was real then and he's real now. He hasn't changed.'"

By the beginning of 1991 Garth could have easily fronted a headline tour. He could command a hefty concert fee and sell tickets in record-setting times. However, he had made many commitments for far less money, and he kept them all, losing millions of dollars worth of offers.

As the *Dallas Morning News* reported, "After 'If Tomorrow Never Comes' and 'The Dance' hit #1, Garth was making as much as $100,000 a show, but he kept a $10,000 gig at the Silver Spurs Gala fund-raiser in Arlington. 'Some acts will readjust their fee after they shoot up into the stratosphere like Garth had done,' says KPLX DJ Steve Harmon. 'Not only did Garth play for the amount which had been agreed upon months earlier, but he turned around after the concert and donated his check to charity, which benefits cancer research.'"

In January 1991 Garth kept a commitment to play two shows at Denver's Grizzly Rose honky-tonk. The *Denver Post* reported that he was the hottest ticket in country music, packing the club

with people in town for the National Western Stock Show. This
was just one month before he shattered the all-time world attendance record for a single rodeo concert performance in February
at the Houston Astrodome, performing for 55,986 fans attending the Houston Livestock Show.

Garth felt that the most important promise he had made was
to open shows for Naomi and Wynonna Judd for what would
be their Farewell Tour through 1991. The Judds' drama had
started while the mother/daughter team was on tour in 1990,
just six months after Naomi had married her longtime love,
gospel singer Larry Strickland. Throughout early 1990 Naomi
had felt sick, to the point that she could barely get to the studio
to sing her harmony parts for the album *Love Can Build a Bridge*.
After Naomi was diagnosed with hepatitis C, a potentially fatal
illness, a news conference was called at the now-vacant RCA
building where the Judds had first auditioned for label head Joe
Galante.

It was a dreary, rainy day and the two women were shocked
at how shabby the old office building looked, with peeling paint
and threadbare carpets. The music press was taken by surprise by
the Judds' announcement, some even questioning whether the
illness was feigned so as to launch a solo career for Wynonna.
But it was very real, and very serious. Wynonna was in a charged
state of emotions as the two started on their final tour. She worried about her mother's health, about whether the tour was
worsening the hepatitis and possibly shortening her life.

Worst of all, from the very beginning, manager Ken Stilts
was pushing Wy to record a solo album to be released soon after
the tour wound up. Wynonna felt so guilty about listening to
demo tapes for her upcoming MCA album that she hid them
when Naomi came to visit. "I felt like a part of me was dying,"
Wynonna said.

The tour, the industry's top grossing in 1991, marched on
with shows opened by Garth and a new act on Capitol, the
Pirates of the Mississippi. Putting a rowdy garage band like the

Pirates out on the Judds Farewell Tour was a stretch, but Ken Stilts also managed them and he was adamant that they get the exposure.

The Judds' pay-per-view final concert was the most successful music event in cable's history at the time, grabbing more viewers than comparable shows by the Rolling Stones and New Kids on the Block. Wynonna, her emotions still wound tight, returned to the studio to work with producer Tony Brown on her solo debut, due out in 1992.

Garth alternated between shows where he *was* the opening act and those where he *needed* an opening act. For the latter, there was never a question in his mind that friend and fellow demo singer alum Trisha Yearwood had the gig. Moreover, when Garth began to record for Capitol, Trisha sang harmony on every album. When asked about the magic the two had in the studio and onstage, Garth told *Music Business International,* "*Anybody* and Trisha Yearwood is a great couple."

By this time, Trisha was an MCA artist, produced by Garth Fundis, who'd made great records with Keith Whitley from 1987 to the year of Whitley's death, 1989. Fundis had learned of Trisha through writer Pat Alger, who first heard her singing backup at a Garth Brooks showcase. As it had with Brooks, it only took Alger one listen to become a Trisha-True-Believer. He phoned his friend Fundis singing her praises. The first thought Fundis had on hearing the Georgia vocalist was of a song he'd rat-holed years earlier, waiting for the right singer with the right image. Enter Trisha Yearwood, all-American girl with a golden voice.

"Let me play you a song I got from this guy in Colorado," he said. " 'She's In Love With The Boy.' "

Now that Trisha had found a producer and was working on an unofficial basis with Bob Doyle and Pam Lewis, Garth wondered if she might find a recording home at Capitol. At the time, 1990, there was some behind-the-scenes tension between

Brooks and Bowen, though nothing to get excited about. But Trisha balked.

According to author Lisa Gubernick, who wrote *Get Hot or Go Home* about Trisha's early career, the singer was suspicious of Bowen. First, she was determined to keep Garth Fundis as her producer and knew she'd be pressured to choose Bowen. Additionally, even if one didn't mind that Bowen tried to get in charge of every artist, it was the way he didn't stay in charge once he took the job. Gubernick explained: "Bowen had come to believe that a performer is primarily responsible for his or her own music. In practical terms, that meant that Bowen supervised from afar, an absentee landlord."

Trisha ended up signing with MCA, by then headed by Bowen protégés Bruce Hinton and A&R ace Tony Brown, who had been looking for MCA's next superstar. He found her in Trisha Yearwood. She decided to break out on her own as far as management was concerned and ultimately decided on L.A.-based Ken Kragen, who handled Kenny Rogers and Travis Tritt.

When Trisha started opening for Garth, her MCA Records debut single, "She's In Love With The Boy," was just taking off. As she later explained, the lack of a track record caused her some concern. "I was intimidated at first," she told *Country Music Special* in 1992. "I didn't think Garth's fans would give me the time of day. I thought I'd be playing to people still walking in or folks talking all through my set. My first single wasn't even Top 20 yet at that point. But they were so accepting and excited. I got great response, partly because my band is so great. Also, we were in a better position than most opening acts because Garth was such a friend and he took good care of us."

Prior to playing the Carolina Coliseum, Trisha told the Columbia, South Carolina, *State:* "We aren't herded in and out for the sound check. Garth always tells the technicians to '. . . make sure Trisha sounds good.'"

But there was also a downside. Rumors of an affair kept cropping up, although both denied that their relationship was anything more than a friendship. Because Garth had been open about his 1989 road fling, people around Nashville were always on the lookout for fresh gossip. And when Trisha and Chris Latham divorced in 1991, it was too easy. Except that it was wrong. Trisha was particularly offended by the talk, since she considered Garth a big brother figure.

Trisha talked about making the tabloids with *Country Fever* editor Linda Cauthen: "My dad wanted to go kill the *National Enquirer,* or whoever it was. The first time that something like that happens, you want to call everybody you know and say, 'It isn't true!' because I've never done anything that interesting! You can't control what people say about you. If there's no dirt to report then they've just got to go make something up. I don't read it. If you sit and think about it, it'll just make you mad. Let them talk. But people who know me, and who know Garth and Sandy, well, most people know it's stupid."

And there was an additional charge that Trisha answered in no uncertain terms with the *Los Angeles Times:* "It's no fun to hear people saying you rode somebody's coattails to get where you are. Okay, I probably wouldn't have made it as quickly without Garth, but I would have made it somehow. I *do* have talent."

The tour got across-the-board raves. Music journalist Michael McCall was among the first to sense that Garth's show was not merely rivaling rock concerts, but had the potential to leave them in the dust. Writing in *Country Music* magazine, McCall described Garth's November 7, 1991, concert at the Murphy Arena in Murfreesboro, Tennessee:

> The spectacle he unleashed that cool November night awed even those who thought they'd seen it all. It was almost as entertaining to watch industry veterans react to the euphoric atmosphere as it was to watch the crowd itself. The hysterical re-

action Brooks draws has long been a part of American culture. It happened to Frank Sinatra, to Elvis, to The Beatles, to Bruce Springsteen, to Michael Jackson, even New Kids on the Block. But when has it happened to an artist who proudly says he plays country music? There are stories about the tens of thousands who lined up for Hank Williams' funeral, and veterans like Minnie Pearl and Chet Atkins say that Roy Acuff's popularity was so massive during World War II that hundreds of fans would line the streets of Southern towns waiting for his concert caravan to roll by. Since the coming of the rock 'n' roll era, though, it hasn't happened to a country artist—not on this scale anyway.

When Garth sold out the Memphis Mid-South Coliseum on September 27, it became the first sellout since ZZ Top the previous January. The *Commercial Appeal*'s Larry Nagar made a prophetic statement: "Country music is pop's poor relation no more."

This kind of press not only benefited Garth, it affected all of country music. Joe Harris said that once the comparisons to rock 'n' roll started being made, promoters stepped up offers for country acts across-the-board. It didn't matter that every country artist didn't put on the high-energy show Garth did, either. The press he began to generate both from his recordings and concerts made country a hot commodity.

If *No Fences* made Garth Brooks a superstar, then its follow-up, *Ropin' the Wind,* reached out and put all of country music in the spotlight. It would have made a splash anyway, but a change in *Billboard*'s methodology brought *Ropin' the Wind* to the fore with a tidal wave. The industry's bible, *Billboard* had previously tracked sales through the stores. What that meant was that an employee, often a young rocker, was asked for a report of what had sold in the past week. The kid remembered pop acts, but country was a big, "Huh?" Because of that, the *Billboard* Top 200 chart, usually referred to as the pop chart, was often a wasteland for country product.

Billboard didn't set out to change the industry's perception of country music, but when they changed to an electronic scanning system known as SoundScan, that's what it did. The change had taken effect during the *No Fences* run, and affected that album's chart position. When the revamped chart was first published in May 1991, there were fifteen more country albums that suddenly appeared on the Top 200 list. Then, when *Ropin' the Wind* was released in September, SoundScan's full impact sent shock waves through the industry.

There is a line from one of *Ropin' the Wind*'s songs, "Against The Grain," that contains the description "go bustin' in like old John Wayne," which sums up what happened when *Ropin' the Wind* met up with SoundScan. The album was released on September 10, 1991, and on September 21 it entered the *Billboard* country *and* Top 200 charts at number 1.

The *Irish Times* described *Ropin' the Wind* as a "revolution," saying, "Late last year, as rock deities Prince, Michael Jackson and U2 loudly unleashed albums . . . Garth Brooks quietly saddled up his horse and rode past them all on the trail to the top of the American charts."

Capitol PR VP Gurley advised Bowen to seize the moment and throw a party for Music Row. Because there were many other country albums showing up in the so-called pop chart, Bowen gave the audience a "rising tide lifts all boats" speech. "We invited representatives from every organization, publishing company, and record label," Gurley says. "The sad thing was, a lot of people who resented Bowen refused to attend. And the other artists who ended up on *Billboard*'s Top 200 were all spotlighted. But Bowen was polarizing, so too many people missed sharing it."

If Bowen noticed the lack of fellow label heads in attendance, he said nothing. He was still smarting from a July 8 article that had appeared in *Music Row* magazine, the insiders' must-read published by David Ross. Publisher Ross and journalist Brian Mansfield interviewed Joe Mansfield about Garth's impressive sales, titling the piece, "Joe Mansfield, The Six Million Pieces Man."

Mansfield was quoted in the article: "When Bowen came to Capitol mine was the only position he didn't bring with him. Originally it was going to be a vice president of sales. I said no, marketing and sales go hand in hand. You don't have one without the other. 'You stay in the studio and make good records,' I said. 'And I'll do the rest of it.' It's worked out just great. I couldn't be happier, he couldn't be happier."

In fact, when he heard about those words Bowen couldn't have been more pissed.

Without meaning to, Mansfield had turned Bowen into "the studio guy" and himself into the brains of the outfit. One promotion man heard the full extent of the anger that same day when he waited in the foyer of Bowen's home for a meeting. The phone rang in the living room and after a short conversation the guy heard Bowen swear loudly. "I'm telling you, that bastard Mansfield is gone as soon as his contract is up. The six million pieces man? He's got a hell of a nerve taking credit for those sales." Bowen listened a moment longer before slamming down the phone. "You think I give a damn what Garth Brooks thinks about anything?"

The pronouncement unnerved the promotion guy to the extent that he almost left before Bowen could get off the telephone. Everyone knew that Garth trusted Mansfield and considered him his key man at Capitol. People knew that Garth and Bowen were often at odds. If Mansfield got canned it could turn into all-out war.

When Bowen took center stage at the Music Row celebration the outward reaction he got from guests was good-natured camaraderie. But right under the surface lurked a fair amount of sour grapes. For some of the record executives who did show up, watching Bowen's artist in the driver's seat of the entire industry was almost too much to take. Unfortunately, that begrudging attitude began to spill out to include the artist himself. Initial grousing involved one of Garth's song picks: "Shameless."

The song was an easy target, playing right into the old pop-versus-traditional bias. Never mind that many country artists at the time were making pop-flavored records, and radio had been balking at playing some of the traditional acts for several years. When stone country singer Larry Boone released the Faron Young classic "Wine Me Up" in 1989, the single stalled midchart. When PolyGram promo chief Frank Leffell tried to get the bullet back, several programmers told him that the song was "too country."

"Hell, Frank," one said. "Randy *Travis* is too country for me these days."

But while some thought Garth was both pandering to certain country programmers and going for pop play, the singer was clear about why he recorded it. From the beginning, Garth had depended on his audience to tell him what worked.

"I know a lot of people thought that song came out of left field," Garth said, laughing at the time. "But 'Shameless' had been one of my favorites of everything Billy Joel wrote, and when I sang it in concert the audiences went crazy."

This presented a dilemma for Capitol. Pop stations began playing the cut, and the logical thing to do would have been to hire an independent pop promotion team to take it to the top of the pop singles charts. Crossover hits had long been sought by country music. Interest in broadening the scope and market for country went as far back as 1933, when the Opry hired the Delmore Brothers hoping their more sophisticated bluesy qualities might attract new listeners. Fred Rose was known to fool around with Hank Williams's melodies hoping to garner pop covers. Patsy Cline had "Walking After Midnight," "Crazy," and "I Fall To Pieces." Cash had a string of crossover successes, the biggest being 1969's "A Boy Named Sue." Lynn Anderson's million-selling "Rose Garden" in 1970 and Donna Fargo's 1972 back-to-back million-selling singles, "The Happiest Girl In The

Whole USA" and "Funny Face," were among the records that confirmed pop play meant sales hikes. And, of course, Crystal Gayle's "Don't It Make My Brown Eyes Blue" had made her a multigenre superstar.

It would have been an easy decision to put together a pop team and work "Shameless," well, shamelessly. Ever since the debacle with "Much Too Young (To Feel This Damn Old)," Bob Doyle had believed in hiring outside radio promoters if needed. But he and Garth agreed that chasing pop radio would be counterproductive.

"Country radio has had my back from the beginning," Garth said. "I'd rather have pop listeners cross over to our side of the dial. Some pop stations played 'Friends In Low Places,' too, and while I appreciated the support, I loved nothing more than to hear about kids switching over to country stations because of the song. So we made the conscious decision not to promote at pop, and I stand by it."

Beginning with "Shameless," *Ropin' the Wind* reflected the large umbrella that was country. There were ballads like "What She's Doing Now" and "The River." "Rodeo" and "In Lonesome Dove" swung to the western side of C&W. "Papa Loved Mama" was a hard-core honky-tonker.

"Rodeo" was originally titled "Miss Rodeo," written as a first-person woman's song. Garth loved it and pitched it to every female singer he knew. When it was turned down he decided to turn it into a more general third-person song and sing it himself. It was a Larry Bastian song that again paid tribute to cowboys like Chris LeDoux. Garth felt honor-bound to include this con-stituency on each offering. "I think country music owes the folks in cowboy hats a lot for stickin' with the music through thick and thin," Garth said.

The last five singles released had all hit number 1, but "Rodeo" broke the streak and only climbed to number 3. The main reason? "Shameless." The song simply couldn't be held back, and as a consequence the label went ahead and released it two months after "Rodeo." That experience, plus the memory of how "Friends In Low Places" had threatened to overshadow "Unanswered Prayers," kept Garth up at night over one of his favorite songs on the album, "What She's Doing Now."

"I'm amazed at the numbers of people who remember every word on this song because I was afraid it was gonna get buried," he said later. "Look at the four other singles from *Ropin' the Wind*— 'Rodeo,' 'Shameless,' 'Papa Loved Mama,' and 'The River.' A quiet ballad could easily get lost in that. One of the things that happens when you are planning the set list for concert tours is that often it's the ballads that get cut because fans want that high energy. But from the beginning, people were singing 'What She's Doing Now' start to finish."

"What She's Doing Now" stayed at number 1 for a month in early 1992, followed by the deliciously sinister Top 5 hit "Papa Loved Mama." This was a song that Garth feared radio might question, but not for any lyric misstep.

"At our recording sessions, the music is always the boss," Garth says. "'Papa Loved Mama' is a perfect example. Bruce Bouton pulled out his lap steel and played this nasty, loud part that was absolutely perfect. I didn't know if country radio would even play it—but you gotta cut what has to be cut."

Garth's co-writer, Kim Williams, laughed when he thought back to the "Papa Loved Mama" writing sessions: "I was living in a little Music Row apartment with so many roaches running around that we had to spray every time we tried to write." The hook line, *"Papa loved Mama, Mama loved men / Mama's in the graveyard, Papa's in the pen,"* came from a list of "Things I Wished I'd Said," and was attributed to Carl Sandburg. But when Williams checked with the Sandburg family, it turned out the poet had heard the line in an old folk song.

Although Kim had been working in Nashville for several years, "Papa Loved Mama" was the first song he had written with an artist. The collaboration offer came from Garth, who had been pitched a Williams song and asked the plugger to put them in touch. Kim was shocked when the request came in and Garth offered to come to his apartment for the session. "I thought I'd have to jump through hoops to work with an established artist," Kim laughed. "That wasn't the way it came down."

That blistering Bruce Bouton lap steel solo on "Papa Loves Mama" is sometimes confused with Chris Leuzinger's slide work. "Ever since we started working with Garth, Bruce has been getting compliments for parts I played and vice versa," Chris laughed.

The album's final single and number 1 hit was "The River," an ode to pursuing dreams against all odds, written by Garth and Victoria Shaw. It was also the final, therefore favorite, song on *Ropin' the Wind*. "This is the first time the tenth cut has been a song where I had anything to do with the writing," Garth said. "I live by this song every day and hope it gives courage to people who have ever been in a fight they didn't know if they could finish."

Even some usually jaded industry types confessed that "The River" affected them. One writer told a Capitol employee, "I had just about given up on this damned business. I honest to God had one A&R person who threw my tape in the trash and spit on it. *Spit on it!* Right in front of me. I was only about a half a fan of Garth Brooks, to tell you the truth. I liked his stuff but didn't quite get all the noise. But when I heard that song ["The River"] I felt like it was talking directly to me. I thought, '*Okay, now I get it.*'"

It generated more fan mail than any other song Garth has released. "I thought 'Friends In Low Places' or 'The Dance' would be the all-time biggest when it came to mail," Garth says. "But 'The River' beats all others maybe three or four to one. It's been amazing. Entire classes have drawn very involved, intricate pictures showing what the river is to them. It's a song for dreamers, and it turns out that a *lot* of us are dreamers."

Ropin' the Wind's impact on country music and the industry was noted in *Billboard,* when chart analyst Paul Grein wrote,

"The other albums to open at number 1 this summer have all been hard rock/metal bands—Skid Row, Van Halen, and Metallica. Such groups appeal to young, active music buyers who are more apt to find the time and inclination to buy an album in its first week of release than are the older, more settled country and pop fans—or at least that has been the conventional wisdom. [*Ropin' the Wind*] suggests it's time to recognize that country fans can also be active and committed."

By the end of 1991 Garth's overall record sales accounted for 40 percent of Capitol's sales. As of 2008, *Ropin' the Wind* has sold over 14 million.

HIGH ON GARTH'S REVENUES, Bowen wrestled control of Capitol Nashville away from New York and L.A. the following year, renaming the Nashville label Liberty Records. It was a coup for Nashville even if few appreciated it and Bowen overestimated his win. New York still held the real power. And most didn't refer to Capitol as Liberty. But still, it made a statement.

If Bowen and Garth appeared to have something of a truce going, it would end when Garth was advised to renegotiate his contract. In late 1990, Bowen had offered him a bump in royalties, from between the 10 and 11 percent he'd been given when he first signed to Capitol, to 16 percent. Garth was thrilled with it and took out a thank-you ad in the trade magazines. But within a year it was obvious that further adjustment was due the artist responsible for the label's sales, over $130 million. What Garth wanted was his own imprint and complete creative control. He would be paid no advance, would pay for his own recordings, but would own them in the end.

Bowen told Garth that he didn't deserve that kind of a deal and that it could only be negotiated in New York, anyway. And so that's where Garth negotiated it. He stayed involved with every step of the deal making. "I did that simply because I couldn't expect somebody to stand up and ask for what I thought was right,' he said. "Especially since what we asked for had never been asked for before [in country music]."

As he explained to *Billboard*, "It's a full incentive contract where we start from scratch every time. If we don't sell any records, we don't get a cent; and if we sell a lot of records, we get a lot of money. It's that black and white."

All artists on major labels, be they country or pop, would be well advised to take a look at the top management in the parent company. In the end, these are the people who will make decisions that affect everything they do. Label heads in Nashville may have control over what goes on within their offices, but Bowen's renaming Capitol to the contrary, New York and Los Angeles executives are the ones who choose country's executives and whose overall business decisions affect country's future.

Jim Fifield had been president and CEO of EMI Music (Capitol's parent company in the United States) since 1988, after having been an executive VP at General Mills and president/CEO of CBS/Fox Video. Although he came from outside the record business, Fifield was a confirmed music lover who tried to balance out the books and the art. Those close to Fifield said he was a rarity at top corporate levels, a man who despised office intrigue and any hint of gamesmanship.

He was deliberate, unaffected—and an unabashed Garth Brooks fan. That didn't mean he was willing to give him anything just to keep him happy. Fifield represented EMI. Garth represented himself, the biggest artist on the label, but one artist, nonetheless. And so their relationship might best be described as cordial, but cautious.

Joe Smith, the man who had cut the deal for Bowen's takeover, was president and CEO of Capitol-EMI Music. Smith was originally a radio guy, who went on to become one of the top music executives in the business. He had run Warner Bros. and Elektra/Asylum before arriving at Capitol-EMI in 1987. Smith had long been close to Garth, spending time at his home and offering advice on keeping his feet on the ground during heady times.

Standing behind those executives, of course, was Sir Colin Southgate, the British chairman of the board who came to power at Capitol's international parent company, Thorn-EMI, in 1987 and hired Fifield soon thereafter. Southgate was not without detractors. *Fortune's* analysis of his business style was that he sold music as he might sell widgets, never quite grasping the volatile personalities and egos involved. *Fortune* referred to the EMI board of directors as "a clubby institution that's thoroughly British, clanking with knighthoods and for the most part clueless about the music business." On the other hand, Southgate took charge of a company that was buried in subsidiaries as disparate as defense contracting to movie houses and turned it into a commanding global music presence. Southgate accomplished the feat with the help of men like the ever-cautious Jim Fifield, who agreed that Garth Brooks deserved a new contract, one that gave him a joint venture. In the end, Garth had his own label, Pearl Records, complete creative control of his music, paid for his own recordings, and ultimately owned them.

Bowen didn't like the new contract, believing it would hurt the label's revenues. But in fact, Garth's joint venture was not heavily criticized in the industry. Many saw it as perfectly justifiable. After all, in 1992 his albums made up more than $177 million of EMI Music's $2 billion-plus annual revenues.

On January 7, 1993, the *L.A. Times'* music business analyst, Chuck Philips, explained one of "the largest and most uniquely structured deals ever negotiated." As Philips noted, "Sources said the 30-year-old singer will receive almost 50% of the profits from each album he sells in the United States. That rate is said to match Michael Jackson's much-touted 1991 pact with Sony Music—and to surpass the Madonna and Prince deals with the Warner Music Group.

"Unlike superstars such as Madonna and Prince who have demanded cash advances of $5 million to $10 million per album, Brooks opted to receive no cash advances and will pay for all recording and music video costs out of his own pocket, sources said. He used to receive a 16% royalty rate and about $500,000 cash advance per album."

Eric Kronfeld, president and CEO of PolyGram Holding, Inc., the company that distributed, among others, country rival Billy Ray Cyrus's multimillion-selling album, told Philips, "Garth blazed the trail for other artists like Billy Ray. If somebody would give PolyGram an artist who sells as many records annually as Garth does, I would be the first to recommend that this company give him a joint venture."

Not to be outdone, and because Bowen was ending his own three-year deal with Capitol, the label head floated a rumor that PolyGram was offering him a high-dollar contract. For weeks on end the staff at PolyGram was on pins and needles, making secret calls to friends at Capitol to see if anyone knew which way the wind was blowing. Bowen loved every minute of it. He even asked his PR staff to prepare two press releases, one announcing that he was staying at Capitol, and why; the other stating that he would move to PolyGram, and why. When asked for quotes about the "why" of either move, he laughed and said, "Who gives a damn? Make something up." Bowen loved running a bluff and he was a master at the game.

Ultimately, EMI offered Bowen an astonishing five-year deal. In his words, "millions in salary, bonuses, and other perks, but also a Christian music deal potentially worth tens of millions through the life of the contract." Bowen was right about the Christian music market, and it is to his credit that he got EMI into that end of the business. It had long been underappreciated and underpromoted. With EMI's machine behind it, the genre moved further into the mainstream.

CHAPTER NINE

"Who in the hell is Garth Brooks?"

Garth drove through Los Angeles on his way to the Universal Amphitheatre at Universal City Walk. He'd been opening for the Judds' Farewell Tour on a California run beginning in Costa Mesa, winding up at the Shoreline Amphitheatre in Mountain View the previous night. He was juggling a tight schedule, fulfilling opening-act commitments as well as headlining his own sold-out tour.

Thinking ahead to sound check at the venue, he pulled up to a stop sign and noticed a bumper sticker on the car ahead of him. He thought he was reading it correctly. Squinting in the bright California sunlight, he took a second look. Yes, he'd been right. There on the car's bumper was a question:

WHO IN THE HELL IS GARTH BROOKS?

Before he could even check out the driver, the light changed and the other car changed lanes, disappearing into traffic.

Garth sat there for a moment, laughing. He knew just how they felt. He'd felt much the same way when all the hoopla started.

GARTH LEARNED ABOUT HIS historic entry onto *Billboard*'s Top 200 chart while he was filming a show at Reunion Arena in Dallas. The idea began with a long-form video in mind, and ended up as an NBC special. By the summer of 1991 it was obvious to Capitol that Garth's show deserved to be seen by a wider audience. Joe Mansfield especially had believed that event marketing, increasing visibility in as big a way as possible, would be particularly effective for Garth.

"Anyone who had ever seen Garth in concert knew that his show was fueling those CD sales figures," Mansfield said. "We wanted to take advantage of what was a huge asset in his career path, his ability to entertain."

Garth wasn't sure. "I loved the idea," he said later. "*Loved it!* I mean, to get the chance to put our show on TV? Who wouldn't? But, and it was a very *big* 'but,' it was a scary idea to think people would tune in. On the other hand, I knew that even though I wasn't the greatest singer in the world or the best songwriter—somehow I'd figured out how to entertain people. I guess I'd been working on that one since I was a little kid singing for the family in Yukon, Oklahoma."

Once the decision to film a show was made, the question was asked. Where? The answer, as far as Garth was concerned: Texas. "That crowd steals the show. If you've ever been to one of our shows you know there are times I can walk offstage and the audience would never know it. They're raising hell, having fun—they're crazy."

"Dallas was the first city to really embrace what Garth was doing," Joe Harris explained. "His whole deal in concert is to feed off the energy of the crowd, and Dallas audiences were always the most excited."

The Reunion Arena show sold out eighteen thousand seats in forty-five minutes.

Some special guests were invited to witness the show: NBC programming brass. Country veteran Gene Weed, VP of Dick Clark Enterprises, had been pushing the network to do such a show for some time. But as Joe Mansfield told *Video Insider*'s Barry Gutman, "What it took was for them to see those live concerts."

Rick Ludwin, NBC's senior VP for specials, variety programming and late night, who attended the Dallas concert with a group
of network executives, said, "I have never heard an audience react
the way this audience reacted to Garth. It was like Elvis was back.
And as I looked around at the crowd, there were teenagers as well
as twenty-, thirty-, forty-, fifty-, and even sixty-year-olds!"

Ludwin was so impressed that he went back to L.A. and hired
Gene Weed to put together a series called *Hot Country Nights,* a
show he vowed would represent the new country attitude—one
that did not include hay bales, corncob pipes, or blacked-out
teeth.

Joe Mansfield had seen that reaction coming. While *This Is
Garth Brooks* was in the planning stages, he described the event
as a win-win for everyone concerned. "This will introduce
Garth's concert to those fans who haven't seen the show yet.
By the time it airs in 1992, *Ropin' the Wind* will have been out
around six months, and I'm betting that the special causes a spike
in sales on *all three* of the albums. Beyond what it does for Garth,
it will show the excitement that country music can summon. I
think it'll help put to rest that old idea that we are the stepchild
of the music industry."

This Is Garth Brooks aired on January 17, 1992, and gave NBC
its best Friday night in more than two years. The show received
a 17.3 rating, and a 28 share. (1 rating point represents 959,000
households and a "share" is the percentage of sets tuned in
during a given period.) It was the number 9 show in the Nielsen
ratings for the week. At the second airing, *This Is Garth Brooks*
remained powerful, receiving a 6.9 rating and a 12 share.

There was one controversy that for a time threatened to overshadow the success of the special: the infamous guitar-smashing
spectacle. To show country's wild side, Garth decided to mimic
rock's tendency to smash guitars onstage. Nervous about ruining
good instruments, Garth ordered two "seconds" for he and Ty
England to break. But as the hours went by and no delivery was
made Garth felt backed against the wall. He weighed his desire

for a scene-stealer against two busted guitars and finally went ahead with the plan. In hindsight, Garth said his biggest regret was that he hadn't secured the flawed guitars well in advance.

The success of *This Is Garth Brooks* reminded music marketers that network television could sell records, and showed advertisers that country was a good investment. And as the special proved: visibility is everything.

On January 30, 1992, Chuck Philips, the *Los Angeles Times* music business analyst, explained what happened when *This Is Garth Brooks* aired: The first tangible result of the special involved record sales, with *Ropin' the Wind* again taking the number 1 spot in *Billboard, No Fences* moving back up to number 2, and *Garth Brooks* to number 10 on the Top 200 chart. This meant that Garth became the first country artist ever to have three albums in the pop Top 10 during the same week. Statistics like that immediately spurred new interest in prime-time television as a music marketing avenue, much like when Elvis Presley had been spring-boarded to superstardom on shows like Ed Sullivan's. Philips's article quoted Mike Fine, CEO of SoundScan, the New York research firm that provides sales data for *Billboard:* "Recent sales statistics prove that record manufacturers can successfully market all kinds of music to a wide variety of audiences without the help of Top 40 radio."

Philips also interviewed Paul Schulman, whose firm analyzed and placed about $175 million a year's worth of advertising on the television networks. "Garth got ratings that astounded everyone," Schulman said. "When advertisers and networks see numbers like he pulled in you can bet they pay attention."

By 1992 country showed a 76 percent increase in revenue over the base year of 1990, the Country Music Association announced. The largest area of growth was in record sales, from $6.6 million in 1990 to $1.4 billion in 1992, and concert revenues from $64 million in 1990 to $126 million in 1992. Additionally, in a sampling of the top one hundred country radio stations, advertising revenues grew from $5.5 million in 1990 to $6.6

million in 1992. On October 3, 1992, *Billboard* reported that Garth was having a "Garthgantuan" effect on the entertainment industry. "Moderate estimates indicate that Brooks has generated more than a half-billion dollars for the industry, from concerts to merchandise, and from record and video sales to music publishing and songwriting."

Entertainment Weekly named Garth one of the top fifty most influential people in the entertainment industry, after he had been signed to a record label less than four years. Garth explained his feelings to *Country Fever*'s Frank Barron: "I've gotta be honest. I'm having the time of my life. When you stand up there next to the people you were with in an old musty basement, just dreaming, and didn't have a pot to pee in, really, and then sitting there and thinking—'My God, it's happening!'"

Although he was quick in pointing to the strong careers of artists like George Strait, Randy Travis, and Ricky Skaggs, many of country's other top acts started looking like also-rans. Most artists just understood that it was the way of the business when "the next big thing comes along." Some in the business resented the seemingly overnight success. But Garth had strong friendships among male artists, notably Steve Wariner and Ricky Skaggs. *L.A. Times* powerhouse music voice Robert Hilburn pronounced, "Garth Brooks is so far ahead of every other male singer in country music sales and concert vitality that's he's going to have to stumble badly for anyone to soon take away his crown."

Country music reigned and Garth Brooks ruled the realm. The national press didn't just jump, it dove headfirst into the tank for Garth. But as Johnny Cash once said, "The higher you climb up the ladder, the bigger the target on your butt."

Garth learned that lesson soon enough.

Jory Farr wrote a piece in the Riverside, California, *Press Enterprise* titled "The Accelerating Decline of Rock 'n' Roll": "Is rock 'n' roll dead? Not yet. But in 1992 there were signs that music as we know it should be put on the endangered species list as country, long considered novelty or hillbilly music, soundly kicked its butt at every turn. And it wasn't just Garth Brooks . . . albums by everyone from Trisha Yearwood to Travis Tritt turned platinum with ease."

The *Orange County Register*'s Gene Harbrecht wrote, "For a handful of music history's superstars, there comes a point when their performances transcend the label of concert and become *events*. Elvis, The Beatles, Bruce Springsteen and Michael Jackson are a few examples. It's uncertain exactly when country music messiah Garth Brooks crossed that threshold, but he most certainly has."

The *Seattle Times* said, "Brooks has almost single-handedly boosted country music to its greatest level of popularity." *Entertainment Weekly* pronounced Garth "the most popular singer in America." He appeared on the covers of *Time,* the *Saturday Evening Post, People,* and *Entertainment Weekly.*

Forbes led with the cover line, "Led Zeppelin Meets Roy Rogers—Country Conquers Rock."

Time described a Garth Brooks concert as "part Jolson and part Jagger . . . more of the Fillmore than the Opry, and the audience hollers for him, feasts on him, lets itself go nuts with him." *Album Network* noted, "Garth Brooks isn't just a superstar country artist anymore, he's rewritten music history."

Well now, it was one thing for Garth to be lauded for setting new standards of success in country, but talk of rewriting music history was unacceptable. And as if it hadn't been bad enough to say that country had conquered rock, *Forbes* heaved heavy metal and rap into the mix. Here's what the magazine reported:

"This phenomenon suggests that American popular culture is taking a new, healthier direction. At [Dallas country dance club] Denim and Diamonds, the clientele is of mixed ages, with a preponderance of the young, but ranging from 21 to 60 and up. The scene is less solipsistic and drug oriented. Dancing becomes a social activity again, with people dancing with each other rather than wrapped in their own private ecstasy. The sexual electricity is there, but it isn't vulgar or violent."

Then the *Forbes* article, with an assist from Jimmy Bowen, plunged a knife straight in metal's and rap's backs:

"One thing country music is all about is everyday life and everyday experience. Rapper Ice Cube writes about burning down Korean grocery stores. The Geto Boys talk about a horrifically violent rape. 'If you don't live in the inner city, you can't relate to those lyrics,' says Bowen. 'There are millions of other younger Americans who are disenfranchised. They don't like dancing to heavy metal music. They've been poking around and they found Garth Brooks.' What they found is an entertainer they can relate to."

The British country bible *Country Music People* added to the conquers-rock meme: "[Brooks's] success has even reached the pages of the British rock press, who usually reserve their country coverage for rebels from California. For them, Garth is the man who toppled Guns N' Roses, destroying a heavy metal hype that had been eighteen months or more in the making. The metal merchants had staged a cunning publicity campaign for their latest albums, delaying the release over and over again until excitement was (supposedly) at fever pitch. Sure enough, their double-pronged assault on the US album charts stole the top two positions—only to be toppled a fortnight later by the singer who had already made history by becoming the first country artist to debut an album at #1 in the States [*Billboard* Top 200]. And there Garth stayed for another two months with *Ropin' the Wind* racking up five million sales along the way."

At MTV's awards show, Metallica's Lars Ulrich echoed the bumper sticker: "Who the hell is Garth Brooks?" Head Candy lead vocalist Mike Sangster questioned Garth's authenticity, saying that he was to country what Skid Row was to metal. *USA Today* pop critic Edna Gunderson believed Garth was stealing the spotlight from artists like Steve Earle, never mind that Steve had moved on from country several years earlier. Gunderson wrote, "If some semblance of taste is to be restored to mainstream pop, this hip hillbilly's reign must end."

USA Today's country critic, David Zimmerman, fired back, saying that "other forms of music are so poor and mindless that Brooks was sucked into the vacuum."

But perhaps the best explanation came from *Billboard* country editor and music historian Edward Morris:

"What most rock critics either don't understand or won't accept as valid are the traditions of civility and self-effacement in country music. Rock seems to revel in 'rawness' and posturing, usually mistaking them for wisdom. Country prefers a more measured and restrained approach, even when the subjects are provocative or violent. The elements in Brooks' songs that Gunderson describes as 'safe' and 'approachable' are absolute virtues to people who prefer not to be lectured to or shouted at. In country music, the singer is always subservient to the song. Brooks knows that and has benefited greatly from that knowledge. It is too bad that he is insufficiently barbaric for Gunderson's tastes. The rest of us can handle his sensibilities."

In public, Garth often made light of the criticism, facing it with self-deprecating humor. As he told *Playboy,* "Three years ago would you have thought that the largest selling artist in the '90s would be going bald and have an eating problem and be doing fiddles and steel guitar?"

But he admitted to a friend, "I am getting real sick of seeing myself on magazine covers. And if I am sick of me, then I have to figure somebody else is too."

Considering his admiration for the sales plans put together by Capitol's Mansfield, Garth was astonished to read that his sales were the result of his own marketing genius. He told *Country Song Roundup,* "I read a magazine article once, and I swear to you, I didn't know who they were talking about. It had my picture on it. It had my name on it. But this guy sounded like somebody from outer space. It was the furthest thing from *me* that could possibly be. This guy sounded like some kind of Einstein of country music, and it was like—'Get a *grip!*'"

CHAPTER TEN

Why should rock 'n' roll
get all the glory?

The guy wearing a baseball cap and sweats wandering around an empty Texas Stadium would have looked confused to the casual observer. He sat in one section for a time, then moved to another, and yet another. He sprinted up to the Crown Suites, Texas Stadium's highest point. Then, astonishingly, he crawled up onto the stadium's catwalk.

What Garth was doing was putting himself in the position of his potential audience. As a high school and college student, he'd attended plenty of stadium and arena rock concerts. And since he never had much money, he always had to sit in the nosebleed section. Scrupulously checking out venues had become a pattern since he'd started playing those stadiums himself. And if a show was being taped, the routine became even more crucial. In the case of Texas Stadium, where he planned to film *This Is Garth Brooks, Too!,* he needed to know everything up to how helicopter shots might work.

Making a big stadium show an intimate experience for every audience member might seem like an impossible undertaking, but Garth was determined to pull it off.

THE CONCERT SEASON OF 1992 was a "big bucks summer," according to Buddy Lee Attractions president Tony Conway.

"The economy's taking a turn and there is big interest in country from a younger audience," he announced. "There aren't a lot of new venues, but the venues are buying more this summer. Sheds [amphitheaters such as Nashville's Starwood] that in the past bought one country show a month are buying three or four a month. If you go back to the 1940s, '50s, and '60s, there weren't twenty-five acts that could play 24,000-seat arenas. We have forty acts and they're all out there working."

Buddy Lee was up 16 percent over its 1991 gross and definitely in a position to profit from country's renewed popularity. The agency booked Garth Brooks, Mark Chesnutt, Emmylou Harris, the Highwaymen (Waylon Jennings, Kris Kristofferson, Willie Nelson, and Johnny Cash), Tracy Lawrence, Willie Nelson and Family, Waylon Jennings, Ricky Van Shelton, Doug Stone, Marty Stuart, Steve Wariner, Trisha Yearwood—and a newcomer named Martina McBride.

In 1992, Garth set off on his first real solo tour, and thus began changing concert history. For the remainder of the decade, pop and rock ticket sales records fell by the wayside with regularity. Garth outsold them all, running the gamut from Elton John, Michael Jackson, and Prince to the Stones, Van Halen, and the Grateful Dead.

For his opening act he turned to Martina McBride, wife of his production manager, John McBride, and newly signed to RCA Records. Martina got her shot with the label in an impressive bit of good-natured duplicity. After the label took a first pass on her demo tape, she famously sent it back with "Requested Material" written on the package, got a meeting, a recording contract, and an opening spot on the Garth Brooks show.

Garth was impressed with Martina even before he ever heard her sing. "She used to come out on the road with John," Garth reflected. "And one time I remember when we were all trying to move the sound equipment quickly, there she was—this tiny brunette, lugging stuff that the guys were huffing and puffing over. Then I heard one of her tapes and I'm going, '*Oh, man!*'

Anyone who ever wonders how all that voice can come out of that little body never saw Martina haul speakers."

Garth and Stillwater had been off the road since December 1991 when the '92 tour started on June 2 with a sold-out show at McNichols Sports Arena in Denver, Colorado. Tickets for the 1992 tour sold in unprecedented time and record numbers, as they had for the concerts Garth headlined in '90 and '91.

The September 22 show at the New York State Fair in Syracuse was a case in point. The Syracuse *Post-Standard*'s Brian Bourke reported: "It was a year of records for New York State Fair entertainment and behind most of them there's a guy named Garth Brooks. Garth Brooks' concert last Wednesday was the fastest sellout in State Fair history. Brooks also did much to help the Fair collect its highest-ever gross receipts from concert sales, more than $2 million."

The *Idaho Statesman* in Boise reported that on April 22, between ten and eleven in the morning, 205,000 attempted calls were logged through Boise Idaho's call switching center. That was opposed to the typical 85,000 calls per day. The December 4 show at Thompson-Boling Arena in Knoxville, Tennessee, sold 25,501 tickets. When Lynyrd Skynyrd played a free concert at Thompson-Boling in 2002, it brought out 17,400 to the show, still not breaking Garth's record.

When tickets went on sale in Seattle for the Tacoma Dome, Garth's show sold out in minutes. The concert at the Minnesota State Fair in St. Paul set a fair record for ticket requests, 160,000. When the Fresno show sold out in twenty-nine minutes, fans petitioned for more. But Garth was booked solid and it was impossible. Garth knew then that he had to consider bigger venues and additional shows.

This breathtaking success presented a serious challenge: the ticket scalping that had become a problem in '91 rose to astonishing levels. After reports of scalped tickets being offered for one hundred dollars or more at the New York State Fairgrounds, the state's attorney general's office began looking into the problem. When the *Post-Standard* phoned the scalpers' office, the man who answered said it was legal and complained that while he was making big money on Garth, he "ate the cost" of the ticket-buy the company had made for a Genesis concert at the Carrier Dome. People writing letters to the paper didn't blame Garth, and most said they'd still wait in line to buy tickets to one of his concerts. One security guard said of the scalpers and line crashers, "In the eleven years I've worked here, I've never seen anything like it."

Garth begged people to reject the one-hundred-dollar tickets. "Do not pay those prices," he announced. "I've seen my show and I promise you it's not worth it!"

Reviewers disagreed. On July 20, the *L.A. Times'* Richard Cromelin wrote, "The country singer is the hottest commodity in creation, and his success was part of the Forum ceremony, which was less a concert than a community celebration."

Garth kept his ticket prices under twenty dollars when many were charging five times that. He believed a family of four should be able to attend one of his concerts, and be able to dine out that night without busting their budget. The concern about fans overpaying for tickets was reflected across-the-board in his concert approach, and it paid off. He not only broke records at the box office, but also with merchandise sales. It was done by strict attention to detail, keeping his prices down and profit margin low. While others were charging upwards of twenty-five to thirty dollars for T-shirts that were often poor in quality, Garth bought Hanes Beefy-T, the "Cadillac" of shirts, and sold them for fifteen to twenty dollars. While other artists made far more money per sale, Garth moved more merchandise. Rondal Richardson ran the concessions at the time.

"For perspective, this is how the concession industry thrived with Garth," he explained. "With 20,000 fans attending a rock concert, it doesn't take long at $30 a shirt for a hot band from the '90s to obtain a gross of about $200,000, or about $10 per customer. That amounts to 6,000 shirts sold in one night for the rockers. Take the same crowd at a typical Garth show of 20,000. Because the merchandise was not only of better quality but also less expensive, fans often bought two shirts instead of one. So it wasn't uncommon for him to have an average of $15 in sales per person sales ratio. That's a gross of about $300,000 but with 20,000 shirts sold. That's how Garth did business, and he did it honorably at every level of his tour. When I think back on working for Garth, I am always reminded that he treated the fans, the customers, like friends. He'd sometimes say, 'If I am the product, would I buy me?' He cared about one fan at a time, and that is how he built a business franchise that will never be equaled."

GARTH HAD BEEN THINKING about a second NBC show even before his debut special first aired in January 1992. In fact, just two months after *This Is Garth Brooks* was filmed at Dallas's Reunion Arena in September 1991, Garth was on the phone inquiring about the possibilities of filming a special at Texas Stadium. He visited the stadium in September 1992, and, again, as he usually does at any unfamiliar venue, he spent hours sitting in one section after another visualizing the concert experience from the fans' perspective. He came away worried that the stadium was too big for fans to truly appreciate the show.

He made the final decision after four visits spent working out the logistics of the event. In May 1993, Garth came to Texas Stadium and firmed up a deal. On June 12 Garth called a news conference, where he admitted to the Dallas press that he was worried about filling the stadium.

"I'm hungry again," Garth said at the Dallas news conference. "I'm going back to being the guy you met in 1989 with a wild look in his eye."

The look in Garth's eyes wasn't anywhere close to being as wild as what happened when those tickets went on sale. On June 12, Texas Stadium sold out in ninety-two minutes, selling over 65,000 tickets and breaking the previous sales record held by Paul McCartney. Dallas fans demanded and got more shows: a second show sold 65,000 tickets in ninety-two minutes, as did a third.

Because of the continued problem with ticket scalping, Garth appeared on the *Crook & Chase* show on July 9 and announced a fourth concert. This one, he said, would be free. As it turned out, because of planned special effects, the show's producers believed Garth needed to lip-synch an entire show for some close-ups. That offered a way he could take the wind out of the scalpers' sails.

When Garth planned the concerts, he kept in mind some advice his dad had once given him: *Leave people with some great memories.* Garth had taken the advice to heart years before. It was in 1989, when he was just starting out, that he told KPLX-FM deejay Steve Harmon on the station's *Harmon and Evans* morning show that country music shows should be able to have some flash, some spectacle: "Why should rock 'n' roll get all the glory?"

Show preparations did not go without incident. While working on what was being called a "supergrid," eighteen crew members were injured as the stage roof supporting lighting and sound equipment dropped to the ground. It was a grid system that had successfully been used for a George Michael show at Texas Stadium, and had previously had no problems. Garth was rehearsing in Las Colinas when the grid collapsed, and he rushed to Texas Stadium as soon as he got word of the accident. "God was with us," he said on learning that there were no fatalities or serious injuries. He stayed at the stadium late helping clear debris. Rather than try to replace the supergrid hanging over the stage, the show's producers essentially turned the entire stadium into a lighting system.

Garth stepped into the show preparations with a more hands-on approach. He has often been accused of micromanaging much of his career, but people who have worked closely with him say that he is just the opposite—*unless* he perceives a problem. Jon Small, who later produced videos and television specials for Garth, explained: "Every time I worked with Garth he first sat down and told me his basic idea. Then I got back to him on how I planned to proceed. If we were on the same page, then I barely heard from him again! Garth only jumps back into a project when something starts to go south, and then, sure, he'll roll up his sleeves and help salvage it. Luckily, with the two of us, that was never necessary."

Overseeing the concert filming was a monumental task. *This Is Garth Brooks, Too!* took 40,000-plus man hours to produce, with 60 semi tractor-trailers bringing in the equipment. Over 3.5 miles of heavy-gauge chain was used to hang the structure that housed the sound, lighting, cables, motors, and special effects. Over 500 varilights were used and over 150,000 pounds of speaker cabinets and cables. A crew of over 600 professionals from engineers to architects to equipment operators and stagehands worked on the show. Over 16,000 gallons of diesel fuel were used to power equipment, with 50 miles of electrical cable and a sound system that used 40,000 watts of power at peak performance. A typical concert uses 2,000 amps of power. Garth's show used 60,000 amps. The entire football field was covered with tarp and plywood, with special risers built to bring the show up close and personal.

Garth's commitment to detail expanded beyond the actual concerts, too. He was hands-on when it came to editing footage from four shows into one television special. He went to Los Angeles to personally supervise the final editing of *This Is Garth Brooks, Too!* As *TV Guide*'s Skip Hollandsworth noted in the April 30, 1994, issue, "[Garth] has already studied all 450,000 feet of film shot from the 14 cameras. He also decided to select the opening sequences for the show." Why the personal atten-

tion to detail? Because, Garth told Hollandsworth, he understood that celebrity is a fragile commodity: "I've seen audiences
get tired of people 10,000 times more talented than me."

When *This Is Garth Brooks, Too!* aired in May 1994 it gave
NBC its best adult (18- to 49-year-olds) rating in the time slot
since the first of the year.

CHAPTER ELEVEN

Country's Big Boom

Billy Ray Cyrus was talking with a trusted Mercury Records executive, a woman with years of music industry experience and a good head on her shoulders. After kicking around playing honky-tonks and dives for years, Billy Ray finally had his shot. He had an album he believed in and a record label that believed in him. Life couldn't have been better. Still, Billy Ray had some concerns.

"Can I talk to you a little about 'Achy Breaky Heart'?" he asked. "I'm kinda worried."

"I can't think why. It's going to be a smash."

"It's about the video," Billy Ray offered hesitantly. "It's not over the top, is it?"

"Nah, don't give it another thought. It's gonna be great," she said, laughing. "This is the nineties. Country *is* rockin'."

BETWEEN 1989 AND 1992 country radio went from 1,800 to 2,400 stations, with more people with incomes of over $40,000 listening to country than any other format. Country was generating over a billion in annual revenue. In January 1992, *Billboard* reported, "Garth Brooks tied his own country album sales record in December, topping the five-million mark with

Ropin' the Wind. His previous album, *No Fences,* hit five million sold just two months earlier. Brooks is only the third male solo artist—after Michael Jackson and Billy Joel—with back-to-back albums over five million. Country music is clearly taking center stage. According to Arbitron, of the Top 100 stations, country tops 47 US radio markets. And 67 have a country station ranked #1 or #2 with the most desired demographic, the 25–54 age group."

Time noted that the new demographics reflected both new music and new artists, the first generation of stars who had been raised on rock but chose to record country. "Today's hot country stars, Garth Brooks foremost among them, are more likely to be college graduates with IRAs than dropouts with prison records." It was hyperbole, of course, given the relatively small number of country singers who actually did time, but it made a point.

The article, titled "Country's Big Boom," included a laundry list of the new Nashville. Vince Gill lived on a golf course and looked like he wore L.L.Bean. Cleve Francis, signed by Jimmy Bowen to Capitol, was a black cardiologist. Mary Chapin Carpenter had a degree in American civilization from Brown University. K.T. Oslin once played Broadway. Reba McEntire studied classical violin and piano in college. Other artists than those mentioned fit the new profile as well. Capitol's Suzy Bogguss had a degree in art from Illinois State. Mercury's Kathy Mattea played in a bluegrass band while at West Virginia University. MCA's Trisha Yearwood studied music business at Nashville's Belmont University, while her labelmate Lionel Cartwright had a degree in business administration. Billy Dean played college basketball in Decatur, Mississippi. Then of course, there was Garth Brooks's advertising degree from Oklahoma State, once more misidentified as a marketing degree in the *Time* article.

These were part of Nashville's new breed, the artists who were drawing in both younger listeners and baby boomers bored with AOR (Album Oriented Rock, focusing on album cuts). As *Time* pointed out, their effect was felt throughout the mainstream. *Nashville Now* host Ralph Emery's autobiography, *Memories,* stayed on the *New York Times* Best Seller list for months. *Country America* magazine doubled its circulation to almost 1 million. The 1991 Country Music Awards show, broadcasted on CBS, landed in the Nielsen Top 10. NBC shot back with *This Is Garth Brooks* and *Hot Country Nights.*

Country had an embarrassment of riches by 1992. The biggest-selling album was Billy Ray Cyrus's *Some Gave All.* Garth took some zingers from the press after his overwhelming success, but Billy Ray was absolutely steamrolled.

The Flatwood, Kentucky, native was the son of a single mother who worked as a maid to support him after her gospel-singing husband left. Billy Ray worked at a succession of jobs— in a warehouse, a car lot—before starting to sing professionally. Besides singing on his own in a lot of small clubs, Billy Ray had opened some big shows and there was a reason he wowed audiences of 15,000 and more: he was one hell of an entertainer. Even so, he had to visit Nashville over forty times before Opry star Del Reeves took an interest and introduced him to a manager named Jack McFadden, who in turn led him to Buddy Cannon and Harold Shedd at Mercury Records. Once the two saw him live, they were sold.

Billy Ray's initial success was stunning, and not without a downside. He liked a tape he'd heard of a song called "Don't Tell My Heart," originally on a 1991 Marcy Brothers record. It was a ditty with an infectious, danceable melody. He recorded the song, renamed it "Achy Breaky Heart," and began the requisite meetings with video directors, press photo shoots, and other pre-release preparations. The label determined that this catchy tune might be turned into a dance craze. Melanie Greenwood, wife of singer Lee Greenwood, choreographed the video and advances were sent out to clubs. The clip featured Billy Ray wearing a torn T-shirt and out-hip-grinding Elvis in front of mobs of young slavering females. It came down to that "over the top" concern Billy Ray had in the beginning: the video had a sex-object look to it that didn't go over with some hillbilly cats.

Travis Tritt, in particular, despised it and went on record with his disdain. Tritt was riding high himself when Billy Ray's debut hit the air. His 1991 album, *It's All About to Change,* had four chart-topping hits including a couple of jukebox naturals, "The Whiskey Ain't Workin'," a duet with Marty Stuart, and "Here's A Quarter (Call Someone Who Cares)." In 1992, *T.R.O.U.B.L.E.* spelled anything but, with hits like "Lord Have Mercy On The Working Man." But maybe *T.R.O.U.B.L.E.* got Travis spoiling for a fight.

Tritt pointed out to the press that Billy Ray's video fan scenes were a hype and his gyrating led one to think he'd once been a Chippendale dancer. Tritt then spouted off on country radio about "ass wiggling," leading his friend Marty Stuart to quip, "Travis, you couldn't have opened a bigger can of worms if you'd said Roy Acuff was gay."

Nevertheless, "Achy Breaky Heart" spent five weeks at the top of the country charts, and hit Top 5 in the pop chart—a rarity in the '90s market—and became a top-selling single. The album, *Some Gave All,* ended up selling nine million copies. The thing about the whole sorry episode is that it was misplaced ado about *something*—a monster success no matter what some Nashville malcontents thought. Billy Ray's second album, *It Won't Be the Last,* rocked a little harder but didn't produce any hit close to the magnitude of "Achy Breaky." He went on to record a respectable catalog that included country, bluegrass, and gospel. And if those didn't cause more than a few to dine on crow, Billy Ray's success with the television series *Doc* and daughter Miley's stratospheric ascent served it up on multiplatinum platters.

Arista's Alan Jackson established himself as one of the industry's biggest stars with 1991's *Don't Rock the Jukebox* and 1992's *A Lot About Livin' and a Little 'Bout Love.* While many critics considered his debut, *Here in the Real World,* the best of the three, his chart-driven sales picked up enormously with the '91 and '92 releases. Singles from *Don't Rock the Jukebox* stayed at number 1 seven weeks, and from *A Lot About Livin' and a Little 'Bout Love* for five weeks, including the monster career recording "Chattahoochee."

Reba McEntire still sat atop the female vocalist roster, but the new Queen of Country had been through a tough year. After playing a private show for IBM on March 15, 1991, the private plane carrying seven of her band members and their road manager crashed, with no survivors, on Otay Mountain near San Diego, California. It goes without saying that Reba was inconsolable.

"At first I didn't want to get close to anybody ever again, 'cause I was afraid they'd be taken away," Reba told CBS News. "Then I realized that can't be the situation. You gotta embrace the people you're with. You gotta take every minute as if it's your last."

After much deliberation, she decided to address the tragedy in song on *For My Broken Heart.* The title cut went to number 1, as did "Is There Life Out There." The final song on *For My Broken Heart,* "If I Had Only Known," is a tribute to the friends she lost. Reba said that the album meant more to her than any album she'd ever recorded.

Wynonna Judd's much-anticipated eponymous solo album on MCA lived up to expectations, with some songs offering a glimpse back into the duo days, while most stretched out to show Wy's power and versatility. Standouts included her first solo number 1 hit, "She Is His Only Need," with startling revelatory lyrics and a melodic break from country. She followed it with "I Saw The Light." Radio also saw the light and held the single at number 1 for three weeks. Her high-energy blues performance on "No One Else On Earth" surpassed even the previous chart foray, holding at number 1 for a month. *Wynonna* sold five million albums and put Wynonna front and center among Nashville's female vocalists.

Two premier vocalists who had directly benefited from the Garth Brooks juggernaut had important albums in 1992. Clearly, country fans heard the same remarkable command in these two women as Garth had. Trisha Yearwood followed her self-titled 1991 debut with the monster *Hearts in Armor*. Critics called it a tour de force, the "most lauded Nashville album since Randy Travis' *Storms of Life*." Trisha's crystalline vocals could turn from passionate on ballads like "Down On My Knees" to tough yet conversational on "Wrong Side Of Memphis." Some in Nashville joked that "Walkaway Joe," the duet with Don Henley, was clearly a case of the Eagles star "marrying up."

Martina McBride's 1992 debut, *The Time Has Come*, established her as another formidable female talent with a vocal maturity seldom found in a new artist. But despite the album's strengths, it yielded little chart action. Only the following year, when Martina blasted back with *The Way That I Am*, containing singles like "My Baby Loves Me," "Life #9," and "Independence Day," did radio fully appreciate her. It didn't hurt that down the line Martina cut her hair short to separate herself from a pack of longhaired brunette beauties vying for attention.

Clint Black came back from a somewhat disappointing second album, 1990's *Put Yourself in My Shoes*, with a powerhouse 1992 release, *The Hard Way*. Clint had taken some criticism for continuing to co-write only with guitarist Hayden Nicholas, and for supposedly selling out by marrying a movie star. Clint more than redeemed himself with *The Hard Way*'s knockout hits, including "We Tell Ourselves," "When My Ship Comes In," and "Burn One Down."

Clint was as happy as Garth was when the press laid off a dueling cowboys theme. Unfortunately, Nashville gossips found a new tabloid tale to peddle. When Clint met and married actress Lisa Hartman, rumors started floating that his management

disagreements with manager and Texas moneyman Bill Hamm
were due to meddling by Lisa and her mother, PR woman
Jonie Hartman. Jonie was portrayed as some sort of Hollywood
Medusa, quietly manipulating Clint while turning his good old
country boy pals to stone. Of course, the truth was that Jonie
was herself a good old Texas girl from Houston, and just happened to help Clint with media advice. But as one of Nashville's
favorite philosophers, big John Cash, used to say, never let the
truth get in the way of a good story.

Vince Gill's 1992 album *I Still Believe in You* contained a
string of chart-topping singles that included the title cut, "One
More Last Chance" and "Don't Let Our Love Start Slippin'
Away," which stayed at number 1 for three weeks. After only
a year as a team, Brooks & Dunn were named the Country
Music Association's Duo of the Year in 1992. Their 1991 debut,
"Brand New Man," produced by Don Cook and Scott Hendricks
for Arista Records, took the airwaves by storm, beginning a
string of number 1 singles that simply wouldn't relinquish the
top spot. "My Next Broken Heart" stayed at number 1 for two
weeks, "Neon Moon" for two more, then the big kicker, "Boot
Scootin' Boogie," refused to budge for a month. The duo was
the brainchild of Arista's Tim DuBois, in an attempt to fill the
void left by the Judds. He asked the two to write something together, and they returned in a few days with "Brand New Man."
DuBois, not one to mince words, gave them this advice: "Keep
your boots on, keep your jeans on, and keep it country."

Marty Stuart continued to carry country's banner with his
1992 MCA album, *This One's Gonna Hurt You*. Critic Karen
Schumer called it "nothing less than a concept album about the
meaning of country music." MCA's stone country stylist Mark
Chesnutt brought out *Longnecks and Short Stories*. Critic and
music historian Robert K. Oermann called the record "as close
to perfect a country album as anything released during 1992."
Another traditionalist to make his name in 1991 was Tracy
Lawrence with his Atlantic debut, *Sticks and Stones*. Atlantic had

two more hot entries in 1992: John Michael Montgomery, with *Life's a Dance,* and country rockers Confederate Railroad, with their self-titled debut.

Given Garth's numbers, Nashville labels were obsessed with signing artists they thought capable of moving records on massive levels. Warner Bros. saw that potential in Travis Tritt while RCA looked to Martina McBride. CBS signed Patty Loveless and Collin Raye to its Epic label. New to the playing field, Arista, under Tim DuBois, had made smart early choices: Alan Jackson and Brooks & Dunn. Mercury had Billy Ray Cyrus with Shania Twain and Toby Keith in the wings. Curb had hopes for a singer/songwriter named Tim McGraw. MCA backed Wynonna and Trisha Yearwood.

A question hung in the air: when it came to big-selling artists, was Capitol a one-trick pony?

Determined to have a superseller other than Garth Brooks, Bowen had expanded his artist roster with amazing speed and diversity, signing some interesting new acts, developing others, and branching into instrumental and songwriter releases. He even decided to make a run at pop rock recording and hired an L.A. A&R vice president, Kim Buie.

The problem was, none of the artists Bowen found had the same success as those his counterparts at other labels were signing. While he had success with Sawyer Brown, Suzy Bogguss, Billy Dean, John Berry, and the Pirates of the Mississippi, none of his acts, despite their talent, hit superstar levels and the rest simply couldn't win over country radio. It was not for lack of trying on the label's part.

Bowen so believed in former PolyGram artist David Lynn Jones's potential that he gave him a budget to remodel his Arkansas studio to record an album away from Nashville distractions. No singles charted from the resulting *Mixed Emotions.* A film crew was hired to follow Texas honky-tonk rocker Ricky Lynn Gregg around in anticipation of a making-of-a-star television documentary. When Gregg's debut single only made it to

number 36 on the charts, Capitol financed a radio showcase in
Florida. Jocks and programmers were flown in from all over the
country, but it was to no avail. He never charted again.

The Pirates of the Mississippi's 1990 self-titled debut album
generated considerable press interest, and a Top 20 hit with
1991's "Feed Jake." *Radio & Records* named the Pirates its Top
New Group, as did the Academy of Country Music. But the
three succeeding Capitol albums made little noise on the charts.
Another group, the Cactus Brothers, was about as close to hillbilly hippie music as could be found in Nashville in the early
'90s, and their self-titled debut album contained a wealth of
tasty musical tracks but no hits. Mississippi band Pearl River had
two albums and one charted single.

Reba protégé Linda Davis, known to be one of the finest
voices around Nashville, released two Capitol albums, but, as
it turned out, divine vocals don't always translate to chart singles. Linda's legacy for Capitol may end up being her daughter
Hillary Scott, who could often be found in the label's offices,
quietly coloring in a corner while her mother held an interview.
Now grown and a top vocalist in her own right, Hillary sings
with Capitol's hot new trio, Lady Antebellum, winners of the
ACM award for Top New Group in 2008.

The legendary swing band Asleep at the Wheel recorded *A
Tribute to Bob Wills and the Texas Playboys,* with guest artists including Garth Brooks, George Strait, and Vince Gill, among
others. The ambitious collaboration was released to great acclaim
and won two Grammy awards. But other established artists did
not fare well. Gary Morris had turned his efforts to Broadway
in the '80s, starring in the 1988 production of *Les Miserables* and
drawing raves from New York skeptics. He charted no singles
on Capitol. Eddie Rabbitt and Eddie Raven made their final
chart appearances. Ronnie Milsap, Crystal Gayle, and Barbara
Mandrell's releases quickly slipped from the radar. Lacy J. Dalton
and former Highway 101 lead singer Paulette Carlson fell by the

wayside. Capitol mainstay Anne Murray met with little success
and left the label.

Artists signed to Capitol during the Foglesong years fared
best. Sawyer Brown's 1991 single "The Walk," from *Buick,* re-
established the band at radio and set up the 1992 hit album, *The
Dirt Road,* although it took the band's management borrowing
a page from Doyle/Lewis's playbook when they hired an independent team to rescue the record.

Along with Garth Brooks and Trisha Yearwood, Florida
native Billy Dean was a regular on the Music Row demo-
singing circuit. Dean's first album, 1990's *Young Man,* showed
off his writing talent and yielded two Top 5 hits, "Only Here
For A Little While" and "Somewhere In My Broken Heart."
His second album, *Billy Dean,* had four more top-five releases,
including his signature "Billy The Kid."

Tanya Tucker relished wearing her '91 CMA Female Vocalist
crown, awarded in absentia because she was in Nashville's Baptist
Hospital where she had just given birth to son Beau Grayson.
Even though Tanya was not married and would not reveal the
name of the child's father, she remained a media darling. When
presenter Roy Rogers announced the CMA win, journalists sitting in the press room at the Grand Ole Opry House leapt to
their feet and applauded.

Bowen decided to co-produce Suzy Bogguss's recordings,
and the records they made together speak for themselves, with
dazzling vocal performances and commanding songs backed
up by radio-friendly tracks. It was 1991's *Aces* that broke her
through at radio. She had hits with "Someday Soon," "Letting
Go," "Outbound Plane," and the album's title song.

Bowen also instituted a series of songwriter and musician
releases. Four from both categories were chosen: singer/
songwriters Pat Alger, Jill Coluci, Kostas, and Kathy Mattea's
husband, Jon Vezner; and musicians Sojoro, Larry Nechtel, John
Jarvis, and Billy Joe Walker Jr. He signed Jason Ringenberg of

Jason & the Scorchers fame, but despite having a loyal following, his *One Foot in the Honky Tonk* charted no singles.

One success that circumvented radio was Garth's old friend Chris LeDoux, who had already proven he could sell records without airplay. Once Garth introduced Joe Mansfield to Chris's music, the marketing VP became a big fan and made Jimmy Bowen aware of the $4 million in tapes sold from the back of LeDoux's truck. The label was also interested in the cult following that could always be counted on to buy any new LeDoux.

It was perfect timing for Chris, who was experiencing tough financial times. All those tapes had been sold over a period of many years, and they no longer covered expenses. "The music career was paying our day-to-day living expenses," he said. "But costs were up and profits were down at the ranch, and my music couldn't make the land payments. For a while I was afraid we were going to lose everything."

Chris resisted the label offer at first, because he was afraid that Bowen might try to change his music. "We won't try to 'Nashville you up,'" Bowen promised. So Chris literally saved the farm by signing with Capitol and licensing his entire catalog to the label. It was a win-win situation for everyone concerned.

Bowen and Jerry Crutchfield produced Chris, with the first album, *Western Underground,* a tribute to cowboys, rodeos, and family. One of his favorite songs on the album reflected his concerns for some of his rodeo pals, the ones who too often lived love-'em-and-leave-'em lives. In "Riding For A Fall," he spoke to freedom, and what it really means. "They [the aforementioned ride-off-into-the-sunset types] need to understand that sometimes you need to sacrifice some of that freedom to find true happiness."

Though Chris's catalog and new releases sold steadily, he had only two chart hits, both from his 1992 gold-selling album, *Whatcha Gonna Do with a Cowboy.* The title cut, performed by Chris and Garth Brooks, produced by Crutchfield and Allen Reynolds, was a Top 10 tune. In 1993, a second release, "Cadillac

Ranch," hit the Top 20. But chart outings were not what kept Chris LeDoux going or selling records. It was his road show. The rough-and-rowdy one that Garth always laughed about stealing from.

They were heady days. Chris saw his entire catalog put out on professionally manufactured CDs, signed with manager TK Kimbrell of Sawyer Brown's organization, had his road show come out of the chute like a wild horse, and finally felt a financial safety net. Everything was going so well that when Chris went in for an insurance company health check, he shrugged off a questionable blood test.

"Might just be a touch of hepatitis," he was told. Probably nothing to worry about.

CHAPTER TWELVE

Damn this rain and damn this wasted day

Stephanie Davis sat on a grassy hill on Garth's farm outside Nashville. She fidgeted a bit, unused to trying to write a song without her guitar in hand. But she understood why Garth had insisted on leaving the guitars at the house and what he was trying to do by writing in such an unconventional manner.

"I think the lyrics to this song are so important that the music shouldn't distract us," he had said. "Let's go out to the hillside and get to the heart of the song before we start thinking melody."

Garth already had the message: tolerance. And Stephanie already had the title: "We Shall Be Free."

GARTH WAS IN THE middle of a six-month break from the road; everybody needed a hiatus. "We've been touring for two and a half years, and I just said, 'Let's take care of family.' My guitar player called his daughter on her first birthday and we figured out that he'd seen her only forty-nine days during the first year of her life. That's when I said enough was enough. I just needed to get my people home and get their family back to being what it was."

By 1992 Garth's sister Betsy Smittle had joined the band on bass and background vocals. A multi-instrumentalist (six-string bass, electric guitar, acoustic guitar, and percussion), Betsy was a veteran of Gus Hardin's Oklahoma-based band and a singer/songwriter in her own right. Betsy had been the most serious about music in the Brooks brood. She was the only child who didn't go to college, attending one day and deciding it wasn't going to help her become a professional musician. And while she became most visible through her baby brother's fame, she'd initially made it on her own.

The other Stillwater players remained: James Garver, lead guitar, background vocals; Ty England, acoustic guitar, background vocals; Steve McClure, steel, electric guitar; Mike Palmer, percussion; and Dave Gant, keyboards, fiddle. Unusual for the industry, Stillwater was on salary, with health insurance and a retirement plan. That meant when Garth took time off the road, rather than scrambling for new gigs, they could spend the time with their families.

Garth spent the time working on a fourth album and taking care of business on the home front. He and Sandy were remodeling a farmhouse they'd purchased near Nashville and living in a trailer on the property until the work was finished. Their first child was expected in July and Sandy was having some difficulties with the pregnancy. In April, when the two were in Los Angeles, where Garth won the Academy of Country Music Entertainer and Male Vocalist awards, the post–Rodney King riots broke out. Sandy's health had taken a turn for the worse. As they left a city in flames, Garth was sick with worry over his wife and unborn child and shaken by the societal upheaval.

Back home, with Sandy's pregnancy out of danger, Garth continued to be troubled about what had transpired in Los Angeles. He called Stephanie Davis, with whom he was already writing "Your Time Will Come," a song addressing racism. Garth suggested that the theme could be expanded. "We Shall Be Free" addressed topics including poverty, homelessness, racism, sexual preference, and class; a testament to inclusiveness, brotherhood, and tolerance.

The song was added to an album that was already the most personal that Garth had recorded. The album had been tentatively titled *Let It Ride.* "I was in a state where it appeared that I'd met all the goals I'd had in life. Then one night in May, I sat up in bed and said, 'You egotistical ass. What makes you think you've met all your goals? If that's true, get up and get some new goals and get back in the chase and run as hard as you can.'"

Despite the enormous effect the Los Angeles riots had on Garth, that experience paled by comparison to his life-defining feelings July 8 when his daughter Taylor Mayne arrived. Garth was with Sandy through the entire ten hours of labor, and when he finally saw his daughter born he says he felt like he'd witnessed such a miracle that he wanted to go down the hall and watch another new soul come into the world. Having a child changed Garth in ways he never expected. For one thing, the career that consumed him lessened its hold and he began to wonder how to balance his life better: "I looked at that little girl and thought, 'From this day on, this is what you are about.'"

From the beginning of his recording career Garth had seen making records as much more than just going into a studio and recording ten songs, hopefully some hits. There had long been something of a divide in Nashville about what albums should be. Throughout its history, the music industry has had artists who paid minimal attention to what songs they were recording. Some left the decisions primarily to the producer, others to their record labels. Results vary.

But there is no question that some of the finest, longest-lasting recordings have been concept albums, built around a common theme. Emmylou Harris's 1985 semi-autobiographical *Ballad of Sally Rose* is widely considered a classic. Waylon Jennings cut an album's worth of Billy Joe Shaver songs and the result was one of his most successful and popular releases: 1973's *Honky*

Tonk Heroes. Willie Nelson brought Columbia Records a tape of *Red Headed Stranger* in 1975 and executives thought he was joking. Not only did the lyrics meander through an outlaw's life of murder and regret, the tracks were acoustic to the point of seeming unfinished. And yet the album is considered by many to mark the beginning of modern country music. Historian/ critic Chet Flippo explained: "It is impossible now to underestimate the impact of *Stranger*—it legitimized country music and intellectualized it and immediately made it mainstream as no album ever had done."

Garth says his way of looking at albums was influenced by something that recording engineer Mark Miller told him early on, that each one should offer some new insight into the artist. Garth took that advice on many levels. It might mean songs that are painfully honest about personal concerns or it might mean being willing to look at human foibles and laugh. The songs Garth wrote and recorded on his fourth album, which was ultimately titled *The Chase,* ran that gamut.

"I opened myself completely on *The Chase,*" he explained at the time. "It's the closest anybody has ever got to getting inside my head. So much was going on. We were expecting our first baby, trying to get our house remodeled, and I was out on the road all the time. The album was recorded during a time that I felt like maybe I couldn't have everything—a career and a family—and do it right. That was the time I thought about giving up the music if it was going to take me away from home too much, and the emotion showed. It was an important album for me to do."

The final song and Garth's favorite on *The Chase* is equal to "We Shall Be Free" when it comes to risky business territory. Tony Arata's "Face To Face" is about looking your fears straight in the eye. The original version of the song spoke to fears of schoolyard bullies in childhood, and adult fears of death.

"I wrote 'Face To Face' in 1987 or 1988," Tony recalls. "Garth heard me sing it in a local club, and liked it. But I don't think it was ever formally pitched to him. Then one night when we were standing in line at the ASCAP awards he started singing it. He said he wanted to cut it, but asked if I could add another verse, one about a male/female relationship." Tony wrote the verse dealing with date rape, and of the girl facing down her attacker in court.

"This song petrifies me," Garth said. "It's about real life—the bad side of real life."

That Garth was drawn to "Face To Face" was no surprise to people who knew him well, and certainly not to Colleen Brooks. The moment she heard the lyrics and message about bullying, she understood. That was Garth the schoolboy making an appearance. From the time he was small he had been on the side of the underdog, the misfit, the last kid to be picked for the team. Garth's women friends knew the side of him that, because of the way he was raised, could see things from the female's viewpoint. This is another of those songs that sounds as if it sprung from his own pen.

Garth often writes from a concept. In "Somewhere Other Than The Night" that idea centered on losing the ability to communicate within a marriage. It deals directly with sexual relations and reviving passions. Co-writer Kent Blazy didn't think it stood a chance in hell of getting airplay.

"Much Too Young (To Feel This Damn Old)" had stopped short of number 1 because of the use of the word *damn*. In "Somewhere Other Than The Night," to describe the hardworking husband's seeming lack of passion for his wife, Garth and Kent wrote the line, "Damn this rain and damn this wasted day." Of course, when the rained-out farmer arrives home to find his wife waiting in nothing but an apron, the day turned out less of a loss than he'd thought. The few offended radio stations didn't balk this time, and "Somewhere Other Than The Night" hit the top of the chart.

Sex was the theme of another chart-topping song on *The Chase*. Pat Alger, Garth, and wife Sandy wrote "That Summer,"

Garth's first Fan Fair, 1989. His first single, "Much Too Young (To Feel This Damn Old)," had entered the charts just a month earlier.

Bob Doyle, Garth, and Pam Lewis in 1990.

Garth and Capitol
marketing/sales VP
Joe Mansfield.

Garth is presented with his first gold record at Fan Fair, 1990.

Capitol chief Jimmy Bowen with producer Allen Reynolds in 1991.

Ricky Skaggs with one of his biggest fans at Dollywood in 1991.

Garth with producer Allen Reynolds, *Billboard*'s Lynn Shults, and engineer Mark Miller in 1991. Lynn encouraged Capitol's Jim Foglesong to sign Garth in 1988. Both Foglesong and Shults were fired by Jimmy Bowen the following year.

Garth and Sandy at the 1991 CMA Awards, where he won Entertainer of the Year, Album of the Year (*No Fences*), Video of the Year ("The Thunder Rolls"), Single of the Year ("Friends In Low Places").

Garth went to
George Strait's
Fan Fair booth in
1991, hoping to
see his idol—but
had to settle for the
cardboard stand-up.

Garth opened for the Judds Farewell Tour in 1991. The emotional pay-per-view
final concert was the most successful music event in cable's history at the time.

Kix Brooks, Garth Brooks, and Ronnie Dunn in 1991.

Garth says that from the time he first started working with Trisha Yearwood her vocals left him wondering how he ever believed he was a singer.

Two of the first major acts Garth opened for, Wynonna Judd and Kenny Rogers.

THE Billboard 200™

TOP ALBUMS
FOR WEEK ENDING SEPTEMBER 28, 1991

THIS WEEK	LAST WEEK	2 WKS AGO	WKS. ON CHART	ARTIST	TITLE	PEAK
1	NEW		1	**GARTH BROOKS** CAPITOL NASHVILLE	**ROPIN' THE WIND**	1
2	1	1	5	META... ELEKTRA	METALLICA	1
3	2	2	14	NAT... LE ELEKTRA	UNFORGETTABLE	1
4	5	4	8	CO... BADD GIANT	C.M B.	3
5	4	3	12	BO...TT CAPITOL	LUCK OF THE DRAW	2
6	6	5	1...	...MOTOWN	COOLEYHIGHHARMONY	3
7	10			...FACTORY COLUMBIA	GONNA MAKE YOU SWEAT	2
8				...TON COLUMBIA	TIME, LOVE AND TENDERNESS	1
9				...OS.	OUT OF TIME	1
					ROLL THE BONES	3

Garth at the Music Row party Jimmy Bowen threw when *Ropin' the Wind* entered the pop charts at number 1.

Garth at 1992's Fan Fair.

Garth at bat in the
1993 City of Hope
softball game.

By 1993 Garth's concert was airborn . . .

Garth credits Chris LeDoux with inspiring his high–energy stage show.

Garth with Jim Foglesong in 1994.

Faith Hill and her producer, Scott Hendricks, in 1994, when her debut album, *Wild One,* topped the charts.

Jimmy Bowen, Chris LeDoux, Charlie Daniels, and Willie Nelson at Fan Fair, 1994.

Jimmy Bowen hosted a Music Row party when *Ropin' the Wind* entered *Billboard*'s Top 200 chart at #1.

Garth's 60 Million party included 1960s icon look-a-likes including Deputy Barney Fife.

Garth and Trisha, 1996.

Trisha Yearwood, 1997 CMA
Female Vocalist of the Year.

Martina and John McBride
in 1997. John was Garth's
sound engineer on tour,
sometimes assisted by his
wife during the early tours.
She opened for Garth
during 1992, after signing
a record deal with RCA.

The Dixie Chicks appeared as presenters at the 1998 CMA Awards. They released their first three number 1 singles that year, and took home the Vocal Group and Horizon awards. The explosion Garth kick-started continued through the decade.

Steve Wariner at the 1998 CMA Awards, with wife Caryn and Capitol label head Pat Quigley. Steve's "Holes In The Floor Of Heaven" won Single and Song of the Year.

Garth with Brad Paisley in 1999. Brad's Arista debut, *Who Needs Pictures,* had just been released.

Garth with Capitol artist Deana Carter, whose debut album *Did I Shave My Legs for This* sold 5 million.

Garth with Brenda Lee at the Source Dinner in 2006.

Garth and Trisha.

which started out to be about an ignored wife who begins an affair. As the song developed through writing process, a more complex story evolved, with the wife replaced by a lonely middle-aged farm widow who seduces her much younger hired hand. It's possible that in country only Kris Kristofferson has written more sex songs than Garth Brooks.

The Chase certainly wasn't an across-the-board societal critique. There's a comical take on pick-up lines with "Mr. Right," backed with Rob Hajaco's hot fiddle, and the breezy "Something With A Ring To It," originally cut by Mark Collie, who wrote the song with Aaron Tippin.

Thematically, the album also touches on two of Garth's tried and true topics: reflecting on old loves and getting past them. "Every Now And Then" speaks to understanding that while people move past relationships, they continue to be affected by them. "Learning To Live Again" describes the difficulty of getting on with one's life. Don Schlitz and Stephanie Davis originally wrote it as a female song, and Garth pitched it to every female artist he knew, to no avail. Finally he asked Stephanie if she and Don would consider rewriting it for a man.

Stephanie wasn't so sure. "It had been written as a woman's song, and I personally related strongly to it. Don first had the idea for it because a woman who worked at his dentist's office was widowed and had to start over. Garth is the one who rewrote the song, although he wouldn't take any of the writer credits. I think he made it a better song. The twist at the end is that both people are feeling the same way."

Garth's friend Randy Taylor had played him Jerry Jeff Walker's cut of "Night Rider's Lament," a perfect addition for *The Chase*. Garth recalled, "I wanted to include a waltz and a cowboy song. 'Night Rider's Lament' was both." As with "The River," the message in "Night Rider's Lament" is one Garth has returned to time and again through his recording career: follow the dream against all odds.

Two more cover songs rounded out the album. When Garth

was in college he lived down the hall from a Little Feat fanatic, and years later he could still hear the strains of "Dixie Chicken" playing in his head. Garth slowed it down a bit and added an all-female choir led by Trisha Yearwood. Every time Trisha came to Jack's Tracks to record with Garth, Allen Reynolds was reminded of something that he'd said to her when he first heard her sing. "I hope that when you get to be a big star you'll still make time to sing on Garth's records, because no one else could add what you do."

With perennial country favorite "Walking After Midnight," Garth faced a quandary: how not to offend Patsy Cline fans. "I knew no one could *really* cover that song," he said. "But I had always loved it and hoped a guy would sing it. I originally cut it for *Ropin' the Wind*, but somehow it didn't fit until we were working on *The Chase*." He cut the song with a jaunty swing touch, and while a few critics questioned its inclusion, most applauded the outcome.

In August, just a month before launching *The Chase*, Garth's first Christmas album was released, *Beyond the Season*. It contained traditional and original Christmas songs, including "Go Tell It On The Mountain," "God Rest Ye Merry Gentlemen," "White Christmas, "Silent Night," and "What Child Is This." At the time Garth said that recording the collection was one of his most fulfilling studio experiences: "I'd make this album every day of the week!" *Beyond the Season* peaked at number 2 on the country charts, sold 3 million copies, and raised $2 million for Feed the Children.

When the question of a first single from *The Chase* came up, Garth felt passionately about "We Shall Be Free" and fought for it. His audiences loved it, and advance press reaction seemed to back up the choice. The *Washington Post* called the song Garth's "Imagine," and *Newsday* touted him as "country's great populist."

Garth was so successful by this time, and radio had expanded so drastically, that it would have seemed that the song could take hold. Country radio now replaced adult contemporary as the biggest format, with 20 million more people listening to country than adult contemporary. The numbers of country stations had climbed to over 2,600, and it was no longer a rural-based industry. In fact, country was the top format in over half of America's urban centers. The listeners were better educated and made more money than any in country radio's history. They were far more sophisticated than, arguably, even radio programmers themselves quite understood.

Bowen was against releasing "We Shall Be Free" as the first single. Singing about poor people in country music was one thing, confronting poverty in America was quite another. And defending gays? Bowen didn't think it was going to happen anytime soon on country airwaves.

Turns out Bowen was right. Radio didn't welcome "We Shall Be Free." Although it made number 12 on the charts, it was the lowest-peaking single Garth had ever had. Part of the problem, it seemed, was the song's categorization. Some programmers thought it was a pop anthem, others considered it gospel, and in fact, it did enter the gospel radio charts.

Garth believed the message was too important to lose. And so, despite the fact that "The Thunder Rolls" had left him wary of videos, he decided to make one. The powerful piece was directed by NBC's Tim Miller, and featured numerous cameos. In addition to celebrity appearances by Whoopi Goldberg, General Colin Powell, Reba McEntire, Elizabeth Taylor, and many others, the video contained news footage depicting society's problems, counteracted by scenes expressing hope. Colin Powell perhaps summed it up when he said, "We're all a family. Let's take care of each other."

"We Shall Be Free" first aired January 31 during the 1993 Super Bowl. It almost caused a controversy. When, at the last minute, Super Bowl officials told Garth they might not be able to air the piece after all, Garth stopped them in their tracks. The video must play, he said. It was part of the package. "We Shall

Be Free" did air, and subsequently received an Outstanding Recording Award from the Gay and Lesbian Alliance Against Defamation/Los Angeles (GLAAD-LA), and won the Academy of Country Music's 1993 Video of the Year.

The Super Bowl performance stopped Garth in *his* tracks, too. Always facing a food problem ("I never met a chicken fried steak I didn't like."), Garth's weight had crept up to almost 240. He knew he carried the extra poundage, but when he saw footage from the Super Bowl he was horrified. Given that he was heading out on a two-year tour soon, he knew something had to be done. "I embarrassed myself," he told a friend soon after the appearance. "I've got serious work to do before August, when we go back on the road." He cut back on carbs, watched fat content, and worked out. By the time he opened his show in Dallas he was down to around 170.

The Chase became the second album in music history to enter both the *Billboard* Top 200 and Country charts at number 1, but initial sales did not match *No Fences* and *Ropin' the Wind.* More than a few were taken aback by the seriousness of *The Chase,* and when sales fell off, industry insiders predicted the end of Garthmania.

After all, Billy Ray Cyrus was out there at number 1 for five straight weeks with "Achy Breaky Heart"—even "Friends In Low Places" had only held the top chart spot for a month. Clint Black's latest, *The Hard Way,* was giving him a renewed career boost. Travis Tritt was still on the hot streak he'd started in '89 with "Country Club," and stalwarts like George Strait and Randy Travis held steady. Many speculated that the mantle was already being passed to Arista Records' Alan Jackson, whose two albums had produced nine hits since 1990.

But the most pressing problem Garth faced was another shakeup at Capitol. Joe Mansfield's contract was up for renewal at the same time *The Chase* was being readied for release. Mansfield had suspected that Bowen might be carrying a grudge over the coverage he'd gotten from "The Six Million Pieces Man" and

other articles. But when he was let go, Mansfield was in shock
and many staffers were outraged. This was the man who had
engineered the marketing that had taken Capitol to new heights
of respect in the industry. By comparison, his replacement, Bob
Freese, the man Bowen called "a nice hardworking kid," was
not considered in Joe's league.

When "We Shall Be Free" failed to hit Top 10, the label cut
back on CD shipments, pulling 600,000 units from Wal-Mart
and KMart alone. Bowen blamed Garth for making a somber
record and for being too candid on television shows such as the
Barbara Walters special, where he had mentioned that he supported the rights of gays, because, after all, his sister Betsy was a
lesbian. Following the show, Garth was crucified for supposedly
outing Betsy. But at a Gus Hardin concert in Nashville, Betsy
told a table of journalists that the whole furor was a joke, that
everyone she knew had long known she was gay. Her real concern had been about the potential for negative public reaction
against her little brother.

Colleen Brooks got off the best comeback. When one reporter asked her if it was true that Betsy was gay, Colleen raised
an eyebrow and slyly replied, "Of course. *All* my children are
gay. They're *all* very gay and happy people."

Garth made another statement on the Barbara Walters show
that was in hindsight a mistake. Talking about the creative process, Garth tried to explain that money had no place in his choices,
that being successful had freed him from worrying about taking
risks. In making his point, he said he made more money than his
grandchildren, or their grandchildren could spend. So it wasn't
an issue. It was an unfortunate statement, a completely honest
assessment, and one that could have only come from someone
with solid working-class roots. The statement of fact was seized
on and parsed to death.

Colleen had this wisdom to share with her son. "I said,
'Honey, let me give you a little advice. When you are talking to
the press don't *offer* anybody anything. If you are talking with a

reporter you think is going to tell the story in the way you are telling it, *let them ask the questions.* You have the right to answer or keep it to yourself.'"

"That's really good advice," Garth said. "Why didn't you tell me that when I first started out?"

By this time Garth's dealings with Jimmy Bowen were complicated. The label head had developed an intense dislike for some of Garth's representatives, including a financial adviser, and refused to take meetings with them, so Garth met with Bowen alone.

Bob Doyle encouraged Garth to do so. "There's bound to be issues between artists and the people who run the record labels," Doyle reflects. "But in the end, every label, every company, has to have a place where the buck stops. Somebody has to be accountable. Garth and I both understood how critical it was to keep communications open."

But the divisions grew with each meeting. When confronted about the lack of advertising, Bowen reacted with what would become a pattern. He blamed the music, countering that Garth had spent too much time working on his new contract and not enough time on *The Chase.*

Garth was willing to take the blame, if that's what was called for with an album that eventually sold over 9 million copies. "I had a real hard time with *The Chase,*" Garth later said. "I got too much into the lyrics, and I got rid of the honky-tonk fun part of the music. If you're serious all the time, people wonder, 'What's he bitching about this time?'" But in the end, *The Chase* is still the album Garth listens to when he feels he needs to get focused.

Despite questions about his latest album, Garth was not merely selling records in astronomical numbers, he was rapidly becoming one of the most awarded artists of all time. Later, after looking over the list of thirty-plus awards he'd received in 1992 alone, Garth had a talk with the record label about the official biographical material being released. "I'm afraid that all these sales and awards are getting in the way of the music," he said. "Is there a way we can separate the two things? Put out a bio that has to do with the music, and a different one—just an update—about sales and all that?"

"It's really becoming two things, isn't it?" he was asked. "There's you and the music, and there's this Garth thing."

"Yeah." Garth shook his head. "I think of it as a GB thing."

He sat staring out the window and finally explained in more detail what he was feeling. "I've said this before, but awards are like Christmas trees. They add some sparkle to the holiday but they are not what Christmas is all about. Plus, these awards and sales involve more people than me. This career is about everything from the songwriters, to the people at Doyle/Lewis and Jack's Tracks to all of Capitol's employees, the fans—radio. This star business gets very complicated. The worst mistake an artist can make is to start thinking of 'I' when talking about a career. I have to make sure I know the difference between *me* and *it*."

But referring to his career, including his team, success, sales, and awards, in the third person as "Garth Brooks" or "GB" would be scrutinized for the rest of the decade.

CHAPTER THIRTEEN

"It's a once-in-a-lifetime thing"

Garth and the band missed the old touring days, even the downside: pulling the van into an empty parking lot and wondering how many would show up, the darkened interior of the bar lit mostly by neon, the stale smell of last night's beer and cigarettes. So the parking lot at Clovis City Limits brought a smile to their faces that night in 1993. The thirty or so who were hanging around were there for the beer, because nobody had ever heard of the bunch of pickers advertised, an outfit called Yukon Jack. That changed when the band stepped onstage and Yukon Jack turned out to be Garth Brooks and Stillwater.

It had all started when guitarist James Garver sat down with Garth and confessed that while he loved the big tours, he really missed the days when Joe Harris was booking them into club dates and fairs. It turned out that Garver wasn't the only one who'd been having nostalgic thoughts of the old days.

The idea of doing some time traveling was just fine with Garth. He was sick of corporate politics, of the feeling that although he'd gotten control of his recording process, there were still career decisions being made whether he agreed or not. One of his regular song collaborators had seen it coming. In 1992 Kim Williams asked Garth what it felt like to be on top of the mountain. "I like what I've got, but I miss what I had," Garth answered.

"I loved the thought of heading back to one of those honky-tonks," Garth later said. "We owed so much to those audiences, and sometimes they were *real* small audiences. Twenty people crowds. *Nine* people! But we got our sound down out there, tried out new songs, screwed up stuff all the time and had fun doing it."

So while they were gearing up for the 1993–1994 World Tour, Garth had Joe Harris book them into the little club in Clovis, New Mexico, under the name Yukon Jack. And what a night it was. Once the band stepped onstage, the word went out. By the time Garth sang "Friends In Low Places," Clovis City Limits was the jumpin'ist joint in the state.

JOURNALISTS USUALLY POINT TO Garth's 100 million album sales as a watershed event in music history. But while those numbers were phenomenal, they have overshadowed his other career landmarks. One of those was the 1993–1994 World Tour. In those two years Garth headlined what was at the time the biggest and fastest-selling concert tour ever fronted by a country act in the world.

Garth's early career was built on performances in the honky-tonks across the country, many of them in the Southwest: Texas, Oklahoma, New Mexico, Kansas, Colorado. The people who came out to hear him had much in common with those Gilleyrats who had captured the nation's attention in 1980. They were from a broad spectrum of the population—blue-collar workers, professionals, young and old. It was like Gilley's owner Sherwood Cryer had once said, a honky-tonk is a place to go to shake off the world. Sure, getting rowdy down at the bar was just a quick fix, but it damn sure was better than sitting home alone on a Saturday night, nursing a beer and a grudge against your swing shift supervisor.

Garth liked the crowds and trusted the people to tell him whether his music worked. He even started using what he called the "Shorty's bar" test for his albums. Garth first learned about the little Southwest Kansas bar when a Capitol employee went home for a visit and played the clientele a copy of *The Chase*. The crowd loved it, especially the tongue-in-cheek pick-up line tune "Mr. Right" and the cowboy classic "Night Rider's Lament." When one recently divorced young farmer heard the line "learning to live again is killing me," he said, "Damn straight."

Not one of the crowd had problems with the socially conscious themes found in "Face To Face" or "We Shall Be Free." Garth thought the industry underestimated country listeners, whether they were tuned to a radio station in Detroit or sitting in a small-town honky-tonk. They were not a bunch of rubes. Even after multiples of millions in sales, he always asked the employee to send Shorty's a copy of each album and report back.

In 1993, around Nashville there were fifteen gold albums, twenty-six platinum, five double platinum, four triple platinum, and, of course, Billy Ray Cyrus's whopping debut, *Some Gave All,* which had sold 7 million and was well on the way to nine. Nashvillians in the business of selling records were ecstatic. But it was a time of cautious optimism for the country concert industry.

Because of renewed interest in the genre, more than two hundred country acts were heading out on the road in the summer of '93. In May *Billboard* reported that the booking industry feared many major markets would be saturated. Garth's tour, which would begin at Cheyenne Frontier Days in Wyoming and end in Aberdeen, Scotland, would not even begin until August, after most road shows had been out for months.

But less than a month after the *Billboard* article appeared it was clear that saturation was not a problem. Mike Combs, events manager for the Tacoma Dome in Washington, told *Variety* that country shows were leading the concert charge, and pointed to Garth's two shows that sold 44,426 tickets within minutes of going on sale.

The *Idaho Falls Post Register* reported that people were standing in ticket lines more than two months ahead of the August 21 concert. As one Pocatello resident said, "It's just a once-in-a-lifetime thing. If you get a chance, you ought to do it."

In fact, Garth sold capacity in all markets, from Las Vegas to Minneapolis. Everybody, it seemed, had a ticket story. The *Bismarck Tribune* reported one of the funniest: A local woman called a police dispatcher to report that her brother-in-law had just left town with a pocketbook she needed. At first the woman was too embarrassed to say why she needed her purse so desperately. But after speaking to a couple of dispatchers, she confessed, "It wasn't so much the pocketbook. It was the eight tickets to a Garth Brooks concert." The dispatcher didn't hesitate: "Oh my God," he said. "That *is* an emergency." A state trooper (obviously a fan) flagged down the brother-in-law's car and made arrangements for the woman's daughter to collect the tickets.

Garth brought in crowds of all ages, not just the college kids who'd considered "Friends In Low Places" a rallying cry. After the Canadian leg of the '93 tour, the *The Ottawa Citizen* published a letter from a woman who said, "I just felt like one of the teenage girls, 20 years younger, singing and screaming."

Ticket scalping escalated to the point that Garth took his case to the Tennessee Senate. "It's the people who pay for it," he told the lawmakers. "It's not me." But the state senate declined to take action, so Garth fought back the only way he knew how, by adding more shows when the market called for it.

"I get letters from people who tell me that they camped out and waited in line for days, and right before the box office opened a van pulls up and twelve guys get out and get all the great tickets," he told *Tune-In*'s Sandy Adzgery. "I feel I have to do something about this situation."

He tried to combat scalpers in several ways. If the long lines presented a problem for some sales outlets, armbands were available to ensure that people could return and get their same place. He also came up with a plan to keep seating fair. Tickets for seats in the first two rows were not sold. Then, about a half an hour before the show started, the crew went to the back rows and handed out upgrades. One audience member from the show in Ottawa wrote to the *Ottawa Citizen,* "Just when you can't get any higher in the Civic Center, someone from the band comes up and gives you front-row seats!"

And what did the ticket buyers get in return?

The *Lewiston Morning Tribune*'s Nicole Peradotto reviewed the Pullman, Washington, show: "Thunder rumbles. Lights flash and descend from the ceiling like tentacles. Is it Madonna in that mirrored elevator rising out of the middle of the stage? Michael Jackson, perhaps? Hang on to your plastic seat. It's Garth Brooks. Brooks's stage show has enough bright lights to land a fleet of 747's. The sound effects range from nasal buzzes to blasting explosions. The biggest explosion is Brooks himself. At Saturday's sold-out concert in Beasley Coliseum, the former javelin thrower from Oklahoma State University sprinted the width of the stage at least a hundred times, stamped the ground almost as often and swung over the crowd on a rope a la David Lee Roth. Is this a *country* concert? Well, yes. Which country is anybody's guess. What everyone in Beasley Coliseum knows for sure was that wherever Brooks was going, they would follow."

Garth took Sandy and one-year-old Taylor with him through most of the dates and drew good-natured ribs from promoters who reported a different sort of requirement. While some touring artists sent demands for elaborate menus and drinks, Garth's first need came in the shape of a question: got any suggestions for baby outings in the city?

The couple often took Taylor out together while in the scheduled cities. Zoos were favorite haunts for Garth, Sandy, and Taylor, and their appreciation remained constant over the years. In 1998, when the fledgling Nashville Children's Zoo needed friends it found two in Garth and Sandy, who donated a million dollars. One of the most important considerations for Sandy was that zoo visits involved learning experiences. It was

left to Sandy to name the children's zoo, and she chose to honor
Mae Boren Axton, the co-writer of "Heartbreak Hotel," and
a beloved figure in Music City. Most who knew her called her
"Mama Mae" and her death in 1997 was a blow to the industry.
Since Mama Mae had been a teacher and champion of educa-
tion, she seemed a perfect fit.

Because Taylor was in bed by eight thirty every night, she
didn't attend the concerts themselves, but sound checks had
made her aware of her father's connection to music. "Taylor can
recognize her daddy when she sees him on television or hears
him on the radio," Sandy explained. "When Garth is on television, Taylor will stop whatever she is doing and get three feet in
front of the TV and she is glued."

On October 1 at his Charlotte, North Carolina, concert,
Garth brought the crowd to its feet when he announced that
the Brooks family was expecting another child in May 1994.
Knowing that Taylor would be but a toddler when the new
baby arrived, Garth and Sandy began preparing her for a new
sister or brother. One worry Sandy had was that her "rocking
schedule" with Taylor would by necessity change with an infant
in the house. Over the next months the couple began weaning
Taylor away from expecting to be rocked to sleep every night,
and to be comfortable sleeping in her own room when at home.
Sleeping was problematic on the road, since Taylor didn't like
the small cribs provided at hotels, preferring to sleep in an adjoining queen-sized bed next to her parents. It was a habit Sandy
knew she'd have to break soon. Unlike many star families, which
come complete with a hoard of nannies and others operating as
surrogate parents, the Brooks method was hands-on.

Even though Garth often had his family on the road with
him, he was still traveling with the band. The 45-by-8½-foot
bus was remodeled to include a room for the family in back;
Taylor's bed had a spring suspension that hung from the ceiling.
The band's sleeping area was in the middle portion of the bus,
and a common area was in front.

"We now have thirteen people on the bus," he said. "But I can't find it in my heart to separate the artist from the band, so we'll all stay together." Then he laughed and added, "As long as we don't kill each other." Also, Garth told *USA Today* that he saw some very practical aspects to staying on one bus. If you don't keep bandmates as busmates, "You never see each other except onstage. And being closer can save a show. Say somebody might be having a bad night [onstage]. Maybe there's an inside joke or something you can scream at them and keep them laughing."

Stephanie Davis opened the 1993 shows for Garth. It was not the first time she played a big concert with him, though. Stephanie was a Montana girl who'd come to Nashville to be a singer, and she saw her writing as being more directed at her own potential projects. She found co-writing somewhat difficult until she started collaborating with Garth. The two had a lot in common. They both had small-town outlooks and values, were both youngest children, and both loved songs that had a depth of meaning. But, she confessed, even after they had some hit songs she often put him off with one excuse or another. Garth knew that in Stephanie's dreams, she would return to Montana someday and own a ranch. That was how he convinced her to continue co-writing: "Come on, Stephanie, we've got a ranch to write."

Stephanie also confided to Garth that her parents thought her music aspirations were just a little crazy. They had no interest in music, didn't even own a tape player. Nor could they grasp that songwriters could earn a living, or what her connection to this country singer meant. The two friends laughed about the family disconnect at various times, until Garth realized that he was playing some concerts in Montana in 1992. He had Stephanie send tickets to her parents and told them that he would be performing one of her songs. Then, without telling Mom and Dad, Stephanie flew in for the show. When it came time to sing "Wolves" Garth brought her onto the stage, saying, "This is our Montana songwriter."

It had been over a year since Stephanie had seen her parents. It was a tearful backstage reunion and they never again questioned her vocation. For his part, Garth loved singing with Stephanie and believed she would be a terrific opening act. For the gig to benefit her best she needed to have a record people could buy, so Garth told her to let him know if she had anything in the works. But when Stephanie signed a deal with Asylum Records and had a self-titled release scheduled for August 1993, she didn't tell Garth. After all, another of his co-writers, Victoria Shaw ("The River") also had an album in the works, and Stephanie was afraid that she'd seem pushy. One day the phone rang.

"Are you ready to open the '93 shows?" Garth asked. "We head out on the road in August, just about the time your album comes out."

"I know that people are coming to see Garth," Stephanie said at the time. "While I'm singing most folks are still finding their seats. But knowing that takes the pressure off me. There weren't great expectations, so we just went out there and said, 'Wow! This is fun!'" So, then, what *was* Stephanie's primary concern in the early weeks? She'd spent some hermitlike years in sweat-pants. She needed to go shopping.

Stephanie got more than passing approval from Garth's fans. When she started opening the show she received standing ova-tions and encores. Stephanie stayed with the tour until early 1994 when Garth brought Martina McBride and Alison Krauss on the road, then, for the European leg, Susan Ashton.

By this time Garth had convinced his brother Kelly to join the team as manager and accountant for the tours. Kelly had a good banking position in Oklahoma City when Garth started asking him to consider coming to work with him. Kelly put his little brother off several times, until finally Garth phoned and said, "Kelly, I really need you." The tours had simply gotten too

big, and Garth knew he needed someone who knew what he was
doing, and was completely trustworthy. Kelly gave notice and
headed to Nashville. Garth's childhood friend Mickey Weber
was also on board running the day-to-day road operations.

One of the most important things about this tour was that it
opened up the European market to country music. Due in large
part to Garth's record sales, the country industry showed a 76 percent increase in revenue between 1990 and 1992, which encouraged both the Country Music Association and Country Music
Television to look to Europe as a much bigger market than had
previously been thought possible. Selling country music to the
European audiences had always been a gamble. Entertainers were
often disappointed because the audiences were not as responsive
as those in the United States. But industry leaders wanted the exposure and they looked to the man they considered their one safe
bet. In 1993 they put it a way they knew Garth would respond
to: his touring Europe would be good for country music.

He had been warned that European audiences might not
show much outward enthusiasm at his concerts. But Garth was
unprepared for what happened during some advance promotion in London. During one set of interviews, several journalists showed up wearing tiny cowboy hats and string ties. One
talk show host warbled country music, accenting the "hillbilly"
aspect, and made every attempt to portray country singers and
their fans as ignorant hicks. Garth later told the *Chicago Sun-
Times*' Dave Hoekstra, "It was the worst I ever felt as a human
being, to have to sit there and take that. I kept thinking, 'I should
pop this person or walk out.' Either way the ratings would have
gone through the roof. So I just took it." Then he went back to
his hotel room and threw up. Despite the embarrassment, when
Garth edited down his world tour footage for his 1995 television
special, *Tryin' to Rope the World,* he left in those incidents.

"It was hard to keep from getting mad on the air," he further explained in private. "I kept having to remind myself that I

was in Europe representing country music, that this wasn't some shootout between me and this guy. There's times you have to swallow your personal ego for something more important."

Garth would have preferred that the critics be up front about it. He could easily deal with criticism, as long as it was out in the open and honest.

As things turned out a few hip critics and the British audiences were entirely different animals. Advance tickets for concerts in Birmingham and London, England, sold out immediately, and at the April concerts fans sang along on every song.

Never in country music's history has an artist so completely won over the world. The international leg of the tour traveled to eleven countries and played to over a half million fans in Ireland, England, Switzerland, Germany, Netherlands, Norway, Sweden, New Zealand, Australia, Spain, and Denmark. Australia's *Courier-Mail* said: "Brooks—Talent Outstrips the Hype." In Barcelona, the crowds paid him their highest compliment, screaming *"Torrero,"* or matador.

But the real love affair was between Garth and the people of Ireland. After his experience with some British journalists, he was nervous. When he walked onto the Point stage in Dublin that night in March 1994, he was wary, with no idea what to expect. He felt numb as he sang his opening number. He guessed it was the way a prizefighter must feel during the first round. Just trying to feel his way.

When the band struck up "If Tomorrow Never Comes" it was as if he'd made it to round two and had his feet under him. Thousands of cigarette lighters lit up the sky as the audience began to sing along, finally taking over the song.

"It's like they don't need me now," he thought. "They want me to start the song and then get out of the way." So that's what he did, partly because he was too emotional to hit the notes.

The audience kept right on singing. When the voices soared even stronger on "We Shall Be Free" Garth's eyes filled with tears. It was a song he believed in and had stood behind when others did not. And it had been on *The Chase,* an album that had gotten off to a shaky start partly because of it.

"That experience may be one of the biggest things that ever happened throughout my career," he later confided. "It's hard to explain how much 'We Shall Be Free' means to me. It spoke to things that mean so much to us all—tolerance, brotherhood. And I'd be lying if I said that the initial rejection of that message didn't hurt. That's why I made the video and got so many other people involved, why I insisted that it be played at the Super Bowl. I hoped that the power of seeing all these prominent faces, of hearing their thoughts on where we all ought to be heading, might help make some kind of a difference. Not all songs have messages—or *should.* But I believed this one did. And hearing people from another country singing it made me believe that it had worked."

By the time Garth was called back for the inevitable encore, he wondered if he had anything left in him or if he was too wrung out. Worse yet, what if the audience was too drained to respond? But when he started singing they jumped and screamed—and got Garth fired back up. When he ran to the side of the stage to reach down and take flowers from an audience member, one of the crew yelled, "Start reading the album's liner notes! I bet they know the words!"

The overwhelming international reception couldn't have come at a better time. After riding a crest for the first few years of his career, the sobering realities of fame had set in. But that night, onstage at the Point, none of those things mattered. And in the future, when he dreamed of audiences, he said that he still saw those Irish faces.

His mother, Colleen, accompanied him on the tour, connecting with her family roots in County Cork. Later, Garth said he believed part of his attraction to the Irish was that the people shared his mother's eternal optimism. But it was difficult to drag Colleen away from home those days. Colleen loved the sprawling brick house that Garth had purchased for his parents near Oklahoma City.

Garth and Kelly had been talking about buying a new home for their parents for some time. Every time they were home on a break, they looked through the classifieds in the *Daily Oklahoman*. When they spotted this house, and saw that it had adjoining property, they figured they had found the perfect gift.

It's hard to know what Colleen's skeptical mother might have thought if she'd lived to see the Brooks's 150 acres, complete with an acre-and-a-half-sized pond, roaming deer, wild turkey, and fox. But when Raymond and Colleen Brooks spoke about the new place with *Believer* editor Tami Rose, they said the success and ability to give such gifts had not changed their son.

Though he seldom spoke of Garth's stardom in public, Raymond explained to Rose that when his son's career started to explode, he had given some advice to Garth. "You will be surrounded every day with people who are positive, 'yes people' that will give you no negatives and that's not the real world. There are negatives involved in everyday living." He also warned his son about the dangers of making compromises. "People compromise each day of their life but when it comes to values, true values and convictions, then you better back off."

In retrospect, Raymond believed that his son never buckled on things involving his value system. In fact, there was just one change Raymond saw. Since starting his career Garth's business sense had sharpened, and Raymond credited that to using the tools from his college years. "Garth told Colleen and I that he didn't think he would ever use his degree. And I told Garth, 'I don't care if you get out on the highway and stick your thumb out the day after you graduate, as long as you get that sheepskin.' We both wanted him to know that he had something to fall back on, some security."

Both parents believed that those four years at Stillwater had been invaluable on many levels. They understood that Garth had learned lessons about dealing with challenges, with people as well as with life-and-death situations, such as when his friends Jim and Heidi had been killed. Through it all, he'd developed a capacity for critical thinking and problem solving—and the ability to keep his feet on the ground.

Colleen explained one reason he remained centered: "A lot of people start believing that they are always right and they take themselves too seriously."

The ability to keep things in perspective was never more obvious than during the time Garth faced that hostile reception from the British interviewers. He rejected the impulse to react in an equally hostile manner, retained the dignity he believed he owed country music, yet returned home with an honest accounting of what had happened.

THE SOLD-OUT CONCERTS drew the largest audience for any event in Dublin since the pope's visit in 1979. By the time Garth's eight Dublin shows wrapped, he had been seen live by one in every fifty people in Ireland. One in four Irish families owned a Brooks CD or cassette. Dublin senator Paschal Mooney attended one of the concerts and said, "Every Irish home used to have three pictures: Jesus, the Pope, and JFK—and now there's a fourth, Garth Brooks."

It was an unprecedented welcome for an American artist.

Garth spent a great amount of his offstage time in 1994 with the Irish people. He used both the city buses and the DART (similar to an above-ground subway system) to sightsee, rode horses, and played golf. He came to love the Irish for their "unpretentiousness" and the connection he felt between their own music and the country music he loved. And he was so pumped up about their enthusiasm for music that he promised to return, and bring cameras.

"The thing about the Irish people is that there is no resistance. There's no clenched fist. It's all open," Garth later explained. "They sing. They just pop their heads back and sing. And they sing so well!"

Sandy Brooks also had a special connection with the Irish performance. Because she was at home, just weeks away from giving birth, Garth phoned her from the stage, and the audience serenaded her. Garth loved his experience at the Point in Dublin so much that he named a spot at his Tennessee farm after the venue.

He later told the *Irish Times'* Kathy Sheridan that he did so because his experience in Dublin had changed his life: "Something happened at the Point that really just—just changed where I was going in my life. Changed my views on myself and on the music. It meant that much. You know, if you're playin' only in your own backyard, you start to think, 'Hey, things are happening here and it's cool'—but only in your own backyard. And you think, 'But it wouldn't go over in that person's backyard.' So you go over there and something like this happens that gives you a faith, gives you a courage to actually not be afraid of the world, to not be afraid of the differences we have."

The World Tour was vital to the industry in that many country stars wait until their careers have cooled somewhat to play extensively outside the United States. Garth's commitment, beginning during peak years of his career, encouraged promoters worldwide to book more country acts than normal, benefiting everyone. Two years later, in May 1995, the Academy of Country Music presented Garth with the Jim Reeves Memorial Award at its 30th Annual ACM Awards show in Los Angeles. Named for the man who thirty-five years earlier had pioneered international country markets, the award is only given when the ACM recognizes an artist who has uniquely promoted and enhanced the image of country music internationally.

When Garth returned, he said he believed that country artists should travel out of the country more in an effort to dispel the stereotype: "A lot of the journalists I spoke with felt like country music was nothing but hats, fringe jackets, hay bales,

cry-in-your-beer lyrics and 'Yee-hah!' The only way to erase
the Hollywood image of country music is to bring the real thing
to the rest of the world."

Garth confessed that much of his time during the world tour
was spent in search of food: "I ate eels in Spain and haggis in
Scotland for the first and last time. What I kept looking for
was a Taco Bell. Unfortunately, there were none to be found.
We had a ray of hope in Melbourne, Australia, because our bus
driver mentioned that Taco Bell was around the corner from
the hotel. The band and I were all excited until we found the
restaurant—Taco *Bill's*."

One leg of the tour lost money, but it was not unexpected.
"All the rock acts told us, 'Take half your show to Australia.' It
costs a dollar and a half a pound to fly stuff down there. And
you're talking about a rig that we've got: 90,000 pounds. You
can't pass that on to the people." Garth flew the whole show to
Australia anyway. "We sold out fourteen shows and *still* lost a
ton of money," he laughed.

There was one period of time when Garth came home
from the international tour to await a much more important
event, the birth of his second daughter, August Anna, born
on May 3, 1994. "Having a second child is an eye-opener,"
he later told friends at Jack's Tracks. "When you're waiting,
you think in terms of the first baby. You sometimes picture
the new baby as a little version of the first one. Then she
arrives and right away you see that this is a whole other person.
August had her own little personality from the beginning. I
don't know how many children Sandy will want to have, but
I'd love a whole house full of girls!"

That July Garth made a special appearance with the
Hollywood Bowl Orchestra in Los Angeles, California. It sold
out in twenty-one minutes, leading Hollywood Bowl events
manager Mark Ferber to say, "I can't remember, since the Beatles,
a longer box office line than this morning for Garth Brooks."

Garth tried something unexpected at the Hollywood Bowl.

He asked a couple of cowboy friends to meet him in Los Angeles and open the show. "I couldn't believe it when Garth called and said he wanted Dan Roberts and me to open a show that important!" Bryan Kennedy exclaimed. "I said, 'Man, you're taking a big chance!' And Garth just laughed it off. So Dan and I flew out to Los Angeles and checked into this expensive hotel where Garth had us booked. We got worried, though, because the front desk kept saying they had no reservations for Garth himself. We tried to call somebody—anybody—who knew what was going on. We wondered if something had happened to the bus, or if the show had been called off. But people at the Hollywood Bowl said no, the show was still scheduled. Then we started thinking he must be checked in under a fake name. *Finally,* I got a call from Garth. 'Where are you?' I asked."

"Oh, we got in late and checked into a motel just outside the city," he answered.

Bryan hung up the phone and turned to Dan Roberts. "This is just *wrong,*" he laughed.

But for Garth it was right, because every day he fought to keep living in the real world. In 1993 he gave *Rolling Stone* one of his most candid interviews ever, laying out what constant touring meant, how stardom had affected him, and why it was often disquieting. In it he refers to his childhood friend Mickey Weber, his brother Kelly, sister Betsy, and college roommate Ty England.

"You wake up at one or two in the afternoon and you see a guy you've known since the second grade, and he says, 'Hey, man, here's your schedule. I've already called these people and set up everything. You wanna go get something to eat?' So we go and if it's a busy place, he runs in and gets it for me, and we sit and eat and talk.

"Then the next guy comes looking for you, and it's a guy you've known all your life—your brother. He says, 'Okay, man, here's the scoop for tonight. We've got this percentage here and this percentage here. We've come up short with this money and come up over with this money.' And then he goes, 'There's dinner, do you want to go eat?' So I go eat with him.

"Then you get ready to go onstage. It's a thing of ours, before we go onstage, all the band members get together, hold hands, and say something that's funny or inspirational. But in that handshake, I look up and there's a woman I've known all my life, my sister. I look at a guy who was one of my college room-mates. And when we finish, my sister comes up, gives me a high five, and says, 'Hey, man, I had a great time tonight. You want to go eat?' I say, 'Sure.' And I go back to sleep and the next day it's the same thing.

"That's not real life. We've had construction on our house for a year now. Seeing those guys showing up at six thirty in the morning—*that's* real life."

CHAPTER FOURTEEN

"A white tuxedo and a lot of red paint"

W hen Garth had told Jon Small he wanted a scene in his video for "The Red Strokes" to be an attention-grabber, the director came up with an extraordinary idea. Garth in stark white would emerge from a sea of red. To accomplish that effect the scene would have to be shot in reverse. And so on the day "The Red Strokes" was filmed, Garth sat dressed in a white tuxedo at the white baby grand and waited until the crew began to lower him into the vat of red paint. Lower and lower he went, doing his best to appear as if nothing unusual was happening. But as the liquid covered more of his body, a thought hit him. The paint had been stored out-of-doors the previous night. It was very cold. Finally his face was covered, and he began to go into shock. Garth had always been a little gun-shy when it came to videos. He believed if you made one it should be unique so that people sat up and took notice. "Well," he thought, "this attention-grabber is going to kill me."

BY 1994, 42 PERCENT of Americans said they regularly listened to country music, and business revenues increased by 13 percent from 1993. Newcomer Faith Hill released her first Warner Bros.

album, *Take Me as I Am,* produced by Scott Hendricks. The debut single, "Wild One," stayed at number 1 a month, making Faith the first female country singer in years to have a debut with that kind of staying power. Only three women had ever kept a debut single at the top of *Billboard*'s charts for longer. In 1952 Kitty Wells spent six weeks at number 1 with the classic "It Wasn't God Who Made Honky Tonk Angels." Jean Shepard's "A Dear John Letter" held out for six weeks the same year. And the record for the longest-running female debut was Connie Smith's 1964 eight-week chart-topping run with "Once A Day."

Toby Keith was introduced to country fans with his 1993 number 1, "Should've Been A Cowboy," and three more hits followed from his self-titled debut on Mercury. Brooks & Dunn's *Hard Workin' Man* had five hit singles between 1993 and 1994, and they continued their reign as the CMA Duo of the Year. Tim McGraw made his Top 10 debut with "Indian Outlaw" from the hit-packed *Not a Moment Too Soon.* Trisha Yearwood had a big '94, with the number 1 "XXX's and OOO's (An American Girl)" and marriage to Mavericks bassist Robert Reynolds.

Ironically, the industry was growing in great part because of Garth's success at the very time the relationship with his own record label was deteriorating. Tension over the label's marketing and other issues had escalated between Garth and Bowen during *The Chase* and climaxed with the next album, *In Pieces.*

"We titled this album *In Pieces* because that's pretty much how it came together," Garth said at the time. "We had more time with this album, and we had fun with it. It's got more of a live feel than any of the earlier albums, and I think that's partly because—while we didn't realize we were doing it—we were picking songs that are truly representative of the live show. The other albums were all nailed to the wall, with a specific plan, and a specific vision. This time we just went in totally free and jumped off the cliff, smiled, and said, 'Let's see what falls together.'"

This change of pace was in many ways a reaction to what had happened with *The Chase*. For that album Garth had opened up, dug deep, and—in some people's terms—come up short. This time he was on the road constantly, less in his own head and more in those of his audience. It didn't mean he shied away from substantial material, but that he could respond immediately to songs that set his fans on fire. And he remained somewhat gun-shy about seeming too serious and message-driven.

One of the most popular with audiences was a Bryan Kennedy/Jim Rushing number titled "American Honky-Tonk Bar Association."

"I had a blast singing this song," Garth laughed. "It's about the guys who drive the trash trucks or plow the fields, then hang out talking things over at the corner bar. And the truth is, they could probably run the country as well or better than the ones doing it now!"

"Ain't Going Down (Til The Sun Comes Up)" is a rapid-fire, in-your-face tune. Garth and Kim Williams were writing at Kent Blazy's new house, which Blazy laughingly referred to as "a real fixer-upper." Since the house was filled with workmen the three sat on Kent's back porch. Garth said he didn't yet have a title, but he wanted to work on something with "shotgun lyrics."

"Once we got the title, he had the complete picture in his head," Blazy said. "He knew how the lines would come—fast and furious at the listener—how the music would sound, right down to where it would be on his next album!"

The team worked through the afternoon and finally adjourned to Kent's home studio to record a demo. That's when, as Garth later laughed, "the critics showed up."

Kent was working on that rapid-fire beat with a drum machine when a swarm of termites started coming out of the floor. "Kim—who has the weirdest sense of humor in the world—told me not to worry," Kent recalled. "He said, 'Hey, when Garth and I wrote "Papa Loved Mama" we had a roach attack, and that song was a hit.'"

So was "Ain't Going Down (Til The Sun Comes Up)," the first single released from the album. The second release, "American Honky-Tonk Bar Association," also topped the charts. Those two numbers are part of the reason Garth now listens to *In Pieces* when he wants to crank up some loud music in the pickup.

One of the reasons Kim Williams loved working with Garth was because of his melodies, and it is a talent that tends to be over-shadowed by the admiration for his skill with lyrics. "I thought I was pretty melodic," Kim said. "But then I found there were people in town that could run circles around me melodically, including Garth. When I realized that, I started concentrating more on lyrics and that became my thing, to write lyrics and try to collaborate with people who were melodically strong."

"The Red Strokes" is a song that had its beginnings when Garth's friend Lisa Sanderson went to the Louvre in Paris. "When Lisa came back she told me that one particular paint-ing caught her eye because of the red strokes in it," Garth said. "They indicated passion in her mind. So we wrote this song, about how passion is a little like the red strokes of a painting. The 'red strokes' of life are those times when you are at your most emotional, when you're hot about something—angry or thrilled, maybe in pursuit of a dream."

Garth wrote "Standing Outside The Fire" with Jenny Yates. The two had first met before he had a recording contract, and although they'd written several songs, none had been recorded. Jenny had once been an artist on PolyGram. Her songs and style were powerful, but not quite in line with the glitzy '80s. When her deal didn't pan out, she returned to California and contin-ued to write, checking back with Nashville publishers as often as she could afford to make the trip for song pitching and co-write opportunities.

Once Garth's career took off Jenny feared she'd never have a chance to write with him again. Too many artists, when they hit, turn to big-name collaborators or start writing solo. But one day she ran into him at a Nashville music event and mentioned a desire to get together. "I'll call you," Garth said.

Jenny was tentatively hopeful. But then just a couple of weeks later Garth called her in Los Angeles and asked her if she could come to his hotel to try and come up with a song idea. She had one in mind, and while it didn't become *the* song, it was the inspiration.

"Jenny was talking to me about her idea," Garth said. "I told her that it wasn't me because it kind of *stood outside the fire*. We looked at each other and said, '*Oh yeah.*'"

Tony Arata was pleased and a little surprised when "Kickin' And Screamin'" made the album, since he thought the lyrics might be too weird for it to ever get cut. But comparing birth and death with a whoop and a holler didn't phase Garth's left-of-field sense of humor. Garth's only problem was in the performance. The song requires tremendous vocal gymnastics and a high-energy *kickin' and screamin'* performance.

The New Grass Revival reunited at Jack's Tracks to help Garth record their classic "Callin' Baton Rouge," and despite some early concerns from New Grass purists, it worked. "Just being in the room with these guys was an inspiration," Garth said. "New Grass Revival's musicianship was overwhelming— Pat Flynn's guitar, Béla Fleck's banjo, John Cowan on the bass, and Sam Bush on mandolin. It doesn't get any better than that." The song remains one of Garth's favorites to perform live.

"The Night Will Only Know" (Stephanie Davis, Jenny Yates, Garth Brooks) is a dark tale of murder and a coverup. As Ty England learned years earlier, when writing with Garth Brooks, a story song must have a beginning, middle, and end. Layers must be exposed no matter how far down in the muck you have to get.

Garth carried his love for gut-level reality through to the final cut on *In Pieces,* "The Cowboy Song," written by Roy Robinson. "Bob Doyle found this song in the trash can at ASCAP," Garth said. "He knew how much I loved western songs, so what better to bring me than 'The Cowboy Song'?

"When I was growing up I always wished I could have a horse. But it would have been way too expensive for our family. Then I went to Oklahoma State, which is an ag school. So I grew up around the cowboy and rodeo world, but was always a little on the outside. I think that's why I built a riding arena out at my house, to make up for lost time.

"I think I first heard 'The Cowboy Song' around 1987, and I've loved it ever since. I'd end up pulling out my guitar and singing it on the bus at one or two A.M.—when all the guys would be playing stuff they loved. But somehow it got lost in the shuffle when we started to record. Finally, we decided that the best way to make this song stand out was to do it acoustically. Roy Huskey was playing bass, Sam Bush was doing mandolin, Hajacos was on fiddle, Bouton was on Dobro, and Leuzinger and Casstevens on acoustic guitars. The sound was perfect for the song and it's my favorite on this album."

In Pieces produced four videos, an astonishing break from Garth's usual avoidance of the medium. "Ain't Going Down (Til The Sun Comes Up)" was a concert video from the '94 tour. Footage from the 1993 Texas Stadium shows was used for "Callin' Baton Rouge." To make the other two, Garth contacted director Jon Small.

"Every so often, Garth would call and talk about video, and say, 'We'll work together one of these days,'" Small said. "Then on January 2, 1994, he asked me to come to California and talk about two songs in particular." The videos were approached very differently, "The Red Strokes" as a concept piece and "Standing Outside The Fire" as a three-minute movie.

"Standing Outside The Fire" reflects Garth's belief that to live life fully you have to be willing to take the heat. With that thought in mind, he started putting together a video script for "Standing Outside The Fire," reaching back to an idea he'd had earlier.

"When I was thinking about a video for 'The River,' I wanted to tell a story of remarkable courage," Garth said. "I'm glad we didn't make that video, because the story line lent itself far better for 'Standing Outside The Fire.' Things happen for a reason."

The story Garth wanted to tell was of a young man with Down's syndrome who decides to compete in the all-school track meet instead of the Special Olympics. "Competition can be the most positive thing in the world, especially if the person you are competing with is yourself. You'll probably be brutally honest, because who knows you better than you do? You have to put yourself to the test, to try when it's not a sure win."

When Garth talked to Jon Small about "The Red Strokes" video, he said that he wanted "a bunch of white pianos, a white tuxedo, and a lot of red paint." Making "The Red Strokes" required eighteen white tuxedos, twelve white Stetsons, five thousand gallons of mud, thirty-five gallons of red paint, and six days of filming. "We'd do a shot, hit the showers, go out and do a shot, and then hit the showers again," Garth said. "I was digging paint out of my ears and eyes for days after we wrapped up the shoot."

DECISIONS REGARDING ALBUMS SHIPPED and promoted were strictly up to the label. Joe Mansfield was now onboard as an independent marketing consultant, but while he had influence he had no real power. *In Pieces* shipped fewer than expected because Bowen decided it would sell around 4 million, half of what it ultimately sold.

Garth understood that this thinking could become a self-fulfilling prophecy if it became a pattern. If the label determined that Garth had a core audience, and could sell a certain number of albums with little effort or expenditure, marketing would continue to be taken for granted.

The used-CD controversy of 1993 became another minefield. The dispute garnered a raft of press—most of it bad—for record labels, and a great deal of discussion in music centers like Nashville. After talking with publishers and songwriters, Garth jumped into the fray and said he stood on the side of the labels. What he feared happening was this: Whereas most used-CD sales had been in mom and pop stores, if big retailers jumped on the bandwagon, it would drastically cut into songwriter profits. There were reportedly some retailers who even considered putting used-CD bins next to artists' recently released product. No writer or publisher royalties would be paid on those, and it would encourage people to trade in their new albums.

"It wouldn't hurt me as much as it would the writers," Garth said. "And I know too many of them who are trying to raise families on royalties." Privately, most artists agreed with Garth, that writers would be damaged if the practice was mishandled. But few ever spoke out on his behalf.

Several years later, Gary Graff asked Garth if he regretted speaking out: "If the issue came out today I'd still take the same stand. My biggest problem was the sitting [used CDs] side by side with new ones."

He also said that before he understood the reality of the problem, he'd bought used albums himself. "I used to do it when we had records. But that was before I got into the business. Don't get me wrong, I understand why people buy them. They're half or a third of the price. But now I know how songwriters make their living."

Bowen became increasingly critical of Garth's recordings in the months after *In Pieces* was released. Meetings might begin with a discussion of overall budgetary concerns, but more often than not, they ended with Bowen deflecting questions about marketing by citing the music. Among other criticisms, Bowen said songs like "Ain't Going Down (Til The Sun Comes Up)" didn't sell records. Yet audiences and critics alike loved it. *USA Today* called the song one of Garth's finest performances ever. "Ain't Going Down (Til The Sun Comes Up)" was the debut

single from *In Pieces,* making *Radio & Records* history by entering the country singles charts at number 25, with 222 stations
adding the song out-of-the-box on its way to number 1.

These kinds of disagreements also underscore the differences
Garth and Bowen had when it came to sales. Although Garth
was often perceived as sales-obsessed; in fact, he paid no attention to sales potential while he recorded. For Garth, two things
mattered: how the song affected him personally and the reaction
from his concert audiences. Like Allen Reynolds, he saw a vast
difference between what happened in the studio and what happened with the record label. While recording, the music ruled.
Once it was finished and turned in, it was up to the label to get
it to the public. But since his key man, Joe Mansfield, was an
outside consultant with little real power, Garth was now in the
position that he had to pay attention to how business was being
conducted.

Garth has often said that his albums are like children to him,
living entities. He is unable to go into the studio and cut ten
tunes for release, then walk away hoping for the best. For him,
that's like not giving an offspring a fair chance to succeed. "I
don't understand this idea of *just throw it against the wall and see if
it sticks,*" Garth confided. "If you believe your music deserves to
be heard, you ought to be willing to fight for it."

In Pieces entered *Billboard*'s country and Top 200 charts at
number 1, and Garth had six songs on the trade publication's
Singles and Tracks chart. It was a first for the chart. The only
time an artist had previously accomplished the feat was in 1948
when Eddy Arnold and the Tennessee Plowboys placed six on
the Best Selling Retail Folk Records chart.

Despite Bowen's concerns, critics praised *In Pieces*. The
Chicago Sun-Times called it "the most expressive of his career."
The *Orange County Register* declared it "a focused, well-paced,
energetic album that incorporates all the best elements that influence and constitute country music."

In Pieces was the third album in history to debut at number 1 on both the *Billboard* 200 album chart and the *Billboard* country albums chart. The Recording Industry Association of America ultimately certified album sales in excess of 8 million units. *In Pieces* was an international hit as well. It went quadruple platinum in Ireland, platinum in Australia, triple platinum in Canada, and gold in New Zealand and the U.K.

Garth and Reynolds still loved the fat, organic sound that resulted from recording on analog before transferring to digital. But in meetings with his staff, Bowen still tried to undercut the producer. He often repeated his original criticism of Reynolds's production as "too old fashioned." And during one encounter with Garth, Bowen said, "Just go fix the damned music."

By this time differences with Bowen had gotten to the point that it was uncertain just how much attention was going to be paid to new music, and Garth was hesitant to start another album. He turned to some special releases while he tried to figure out what position he was actually in with the label, and how to fix it.

The Garth Brooks Collection was released on September 2, 1994. This album was not sold in record stores, nor did the 50 million in sales certified by the RIAA on Garth's studio albums reflect this project's 4 million sold. This was an album compiled for McDonald's first music promotion, benefiting Ronald McDonald's Children's Charities (RMCC). The album sold for a limited time in McDonald's restaurants, and RMCC received one dollar from each sale. The album contained tracks from Garth's previous albums. Tina Turner, Elton John, and Roxette also participated in the program.

Garth had the power to make *The Garth Brooks Collection*, but Bowen had the power to set the price. Angered at the extra dollar taken from Capitol's coffers, he jacked up the price by a buck. Because the release was for charity, raising the price angered Garth.

Another package, *The Hits,* was released in December 1994. It was an eighteen-cut album of Garth Brooks's hits, available for a limited time only. The masters were then buried in front of the Capitol building in Los Angeles, underneath Garth's star.

The album sold 10 million copies, making it the biggest-selling greatest-hits package in country music history and the best-selling greatest-hits package in any genre for the 1990s (domestic). *The Hits* was accompanied by a promotional CD Zoom, which allowed listeners to hear thirty seconds of every cut on all Garth's albums. The CD Zoom was hosted by Garth and included free in the package. *The Hits* peaked at number 1 on both the *Billboard* Top 200 chart and the *Billboard* country albums chart.

Garth backed the release with a new NBC Special. *Garth Brooks—The Hits* aired live in January 1995, with Garth taking phone calls from fans while showing clips from *This Is Garth Brooks, This Is Garth Brooks, Too!* and footage from the 1993–1994 World Tour. *Garth Brooks—The Hits* won its time slot for NBC and gave the network its best adult rating in that time slot since January 1994.

Despite the success of *The Hits,* Garth remained uncertain about the wisdom of these types of packages. First, he remained convinced that each album was an entity unto itself, and, like Joe Mansfield, he believed that hits packages might deter fans from buying catalog albums. That, of course, had been the reason for the CD Zoom highlighting every song from the albums included in *The Hits.*

One could (but probably shouldn't) say that *The Hits* package hit stratospheric heights. In November of the following year, Colonel Bill MacArthur, chief of the Astronaut Office Flight Support Branch, took his copy of *The Hits* with him when he visited the orbiting Russian Mir space station as a space shuttle mission specialist, meaning the disc traveled 3.4 million miles. The mission commander stamped the CD, as did the pilot and third cosmonaut of the Russian crew on Mir, and Garth was presented with the collection at a show in Houston.

Still unsure of label commitment, Garth did not release a studio album in 1994. The thrill of the 1993–1994 World Tour was offset by worries about future recording as well as management concerns. In '94 Pam Lewis and Bob Doyle decided to part company and disbanded their firm. Garth briefly considered finding an existing firm to manage his career, but quickly abandoned the idea and formed Garth Brooks Management, bringing along several staffers from Doyle/Lewis, including media specialists Scott Stem and Karen Byrd.

After the backbreaking '93–'94 tour schedule, the label difficulties, and management reorganization, Garth decided to take 1995 off, keeping the band and crew on salary and medical benefits. And since he was no longer required to release an album every year, he decided to continue to hold off recording. It was really the one card he had to play, because despite his status at Capitol, he could not control the level of label support. If the albums were going to be undermarketed, why release one?

Meanwhile, Capitol's parent company, EMI, had been undergoing change. Joe Smith had left EMI in 1993, replaced by Charles Koppelman, a publishing mogul who had sold his empire to EMI in 1989. Koppelman's heart was always with songs and publishing. When he accepted his new position, Koppelman told Chuck Philips from the *L.A. Times,* "No matter what anybody says, all that matters to me is the music. What people forget is our business starts with the music. If you have the belief in your gut about a song and an artist, you have to have the nerve to stand behind the thing, to stay the course."

Bowen respected Koppelman's love of music, but remained skeptical of his relationship with Jim Fifield: "[Fifield] was fascinated by Koppelman's elegance, wealth, the way he schmoozed artists and flew in private jets." Plus, Bowen said he believed all New Yorkers—and that would include Koppelman—looked at country music and thought, "Yee-haw."

Koppelman *was* a bit of a grandstander and more than a little egoistic about his considerable publishing successes. "You know what my image is? Hits," he told *Musician* magazine. On one trip to Nashville, Koppelman was accompanied by his two bosses, Sir Colin Southgate and Jim Fifield. Prior to the trip, Koppelman's representative phoned Capitol to make sure that he had secured the most luxurious of the three suites booked at Loews Vanderbilt Plaza.

Bowen had yet to find another star who could begin to compete with those signed by label heads such as MCA's Tony Brown or Arista's Tim DuBois. Capitol had two potentially important projects in the works when things finally came to a head in late 1994. One was by a new female vocalist named Deana Carter, the daughter of top guitarist Fred Carter. Deana, an edgy songwriter, had a whispery vocal style that belied her strong persona and wry sense of humor. Her debut album, *Did I Shave My Legs for This,* had been finished for months and released in the U.K. and Australia, but not in the United States.

Another artist in limbo was a Portland, Oregon, native named John Bunzow, a singer/songwriter and guitarist whose work drew considerable interest around Nashville in the early '90s. After a few Nashville trips, interest was high enough that Bunzow was asked to do a showcase in his native Portland. Two label reps were after him, MCA's Tony Brown and Capitol's Renee Bell. In what turned out to be one of the worst bits of luck in music history, Tony Brown's flight was delayed, and Renee clinched the deal for Capitol.

The John Bunzow saga is one every fledgling artist should consider, because similar tales are told in every form of music. It illustrates what Garth Brooks had learned early in his career: getting a recording contract means very little. No matter how much the critics and the audiences love them, artists are at the mercy of the whims of labels, executives, timing, and trends. And in the end, they discover that the music they've made isn't even theirs.

Bunzow was given a big budget to record in Los Angeles with guitar guru Pete Anderson producing. Capitol determined that the album belonged in a relatively new radio category, Americana. It has been called a merger between roots rock and country, citing in hindsight Creedence Clearwater Revival as the first Americana act with its debut in 1968. But in recent times, this subgenre had grown out of artistic frustration over country airplay opportunities.

When the advance CD of *Stories of the Years* was sent to press and radio, the response was nothing less than astounding, a press agent's dream. The *Chicago Tribune*'s Jack Hurst: "John Bunzow mixes the rootsy with the revolutionary. It's an energetic collection of individualistic lyrics and delicious melodic surprises that is often reflective of Buddy Holly, Ricky Nelson or Jim Croce." *Good Times* listed the album as a must buy for college students.

Bowen resigned before it was released, and all the encouraging news would turn sour.

In late 1994, Jimmy Bowen reported that he had been diagnosed with thyroid cancer. After undergoing successful surgery at the Mayo Clinic, he reevaluated his life and career, then decided to go for one more negotiation: a severance package. Bowen resigned effective March 31, 1995.

To the end, Garth continued to give Bowen credit when he spoke publicly. Not long before Bowen left, Garth talked to journalist Gary Graff about the juggling of family, big tours, and making music: "I have lots of people around me, Jimmy Bowen and Allen Reynolds included, who tell me, 'Don't try to outdo yourself to the point where you explode.'"

The Bowen/Brooks dispute was both predictable and tragic. It was tragic because the two might have forged one of the most powerful teams in music history, not as artist/producer, but of artist/label head. It was predictable because of the personalities. Bowen's power-driven maneuvers had worked on almost every artist he'd dealt with in the past. Artists he couldn't charm could be backed down. Only too late he understood that Garth was impossible to intimidate. Bowen loved calling Garth the eight-hundred-pound gorilla in the room. In fact, if there was one, there were two.

Likewise, Garth didn't anticipate a whisper campaign that would still be around long after Bowen was hitting the greens in Maui. Bowen portrayed himself as a music guy who came to town to make great records and Garth as a control freak. According to Bowen, his contracting for multiple millions in salary and bonuses was just good business, whereas Garth's new contract, which had been worked out with EMI, gouged the label. And, according to the former label head, Garth resented the fact that Bowen had turned him down when he headed MCA.

Worse yet, the flurry of Bowen-instigated press releases about Garth's sales were dumped squarely on the star's doorstep, leaving the impression that he was concerned only with selling records. In fact, sales were *very* important to Garth, but not sales for sales' sake: "For me, sales mean people are hearing your music, that somebody is being affected by it."

Garth refused to defend himself in public. In private he was confused on one level and angry on another. "To say I carried a grudge because Bowen turned me down in 1988 makes no sense," Garth said to a friend. "It's almost a point of honor to get turned down at least once by every label in town. Foglesong had turned me down once before he offered me a deal at Capitol. If I didn't trust Bowen when he came to the label, it was because of all the stories floating around and the friends who'd been fired when he took over. But I was ready to work with him, anyway. I appreciated the freedom he initially offered about our recording, too. But did I resent how he approached *The Chase* and *In Pieces*? Yes."

He paused, and shook his head. "You know the wildest thing about this mess? All the time we were having those arguments,

I still went out to Bowen's house to meet with him. For some reason—call it charisma or whatever—but you can mistrust Bowen, you can get mad at him, you can want to punch him in the face, but you're still drawn to him. You want to hear what he has to say even if you disagree with it."

"I looked like hell and smelled worse, but the song was finished"

llen Reynolds hung up the telephone in disgust. It had been an industry observer relaying more complaints about Garth and his dealings with Capitol Records. "A lot of the people blaming Garth for disagreements with Jimmy Bowen are the very same people who have been bitching about Bowen for years," Reynolds angrily told a friend who was sitting there in his office. "As far as I'm concerned, what Garth has done in trying to take control of his music is simply an extension of what the Outlaw Movement did in the '70s. People ought to be thanking Garth for taking a stand."

At the moment Capitol didn't even have a label chief. Reynolds believed his job was twofold: to offer a creative oasis and to get Garth's mind right for making a new album. "This is insane," Reynolds said. "You hear all kinds of rumors about what's going on. First you hear that Mansfield is coming back, then you'd hear that the idea is off the table. It's difficult to work when things are that unstable."

Garth stopped by the studio later that day and Reynolds had a talk with him.

"You can break your neck for country music," Reynolds said. "You can wave the flag for country music. Hell, you can even die for country music. But the most important thing you can do for country music is to take care of your *own* music."

IN THE YEARS SINCE *The Chase* was released Reynolds had seen the toll that label battles had taken on Garth as well as the damage done by Nashville's critical attitude. The carping most hurtful to Garth involved what he had or had not done to country music. After his years of steadfast rejection of the Pro Tools that keep vocal performances on pitch, his refusal to release singles to pop radio, and his insistence on using Nashville writers and pickers on every project, he was being accused of weakening the genre. Sometimes people even questioned the fact that fans at his concerts wore rock T-shirts.

"I never understood how a Metallica fan getting interested in country and buying a George Strait album was a bad thing," he said. "I thought it just helped widen country's audience."

In early 1995 Garth began making a new record, *Fresh Horses*. Even though he was supposedly taking a year off, it wasn't easy to find the time. For one thing, he was getting ready for a three-year tour set to kick off in March 1996. He had put together a new stage and light rigging, all designed to make the shows more fan-friendly for stadiums and arenas.

He was also trying to spend as much time as possible at home with Sandy and his daughters. The intense career demands had resulted in the couple spending more time away from each other, and both Garth and Sandy felt they needed to shore up the marriage. And Garth also wanted the experience of having some around-the-clock time with Taylor and August while they were small. He was thrilled when he was able to see August take her first steps and hear her say her first words.

On March 10, he officially became the fastest-selling artist of all time, with sales of 50 million albums in just six years, according to the Recording Industry Association of America. Appropriately, he was honored at the EMI manufacturing plant in Jacksonville, Illinois. Garth and his mother, Colleen, hosted a luncheon for over a thousand employees, at which Garth said, "Behind every extraordinary achievement what you'll find is no big secret—it's a bunch of people working their butts off."

In private, however, Garth was getting tired of sales comparisons. He was trying to make his girls his priority, and yet people from journalists to some EMI executives were reminding him that he just might surpass the Beatles' numbers. "It's fun to see numbers and all that," he confided. "I'd be lying if I said anything else. But every time I get asked those questions, and *admit* that it's great to see, then I look obsessed. You have to fight to keep music the priority."

When Garth was in Nashville, he and Reynolds spent hours in the studio, and soon found an unexpected pattern. This album was moving full circle, back to the more straightforward country of Garth's debut. In thinking back to the early years, Garth was moved to write "The Old Stuff."

"George Strait's movie *Pure Country* inspired that song," Garth said. "The film reminded me of those first road trips. The fans love this song. People will yell out what clubs they saw us at back in the old days—some of those shows only had twenty or thirty people in the audience." Thinking back to the older, simpler times was something Garth often did. By this time he had a $3 million annual payroll and a lighting system for his show that cost $4 million. Everything was big and getting bigger.

"Material like 'That Ol' Wind' and 'Cowboys And Angels' both remind me of the first CD," Garth says. "And the fiddle and steel exchange in 'It's Midnight Cinderella' also takes me back to the beginning. 'She's Every Woman' reminds me of 'The River' [from *Ropin' the Wind*]. Maybe that's because it was written with Victoria Shaw and was written around the same time 'The River' was done."

"Beaches Of Cheyenne" started out to be a story about a guy who lives at the beach but dreams of being a cowboy. It ended up a dark tale of doomed lovers and a ghost that haunts the beach by night. By the time collaborator Bryan Kennedy finished writing with Garth and started home late, he was so into the idea he feared seeing the apparition somewhere in the middle of the road.

"The Change" by Tony Arata speaks of an individual standing firm through hard times, of not allowing the world to change him for the worse. It is a song that almost slipped by Garth, only to be brought back to the table by Allen Reynolds. "It's a noble song in my mind," Reynolds explained. "One small deed juxtaposed against the enormous voice of cynicism." Ultimately, this became the favored final cut on *Fresh Horses* and a powerful video.

Garth's belief in sometimes letting a song stand despite mistakes affected one cut, "Rollin'." Recording the entire song in one take, Garth missed a line and some harmony wasn't exactly on target, but it was all left in. "I don't make perfect records," Garth explained. "That's not to say I never go back and work on a line or overdub guitar parts, because I certainly do. But if we do something in one take and the energy is right but I've screwed up something here or there, I'd rather leave it. That song is about a tough young woman who's out there driving a truck and raisin' hell. I thought I owed her a tough performance."

"There's a lot of rodeo and cowboy culture in *Fresh Horses*," noted producer Reynolds. "'Cowboys And Angels' has those classic campfire harmonies. It's a wonderful cut." Written by Garth, Kent Blazy, and Kim Williams, the song speaks of a proud and reckless cowboy who God realizes needs help, because he will never make it on his own.

Thinking back on how his first single, "Much Too Young (To Feel This Damn Old)," had been rewritten to represent rodeo riders instead of musicians gave Garth an idea for reviving one of his favorite Aerosmith songs, "The Fever."

"I'd been on the bus, thinking that even though the Aerosmith song was about a band, it could fit the traveling life of a rodeo rider," Garth said. And when he took the idea to

Aerosmith's Steven Tyler, the rocker said, "Go for it." Garth got Bryan Kennedy and Dan Roberts involved and replaced screaming guitars with high-powered fiddles.

The song "Ireland," about a doomed soldier far from home, reflected the emotional high experienced during the European leg of the '93–'94 tour. It almost didn't get finished in time to make the album.

"I couldn't get the last verse right," Garth said. "So the last night before the last day of the recording sessions, I stayed up faxing and phoning my co-writers. I was so anxious that I threw up twice. It was dawn when we finally nailed it. I had just fallen into bed when the phone rang. My neighbor lady said, 'Garth, I have a yard full of horses and they all look like yours.' So I ran over there and rounded them up, then headed straight to the studio. I looked like hell and smelled worse, but the song was finished."

Garth had a change of attitude during this time: "I never claimed to be a great vocalist, but for the first time I *fully* understood that I really was just an entertainer who could sing. That freed me up. I lightened up in the studio. I had so much fun that I felt like crying when the album was finished. I wasn't ready for it to be over."

When asked about the title *Fresh Horses,* Garth explained, "It's all about giving one more bang for the buck. It's about being on your toes."

Capitol was leaderless from March until May 1995. Speculation had been running high through the spring. Many were convinced that Garth had the clout to insist on Joe Mansfield. Others thought the mantle would be passed from within the company, to the chief financial officer, Wayne Halpurn, or VP of promotion Bill Catino. Lawyers representing half the producers and executives in town had been circling the label through those months. Many times the person tapped to head a label after an abrupt resignation is the one who has hired the most high-powered mouthpiece.

In the end EMI hired Faith Hill/Brooks & Dunn producer
Scott Hendricks to try to fill Bowen's shoes. An Oklahoma
native, Hendricks was a top-flight producer with very specific
musical tastes. Some around him said the difference between
Hendricks and Bowen was that Hendricks was less experienced
and more opinionated.

Garth would have preferred Joe Mansfield but it was not his
decision to make. Truthfully, it wasn't Hendricks's idea either.
Although the producer liked the idea of being the creative head
of a label, he had never run a large company and was said to
have suggested a sharing of power with an experienced player
like Mansfield. That didn't happen. It was widely thought that
Koppelman was absolutely convinced that record producers
should run record labels.

One of the early decisions was to change the name Liberty,
the historic name Bowen had resurrected during his tenure,
back to Capitol. It made little difference, because the name had
primarily only been used in print materials. Around Music Row
it had stayed Capitol all along. Two of the most respected professionals in town were let go, A&R VP Renee Bell and PR chief
Cathy Gurley, as were the heads of the international and creative
divisions, Cindi Wilson and Sherri Halford respectively.

Hendricks dropped dozens of artists, including John Bunzow,
the man who had been wooed away from MCA and whose debut
album had generated such press interest. It wasn't Hendricks's
kind of music and the promotion team seemed to have problems working *Stories of the Years* at the Americana record charts.
Ironically, Americana was a format Garth had recently discovered and loved, saying it was presenting a fresh, important side
of country music.

Unfortunately for Bunzow, the project had been very expensive, and the Bunzow buzz had died down while he languished
in Capitol's no-man's land. *Stories of the Years* would prove too
costly for another label to pick up, leaving many of his best songs
and an impressive album on the shelf.

Still, most around Capitol were hopeful that the new team would be effective. Those who had heard parts of Garth's new recording were ecstatic about the music, and it seemed like Garth and Hendricks were a natural fit. After all, they were both Oklahoma boys.

CHAPTER SIXTEEN

"I guess we can work with it"

Garth wasn't in Nashville on the day Capitol called people together to listen to the new album, *Fresh Horses*. His personal representatives, including Joe Mansfield and Allen Reynolds, stood along with label employees in the lobby of a Music Row mastering facility. A few of Capitol's established executives were secluded in the facility's soundproof room with the new team.

The distancing from the rank and file didn't surprise the people at Capitol. The staff knew that big corporate changes were fraught with tension, and, in reality, were glad that Hendricks hadn't pulled a Bowen and put them on the street. But on the day of the listening event they were surprised to see people from the artist's contingent left out of the inner sanctum.

Staffers cheered for rowdy tunes like "The Fever" and were nearly in tears at the emotion in "Ireland." But when the execs emerged, only one of Hendricks's crew had anything to say: "I guess we can work with it."

DESPITE THE NEW REGIME'S initial lack of enthusiasm, the first single from *Fresh Horses,* "She's Every Woman," was a number 1 record. *Fresh Horses* was released on November 21. The *Pittsburgh Post*'s Jerry Sharpe called it Garth's best album to date. The New York *Daily News*' Bill Bell said *Fresh Horses* punched all the buttons: "There is some stripped-down, barn-burning boogie, a graceful waltz, a Chuck Berry riff or two, a couple of things with strings, a dramatic ballad, a bit of mad surrealism, and a sentimental bagpipes-and-all tribute to Ireland."

The one song that had trouble at radio was "The Fever," which only made it to number 23 on the charts. Even with the stripped-down band—guitars, bass, drums, and fiddle—the song was too close to rock for country radio. It was ironic that on this, Garth's most country album since his debut, rock charges surfaced over one song.

Some questioned the rock anxieties. J. D. Considine wrote in the *Baltimore Sun* about what Garth was doing. Considine said he didn't simply crank up the guitars until his music was more Lynyrd Skynyrd than Lester Flatt. "The rock and roll element in Brooks's music is more a matter of attitude than instrumentation, a sort of go-crazy delivery that's miles away from the well-mannered reserve most country stars convey. That's why Brooks seems so at home in arenas."

A few years down the line "Fever" would gain two very passionate fans: Garth's daughters, Taylor and August. "The song they first started singing—they were about the right age and it was easy for them, both of them—was 'Fever,'" Garth said. "They knew the one word and they'd run around the house naked screaming, '*Fever!*'"

Hendricks's favorite, "The Beaches Of Cheyenne," was released in January 1996 and topped the charts. Then "The Change" was released and suffered a fate similar to "The Fever," reaching only number 19. The next two singles, "It's Midnight Cinderella" and "That Ol' Wind," hit numbers 5 and 4 respectively.

Fresh Horses enjoyed the biggest first-week sales of any of Garth's previous albums, nearly half a million copies. After the first week of its release, eight of the ten songs on the album appeared on the country singles chart, a first in music history.

But Capitol pulled back on advertising in many major cities. The radio ad budget was cut. It couldn't have been a worse time to neglect marketing because *Fresh Horses* was competing with new albums from Whitney Houston, Tom Petty, Bruce Springsteen, and Vince Gill. Predictably, sales flattened. (*Fresh Horses* sales are now at 7 million.)

As the train jumped the tracks, Garth's hopes for a happy ending to label issues were quashed. The mishandling of his albums during this time raises the question: was Nashville prepared to deal with a career of this magnitude?

One artist who offered insight into Garth's dilemma was Gary Morris, whose successful venture onto Broadway had hurt him at country radio. He remained a player in Nashville, one of the greatest vocalists in any genre, and the publisher who'd first hired Faith Hill. When *No Fences* began to sell in astronomical numbers, Morris foresaw a predicament: "When somebody sells on that level early in his career he's going to be forever judged by those numbers. Ten million in sales is staggering in country and Garth probably won't match that every time out. Unfortunately, he'll be in a situation where three or four million will be considered a failure."

At first, Garth had no plans to make a video for the album. But then came the morning of Wednesday, April 19, 1995, when a rented Ryder truck was parked in front of the Alfred P. Murrah federal building in downtown Oklahoma City. At 9:02 A.M., five thousand pounds of explosives detonated a blast that was felt for thirty miles and damaged over three hundred buildings. The attack killed 168 people. Nineteen children were killed and thirty were orphaned. Eight hundred and fifty people were injured.

The Oklahoma City tragedy put the world's spotlight on countless American heroes, with over twelve thousand volunteers and rescue workers participating in the rescue and recovery. In large part because of these heroes, over one thousand people survived the attack.

Utilizing the message contained in "The Change," Garth attempted to find a new way to deal with senseless tragedy. In the horror of the day he discovered heroes, proud Oklahomans who, when faced with terror, refused to be terrorized. Finally, he decided to make a video as a tribute to the victims, survivors, and the people who acted so courageously on that day.

IN AN EFFORT TO pull the new and old staff together Hendricks decided to hold an all-employee weekend at Tims Ford Lake near Winchester, Tennessee. People were excited, anticipating that this lake sojourn might help develop a close-knit crew. It was an opportunity for everyone to interact in a casual setting, not to mention a chance to stay in lakeside cabins with free food and free beer.

The afternoon that people started arriving looked promising. The revelers included more than Capitol staff members: friends, producers, writers, and others connected to Hendricks or his executives. The mood was genial, welcoming, and open. People water-skied, fished, and soaked up sun and suds. But it turned out to be a little too casual.

As the day turned into night and the liquor level rose to high tide, two worrisome trends emerged. First, there were some highly suggestive and public sexist comments that circulated, to the extent that some worried about the potential for harassment charges. Second, it became very clear that some newcomers very high in the organization had sizable chips on their shoulders. Some began making derogatory remarks about several of the artists already signed to Capitol, including its biggest artist, Garth Brooks. Why? From the comments made, the artist's biggest crime appeared to be that he didn't "hang" with the new executives, that he'd actually declined an invitation to go out drinking in Nashville. By morning, after stories were traded among the cabins, some employees packed up and drove back to Nashville. "Oh good," one female staffer said sarcastically on the drive back. "The frat boys are in charge."

After the shaky start, Garth worked with his own team and virtually ignored the label. Some of the executives began publicly deriding him, holding court late nights at Nashville's Sunset Grill, talking down Garth as well as other artists, including Tanya Tucker. The tales were told all over town.

Most of Capitol's rank and file took the Sunset Grill insults personally, because in the end, they were on Garth's team. The overwhelming majority of them loved Garth. He knew everyone's name, the names of their spouses and children. He somehow knew about—and *asked* about—a son who'd suffered a football injury, a recently deceased pet, a friend in Minnesota who'd been unable to get concert tickets. They liked the fact that he didn't bring a "star" aura with him during label visits and that small things still seemed to excite him. Once, during the days when he and Sandy were living in a trailer while their home was being renovated, an employee had asked him how things were progressing. Garth suddenly lit up. "Can you believe it—this is the first house I ever lived in that has a doorbell!"

The trashing of Tanya Tucker also angered many. They felt that her latest album, *Complicated,* had received short shrift. One of her finest efforts, it produced only one charted single, the Top 10 "Little Things." In some meetings it became obvious that the record label was counting on her best-selling memoir, *Nickel Dreams,* and the marketing prowess of its publisher Hyperion to pick up Capitol's slack.

As time went by, Hendricks settled into his role as president of the company, making inroads with most of the original staff. In truth, many felt sorry for him, figuring that part of the aloofness they had felt involved his deteriorating relationship with fiancée Faith Hill, whom he'd begun dating while producing her first Warner Bros. sessions. On tour now with Tim McGraw, the rumors about Faith's affections, and lack thereof, flew fast and furious. And Scott Hendricks often appeared ghostlike as he walked through Capitol's halls.

To the extent that it was possible, Garth left his own marketing in the hands of Joe Mansfield and the New York office. Once the three-year tour started in 1996, he had no other option. With a schedule that would include playing over 350 shows, he had no time to fool around.

A Capitol promotion executive who had been with the label since 1989 told about Garth's tour launch. "From the time the new team came on board there was a split between the old and the new. We thought Garth was the biggest thing in the business, and the new guys acted like he was over. When Garth started the 1996 tour in Atlanta, I was the highest-rank person at the opening night. Garth asked me if anybody else was coming to any of the Atlanta shows. I had to say that I was pretty much it. Then I got on the phone and asked Scott Hendricks and the general manager, Walt Wilson, to try to attend. After all, this was our biggest act and the beginning of a three-year tour. So the next night they came backstage and that's when Garth was handed a CD of Trace Adkins with this line: 'Here is our new lead horse.' Garth didn't act arrogant or angry. Just shocked at that statement. Then, I was told, Walt and Scott left the arena. It was stunning."

In 1996, Joe Mansfield accepted the presidency of Asylum Records. Joe had been with Garth for the past six years. After leaving Capitol, he had formed the Mansfield Group, marketing records by artists including Garth, Mark Chesnutt, and Willie Nelson. In 1994, he expanded, joining forces with former CBS Records VP Mike Martinovich, another of Nashville's most respected marketing minds. Mansfield/Martinovich quickly became the hottest company in town, working with companies like Anderson Merchandisers (Wal-Mart), and Movie Tunes, as well as with Garth, Wynonna, John Berry, the Charlie Daniels Band, Toby Keith, and others. When Joe took the job with Asylum, it was under the condition that he be allowed to continue advising Garth and Wynonna.

Scott Hendricks was far more effective with some other careers. His tough takes on various albums turned out to be spot-on in some cases. Hendricks reviewed Deana Carter's album and determined that she needed one big smash single. They found it with Matraca Berg's poignant "Strawberry Wine," which stayed at number 1 for two weeks in 1996. A second Berg-penned song, "We Danced Anyway," also hit number 1. Her debut album, *Did I Shave My Legs for This,* also had hits with two of Deana's songs: "Count Me In" and "How Do I Get There." The album sold 5 million copies.

Trace Adkins was a strong Hendricks signing, yet another of the college-educated country singers *Time* had written about, a singer/songwriter who started working in the oil fields following his graduation from Louisiana Tech. After a rig accident, Trace moved to Nashville to play music full-time, and it was at a local honky-tonk that Hendricks saw and signed him. Trace combined a big country voice with a shrewd wit and larger-than-life personality that made him attractive to both television and print media. His Hendricks-produced debut album, *Dreamin' Out Loud,* produced three big hits, including the number 1 "(This Ain't) No Thinkin' Thing."

But the most important act Hendricks signed was a young New Zealand native named Keith Urban. Keith was already a signed artist with EMI in Australia, charting four number 1 records before he moved to Nashville in 1992. A top guitarist, he played with Brooks & Dunn and others, formed his own group, The Ranch, and eventually went solo. Capitol attorney Ansel Davis was the person most responsible for the Capitol signing. Although Hendricks would not be around to develop Urban's career, it would be one of Nashville's biggest by 1999.

★　　★　　★

ON MAY 21, 1996, Garth was the guest of honor at a 1960s theme party held at Nashville's Sunset Studios, attended by family, friends, and members of the music industry. The event celebrated a new milestone, sales of over 60 million of his albums since 1989. As EMI chairman Charles Koppelman said, "To sell 60 million albums in seven years is an extraordinary accomplishment, even for a performer who has made a habit of breaking records. Garth has proven that a great artist with talent, vision, and dedication can achieve the unfathomable."

What was unfathomable to his long-term associates was that the Garth Brooks who showed up that night was pretty much the same one they had gotten to know years earlier. In a celebrity culture where artists like Elvis and Michael Jackson were so overwhelmed by megastardom that they retreated into a form of isolated madness, insulated by troops of paranoid bodyguards and handlers, Garth had come through damn normal.

Loyalty was a trait that had defined Garth's career, and it was evident in his choice of a master of ceremonies for the 60 Million Party: Gentleman Jim Foglesong. Applause for Foglesong was deafening, because he was still a much-beloved and respected figure in the business. However, the shadow that hung over this event was long. In January Joe Harris had passed away at his Nashville home. His experiences in Vietnam had been problematic for years, but his death was unexpected. He'd been driving through snowstorms for two days, returning from the Northeastern Convention of Fair Buyers in Syracuse, New York. He returned home exhausted, sat down in his chair, and did not get up.

In terms of his life and career, Joe Harris died with his boots on, doing the job he loved. Many artists attended his final service, with some, including the Oak Ridge Boys, performing. Per the family's wishes, Garth sang "The Dance" at the memorial service. Joe Harris would have loved the 60 Million sales event. He was one of a small cadre of professionals who had helped most to make it possible.

Billboard's Eric Johnston later wrote about the sales numbers and the viewpoint with which many on Music Row saw Garth. "Frankly," Johnston said, "the Garth Brooks phenomenon baffled the hell out of most in Nashville." What's he really like? Is he a marketing genius? Is he setting the bar too high for other artists? Is he a megalomaniac consumed with a desire to control? And what is going on with this new Capitol regime?

But, Johnston said, the success that Garth enjoyed was due in large part to the fact that he *had* taken control of his career at a crucial time, and doggedly held on. Johnston summed it up:

"Brooks is one of the few artists who fully understands that he alone is ultimately responsible for his career, and therefore, he better oversee what goes on during his watch. He's frequently criticized for being involved in the business side of things, but the roadside is littered with artists who were screwed out of every cent they made because they focused only on their art."

CHAPTER SEVENTEEN

"Who the shit is paying for all this?"

It was the end of July 1996, and Garth had just finished playing three nights at the Rose Garden Arena in Portland, Oregon, where ticket sales had broken records set earlier that year by Neil Diamond. The tour was beginning a Canadian run that would last through September. All those shows had sold out in unprecedented numbers, too. The first show scheduled was at the General Motors Place in Vancouver, British Columbia. Tickets there had outsold AC/DC's recent appearance.

Garth sat on the bus, waiting to cross the border. When he turned and looked back at the lines of buses and tractor-trailers all transporting concert personnel and equipment, he was suddenly alarmed at the enormity of it all. Speaking to no one in particular, he asked, "Who the shit is paying for all this?"

IN 1996 GARTH LAUNCHED a three-year tour that *Amusement Business* said was "easily the top country music tour of all time." Between March 1996 and November 1998, Garth played to over 5.5 million fans at 350 shows in 100 cities.

Just prior to tickets going on sale, Garth worried that he might face a tepid market. *Fresh Horses* had sold 2.5 million since its release, and had fallen out of the pop Top 10 after seven weeks.

And it wasn't because country music was out of favor; in 1995 country had twenty-seven platinum and seventeen gold albums. As usual, Garth was candid about understanding that celebrity is a fleeting commodity. "My dad has always warned me that what you get fast can disappear fast," he said. "I've stayed off the road for over a year, and it's a new world out there."

Garth's biggest single of 1995, "She's Every Woman," was only number 24 on the year's top impact singles: Tim McGraw, Alan Jackson, Pam Tillis, Collin Raye, and Wade Hayes headed that year's list. Mainstays like Brooks & Dunn and Wynonna were at the top of the charts. The biggest news of '94 and '95 had been Tim McGraw, and by 1996, Shania Twain and Kenny Chesney.

McGraw's 1992 self-titled album on Curb hadn't generated any hits, but he was a favorite among songwriters who believed that the singer could be a star if he could just catch a break. The A&R man who came with Bowen to Capitol, James Stroud, turned out to be the break Tim needed. In 1992, Stroud, who had left Capitol to work with Clint Black, was chosen to head the newly opened Giant Records. Part of Stroud's agreement included producing outside acts, and Tim McGraw was the beneficiary of the deal. His first project with Stroud producing, *Not a Moment Too Soon,* contained McGraw's breakthrough single, "Indian Outlaw," and was the biggest-selling album of the year. The soulful follow-up ballad, "Don't Take The Girl," went to number 1, proving that McGraw could deliver far more than novelty tunes, and making him a star. *Not a Moment Too Soon* topped both the country and pop charts and won McGraw the ACM Top Album and Male Artist awards.

In 1996, while Garth struggled to get Capitol behind *Fresh Horses,* Tim, touring with Faith Hill, released his next album, *All I Want,* which produced hits including "I Like It I Love It" and "All I Want Is A Life." Five top-charting singles in all. Faith finally broke off with Scott and married McGraw on October 6 of 1996.

Shania Twain was making news and hits with her first Mutt Lange–produced album, *The Woman in Me.* Propelled by slick and sexy videos, the hits just kept on coming in '95 and '96. "Whose Bed Have Your Boots Been Under?" "Any Man Of Mine," "(If You're Not In It For Love), I'm Outta Here!" and "No One Needs To Know" transformed the Mercury hopeful into an international superstar.

With 1995's "You Ain't Much Fun" and 1996's "Me Too" Toby Keith was showing glimpses of the powerhouse he would become. Kenny Chesney, too, stood poised for stardom with breakthrough singles coming from his 1996 BNA album, *Me and You.* A Nashville-based group named Lonestar had its first number 1 in 1996 when "No News" stayed at the top of the charts for three weeks. One of the biggest stories in country music was the seemingly overnight stardom of Capitol's Deana Carter. Labelmate Trace Adkins also hit big with "Every Light In The House" and "(This Ain't) No Thinkin' Thing."

LeAnn Rimes had an auspicious Top 10 debut in 1996 with "Blue." LeAnn was just five years old and had won her first talent show when Garth got to Nashville in 1987. Her astonishing vocals had been well known around Nashville for years, but even given the success of child stars like Brenda Lee and Tanya Tucker, many were skeptical of signing someone so young. After first hearing her sing, Jimmy Bowen had said, "Great voice, but she's too young to sue." Mike Curb took a chance and introduced a monster talent to the world. Her second 1996 release was the number 1 career-builder "One Way Ticket (Because I Can)."

And because in 1996 the hottest country tour on the road was Tim McGraw and Faith Hill, for all intents and purposes, Garth Brooks was coming out of his time off as an underdog. To make up for it, he was determined to make each show a mind-blowing experience. It was also a study in contrasts.

Over the years Garth's stage show went from busting the occasional guitar to flying over the audience in a harness to the high-tech spaceship special effects of the late '90s. But lest people think he was attempting to turn the Garth Brooks show into a KISS concert, in 1996 he came up with an unusual show opener.

"Did you ever see Rod Stewart's show when he was having a three-piece bagpipe group open for him?" Garth asked a friend, who hadn't the vaguest idea about Rod's pipers.

"It got me thinking," Garth went on. "I love picking guitars around a campfire out on the farm. Why not open the tour that way—a couple of guys sitting around a campfire playing acoustic guitars and singing."

"It sounds pretty low-key. Will your audience go for that?"

Garth grinned. "I think they will. We already gave it kind of a test run in 1994 at the Hollywood Bowl, and people seemed to love it. I think the *contrast* is the reason they'll go for it. I've already talked to Bryan Kennedy about him and Dan Roberts coming on the road with me. Bryan said, 'I guess you know it'll be like your old uncle pulling his guitar off the wall and asking if you'd like to hear a tune.' I said, 'That's exactly what I want, *your old uncle*.'" And so country's most rocked-out tour opened with a couple of cowboys with guitars. It was unexpected, unscripted, and overwhelmingly accepted.

Raising the stakes for a series of shows in Texas, Garth decided to sail over the audience strapped into a harness with guide wires and have a face-to-face with fans on the back rows. He planned for the show opener, "The Thunder Rolls," to include thunder, lightning, and rain. A robed choir was to make an appearance on "We Shall Be Free," and Garth had been taking lessons from the legendary Jim Horn so he could play saxophone on "One Night A Day." But the big spectacle would come with "Standing Outside The Fire," when flames would billow from the stage.

Garth thought he had it all planned out. But he learned that even the best-laid plans can fail to ignite. During the first Texas

show he stood with his arms flung skyward expecting flames
to shoot up in front of him, setting up "Standing Outside The
Fire."

Nothing happened.

Garth glanced around, nervously trying to cover up the stag-
ing error, but it was obvious something had gone wrong.

After the show he asked his tech man, "Why no fire?"

"Because you were standing on the gas pipe. Good thing I
noticed because I damn near torched you."

The crewmember wore a shirt that read, "I work for a
madman."

By '96 only two hundred markets in the United States could accommodate the Garth Brooks tour, a reality Garth regretted: "Two
of our best markets are Fort Smith and Little Rock, Arkansas, and
we couldn't play them because they didn't have the right buildings.
We never went back to Oklahoma State [in Stillwater], but we
probably covered those people in Oklahoma City and Tulsa. We
never got back to Boise [Idaho] and that's a great market for us.
There were a lot of places we didn't get to this time."

Before the tour started some speculated that the special effects Garth had become known for were too extreme for country concerts, and in late 1995, Garth talked with *New Country*'s
editor Brian Mansfield about it. "A lot of people are saying that
we're going to take it over the top, and for the first minute and
a half, they're right. But for the other hour and a half or whatever, it's going to be focused on the music. Entertaining is about
making an entrance. So we're going to make an entrance. We are
going to MAKE an entrance. And we're gonna have fun . . . but
probably 95 percent of the gags we'll do will be in the entrance.
Then, of course, if we're lucky enough to get encores in certain
places, we're going to do some stupid stuff, simply because that's
what GB does."

And what an entrance it was to be. *Country Weekly* described
how Garth kicked off the first show of the tour: "Thick smoke

gushed from all corners of the stage. Multicolored lights turned, twisted, flickered and finally framed the stage with beams. The band's drum set then rose in a slow, full-circle spin, encased in a glass pyramid that looked like a spacecraft. Garth then made his entrance—through a little sleight of band. Fans heard the opening chords from the slow-building song 'The Old Stuff,' then saw a white baby grand piano rise from below stage level. Seated at it was a man dressed in a white suit topped with a white cowboy hat. At first glance it looked as if Garth had decided to act out the all-white scene from 'The Red Strokes.' Then the surprise. As Garth's voice rang out, fans realized he wasn't in the white suit—he was in the piano! A mechanical lift delivered a fist-pumping Garth through a hole that opened in the middle of the piano. To screams and a standing ovation, he bounded onto the stage and belted out the first of 19 songs."

By 1996 Stillwater had expanded. Two longtime members, Ty England and Betsy Smittle, who were pursuing solo careers, had been replaced. Mike Palmer was on drums and Mark Greenwood replaced Betsy on bass. James Garver played lead electric guitar as well as percussion, banjo, and acoustic guitar. Steve McClure played steel. Dave Gant played keys, Jimmy Mattingly was on fiddle, and Debbie Nims took Ty's place on rhythm guitar.

Garth talked to *Country Song Roundup* about the new band: "It's got a big smack. Debbie came in and whipped the hell out of all the boys, like a little sergeant in there. Then there's this kid named Jimmy Mattingly on fiddle who came in, and I think everybody stepped up to a new level when they heard him play. They want to show what they can do. The additions are nice and the remaining original members are rougher than I've ever seen them. They're strong as a rock." To fully appreciate the sound of this tight group, listen to their stellar work on *Double Live*.

After taking a few weeks off for the holidays, Garth kicked off the 1997 leg of his world tour with three sold-out shows at Hirsch Memorial Coliseum in Shreveport, Louisiana, on

January 16. Reports of record-shattering ticket sales started stacking up. On January 25 fans bought over 51,000 tickets for six upcoming Garth concerts at the Jacksonville Coliseum in Jacksonville, Florida, in less than four hours. The previous record holder was Elvis Presley in March 1975. Also on January 25, fans bought over 31,000 tickets for three upcoming Garth concerts at the Richmond Coliseum in Richmond, Virginia, breaking the 1985 record of the Grateful Dead. The January sell-outs were just the beginning of a long list.

In February the Country Music Broadcasters' Association UK named Garth the Most Popular Artist for 1996. On March 11 he received Blockbuster Entertainment's Artist of the Decade award on a televised broadcast hosted by Vanessa Williams. But there was one award Garth did not feel right in accepting. On January 29, 1996, at the twenty-third annual American Music Awards, Garth was shocked to hear his name called as the Top Artist of the Year, over Boyz II Men, Green Day, Hootie & the Blowfish, and TLC. Since he had not released an album, Garth felt foolish to have been chosen over artists who'd had successful recordings. And so he walked to the podium, tipped his hat to the accomplishments of his competitors, and declined the trophy.

"I thought I was dreaming when they called my name," he said when returning to Nashville. "Hootie & the Blowfish? Come on, they should have had that. Look at what they've done. After all those years of kicking around and making great music they just busted in and killed everybody—won a Grammy and sold four million albums."

The most important milestone of 1996 was closer to home, when on July 28 Sandy Brooks gave birth to the couple's third daughter, Allie Colleen. Three months earlier, on the tenth anniversary of their marriage, the couple had renewed their wedding vows. The newest Brooks baby weighed in at eight pounds, ten ounces, and was twenty-one-and-a-half inches long. Garth said, "People are telling me that if we have two more, I'll have a basketball team!"

Given the enormity of Garth's success, the couple took a serious look at the way the girls would be raised. One thing they wanted to avoid was for Taylor, August, and Allie to see themselves as "star kids." It was a widespread problem in the entertainment industry, with too many youngsters developing a sense of entitlement because of their parent's celebrity. Nor did the couple want their girls to be spending time on the road in future years.

It was one thing for the children to travel with Garth when they were small, but Garth completely rejected the idea when it came to preteen and teenage years. He wanted them to be raised as closely as possible to the way he and Sandy had been. He talked to *Country America*'s Neil Pond about it.

"Sandy and I won't be doing them any favors by giving them an easy road. Life is not an easy road, thank God. The best roads I have traveled have been ones that, with God's help, I have cut down the trees and laid the gravel and poured the concrete myself. Then, it's just as smooth a ride as can be. If somebody gives you a ride it ain't half as fun. Some of my favorite years were 1989 and before, when Sandy and I together didn't clear more than ten or twelve thousand dollars a year. But we thought we were on top of the world. And we were."

Garth and Sandy knew they walked a fine line when it came to determining what behavior was "normal little girl stuff" and what was "spoiled little girl stuff." As he told *USA Weekend,* "When Taylor leaves half a sandwich on the plate, I start thinking, 'Oh God, don't let her get used to taking just a bite out of something and think we'll just get some more if it runs out.'"

Concerns about how the children viewed their father and his star status turned out to be something in need of continual attention. Just a year later Garth and Sandy were with the girls outside of their home one afternoon when a group of fans showed up at the gate. Taylor was five years old, and fans shouting "Garth Brooks!" confused her.

"Why are those people screaming my dad's name?" She asked Sandy.

"Well, they came to see him and just want to know if he's here," Sandy answered.

"That's crazy," Taylor mused. "He's just Dad."

When they were back at the house, Garth told Sandy that he hoped the girls could keep that "just Dad" attitude.

But that night at dinner Taylor called her father "Garth Brooks."

"We're gonna have to have a long talk," he said. "My name is Dad."

GARTH'S BIGGEST PUBLIC NEWS of 1997 came on March 26, when he held a press conference announcing that he would play a concert at Central Park in New York City on August 7. Less publicized, but equally important to Garth, were his plans to travel to Ireland to film a television special in May.

When Garth had played eight sold-out shows at the Point in Dublin three years earlier, he had promised the Irish fans that he'd return and that the next time he'd bring cameras. And that's what he did.

Three shows quickly sold out for Dublin's Croke Park May 16 to 18, 1997. Polls showed that one in every twenty people in Ireland wanted to attend the concerts. Mary Arnold, writing in *Country Music News* (Ireland), put it this way: "Garth Brooks had played Dublin in 1994, so in effect, this was the second coming. And if it had been the *real* Second Coming, I don't think a lot of Irish people would have been more excited."

Producer Jon Small utilized an international film team: over four hundred professionals from Ireland, the United States, Great Britain, Canada, Belgium, France, and Australia. In addition to veteran U.S. director, Michael Salomon, Small brought on board Australian director of photography Toby Phillips, considered one of the best in the business for multicamera concert shoots, British lighting designer Patrick Woodruff, and line producer Tom Forrest.

One of the most formidable challenges Small and Forrest faced was Garth's desire to use two helicopters with cameras, one flying over the audience and a second hovering just above the first. The normal minimum air space requirements were finally waived when the production team found a Vietnam veteran and Europe's premier helicopter pilot. "The noise and the downdraft was unbelievable," Small said. "It was wild and the crowd loved it." *Ireland and Back* was later nominated for an Emmy for Multi-Camera Picture Editing for a Miniseries.

Transporting the equipment needed for the show was a major undertaking. The supplies, shipped by air and sea, filled 60 trucks and had a weight of nearly 2 million pounds. The equipment required for the shows included over 100 miles of cable, ten 35 mm cameras, 300 pounds of confetti, 6 generators, 350,000 feet of film, a 70-foot crane, and the 2 helicopters. Each show (recorded on 96 audio tracks) required 24,000 amps of power (a normal house runs on 200 amps). The stage measured 460 feet wide and 65 feet tall.

The first ninety minutes of the special was primarily concert footage and filmed completely in Ireland. Trisha Yearwood, Stephanie Davis, and Susan Ashton provided harmonies.

Garth was filmed visiting Brazen Head (Dublin's oldest pub) to record two songs for the special. He enjoyed the company so much he stayed several extra hours to talk with the customers, and sang "Dublin In The Rare Auld Times" with one of the pub's regulars. The *Hollywood Reporter*'s Tony Gleske pointed to the outstanding performance filmed when Garth and fiddle player Jimmy Mattingly performed "That Ol' Wind" on the waterfront in the fishing village of Howth, about thirty minutes outside Dublin. The final portion of the special was filmed in the United States, and included duets with Garth's friend Steve Wariner.

When Garth arrived in Dublin for the concerts, he sented with a million-seller sales award from EMI (for UK sales), then talked with the press.

"The whole tour this year is the Circle Tour with the UFO—we have this huge UFO that actually launches and lifts off at the start of the show. The theme is one of NASA space gear that includes all the crew, everybody.

"It's not a completely new image," he laughed. "I'll still be in the Stetson wearing those ridiculously tight pants!

"This whole game is built on confidence," he continued. "Confidence only comes through God and people. And only confidence is gonna get you through that first night. What happened at the Point [in 1994] gave me the confidence to believe that music can travel across the water, and that somebody other than in your own country can get what you're trying to say. If I can feel like I did when I walked out on stage at the Point—that's what I'm hoping for. That's magic."

The trip had strong family connections. When Garth had played for Irish crowds in 1993 the audience had serenaded Sandy Brooks over the telephone. This time Garth was able to introduce her to the Irish fans. The response was overwhelming, even to Garth and Sandy, who had both seen plenty of screaming fans. Colleen Brooks, whose family is from County Cork, south of Dublin, was unable to attend the shows because of health concerns, but the people of Cork gave her a citation as an honorary citizen in absentia.

Garth explained the experience to the *Today* show's Katie Couric: "What happened was . . . it shocked Sandy. That night in bed, Sandy's laying there, two in the morning, her eyes are wide open. She goes, 'I see why you do it now.'"

Garth's fiddler extraordinaire Jimmy Mattingly (now with the Grascals) later reflected on returning to the United States during an interview with PlanetGarth.com. When he boarded the plane for the return flight, it seems Jimmy spotted an empty seat with a pillow and blanket. He commandeered it and quickly fell asleep. When he awoke hours later he found the entire band and crew asleep. Garth was on the floor using his jacket for a blanket and his bag for a pillow. In an instant, Jimmy realized the plane was a seat short to accommodate the crowd and he'd grabbed Garth's seat. Chagrinned, he awoke Garth to tell him he could have his seat back. "It's okay," Garth said. Only after Jimmy insisted the two switch out for the remainder of the flight did "the boss" crawl back into his chair.

The tour broke the sales records of several other acts, including AC/DC, New Kids on the Block, Elton John, Aerosmith, Journey, Van Halen, Elvis Presley, Billy Joel, Foreigner, Neil Diamond, the Grateful Dead, Huey Lewis, the Eagles, Pink Floyd, Genesis, Def Leppard, KISS, Paul McCartney, and Michael Jackson. Having one of their own knocking down ticket records set by rock's biggest stars provided a powerful promotional tool for the Country Music Association.

The buzz helped make country even more attractive to promoters, advertisers, and sponsors. His concerts influenced the road shows of numerous stars, including Tim McGraw, Kenny Chesney, and the Dixie Chicks. But on the downside, Garth had not released a studio album since *Fresh Horses,* and it affected the genre's overall sales. In 1993 country had accounted for 19 percent of all records sold, but by 1997 that percentage was down to twelve. A big-selling album was sorely needed, and in fact, Garth had one ready to go.

CHAPTER EIGHTEEN

New York shows up
to kick some ass

I came here to play some music, raise some hell, and have some fun!"

That was just what the audience of nearly a million wanted to hear Garth say when he hit the stage in Central Park that night in August 1997. The masses of screaming fans seemed to overwhelm Garth.

"Not only did you show up," he said. "You showed up to kick some ass!"

GARTH'S NEW ALBUM WAS finished. It was titled *Sevens* for several reasons, one being that Garth had been born on the seventh of February in 1962. So, on November 25, 1997, the seventh year of the decade, he would release his seventh studio album (not counting his Christmas recording). But after the *Fresh Horses* experience, he was not prepared to entrust the release of another album entirely to Capitol in Nashville. The label had done well with artists like Trace Adkins and Deana Carter, and had signed Keith Urban, but not so well with its established artists such as Garth and Tanya Tucker.

Then New York–based EMI executive Pat Quigley brought an idea to the table: a free concert in Central Park as part of the album's launch. This was not a new idea. Joe Mansfield had first broached the subject with Garth in the early 1990s because he'd worked with CBS artists who'd had wildly successful Central Park experiences—Barbra Streisand, Paul Simon, Diana Ross, James Taylor. But at that time, Garth wasn't sure he could draw that kind of a crowd.

Quigley hadn't come up through the music marketing ranks, but had a background in sales with companies such as Rolling Rock beer, Swatch watches, and various winter sports companies. He had made a name at EMI as a sales wizard who thought outside of the box. There was a constituency at EMI who considered Quigley's management style abrasive. But it was a side Garth Brooks never saw.

Garth and Pat had become friends over the past year. When Quigley's father died, Garth attended the funeral, even held Pat's crying child during the service. That shared event solidified Quigley's loyalty to the Nashville-based artist; he later explained: "How do you repay a guy like that? You work hard for him."

As he had when Mansfield first brought up Central Park, Garth hesitated when Quigley broached the subject, unsure if he could bring out New York audiences on that level. When he finally did agree, it was more about the challenge, and promoting *Sevens* would be the added benefit. Working with Quigley, Charles Koppelman, and EMI executive VP Terri Santisi, Garth began to put the event together. In many ways, the Central Park story, with its upfront highs and behind-the-scenes lows, becomes a paradigm of Garth's career pattern—disciplined risk taking.

He took flak for the decision to play Central Park. The New York *Daily News* asked if this had the potential for a "Garthgantuan flop." The *New York Times* asked, "What's New York about Garth Brooks?" And there were other digs. Garth laughed when he heard that the Stage Deli had named a sandwich after him: turkey on a kaiser roll.

"The very first Macy's Thanksgiving Day Parade I participated in I was asked to ride on the turkey float," he joked. "Do
you think there's a pattern here?"

Underneath, despite an unbelievable amount of careful preparations and extensive promotion, Garth was nervous about
the outcome. "I have nightmares about this show," he said. "I
dream that I run out on the stage and Central Park is completely
empty."

Garth again handed production control to Jon Small, who
was just wrapping up work on *Ireland and Back*. The first meeting in New York was held outside Mayor Rudolph Giuliani's
office at city hall and involved Small, his two associates, and an
incredible lineup of city departments. "Central Park is under the
jurisdiction of four or five various police and fire departments,
each one dealing with separate areas—that's even before you get
to the various divisions of the Parks Department," Small ruefully reported.

Many of Central Park's big events had been held on the
Great Lawn, but it was being renovated. So Garth's concert was
to be held at the North Meadow. But neither the Great Lawn
nor the North Meadow had an infrastructure, so everything
had to be brought in. Exits and entrances had to be established,
toilets, handicapped facilities. The area in question was larger
than nine football fields. "It took six months to work out the
logistics," Jon Small said.

Ultimately, Small used over one thousand speakers and four
thousand lights. In addition to a one-of-a-kind Russian-built
crane for aerial shots and twenty-four cameras, a "rail cam" was
used to allow viewers to track every move the entertainer made.
Director Marty Callner told the Associated Press that even on
a platform sixty feet longer than a football field, the rail cam
would be able to track Garth's every move on five JumboTron
screens so the Central Park audience could see the entire show.

"No man can run that fast with a camera in his hand," Callner
said. "Also, we have a satellite stage, which is going to come out

to the middle of the house. It's going to be unbelievable because he's going to be out there with all these people around him."

Callner told the *New York Times* that the Great Lawn, with its grand view of the New York skyline, would be sorely missed on the HBO show. To give television viewers a sense of being in the city, cameras would cut to shots taken from blimps and helicopters.

But, as the *Los Angeles Times'* Steve Hochman later wrote, other than those shots, and the appearance of Billy Joel, Garth "did little to tailor his show to the setting. That was smart. Brooks' greatest gift is as a natural entertainer, and that's where he kept the focus."

Fans from all over the world showed up at what by now was being called "Garthstock." The crowd quickly overflowed into a field west of the North Meadow and into the East Meadow. Initial attendance estimates went from a quarter of a million (from the police department) to over a million (from the park service). But in May 1998, the New York Fire Department officially announced the final attendee numbers at 980,000. This made the concert the largest ever held in Central Park, beating out attendance for Simon and Garfunkel, Barbra Streisand, James Taylor, Diana Ross, Elton John, and others. When told of the fire department's announcement, Garth said, "There's something we've never said before, and now I'm glad it's out. I was handed a piece of paper right before I walked on stage from the parks department. It said 1.1 million people. But then we got the reports of a quarter of a million people. I didn't know why it came out that way."

And for those who had speculated that country music wasn't for New Yorkers, Garth led with "Rodeo" and followed it with "Papa Loved Mama." It was rough and rowdy country music and the crowd went nuts. After the initial rousing numbers, Garth turned serious and delivered an inspirational version of "We Shall Be Free."

Other concert highlights included Garth's walking through the crowd during his performance of "The River" and "Fever," with fiddle player Jimmy Mattingly taking the instrumental lead. Then, of course, there were the special guests. New York's own Billy Joel not only showed up, he sang along on "Ain't Going Down (Til The Sun Comes Up)." Then he and Garth collaborated on a moving version of "New York State Of Mind." The New Yorkers loved it. In an encore that beat all encores, Don McLean walked onstage to sing "American Pie" with Garth.

The HBO live concert ended, but the audience still wouldn't let Garth go. He stayed and performed song after song, some of which are included on the home video.

HBO's Nancy Geller summed up the cable network's feelings at the end of the day: "My job is to give HBO viewers something they can't get anywhere else. I've done that. I've given them one hell of a show."

Garth even convinced the skeptical New York press. The *Daily News* wrote, "No country star has pulled this kind of crowd anywhere, and to do it in New York City, well, anyone who thinks they can do better is welcome to try."

Garth Live from Central Park was HBO's highest-rated original program in 1997, as well as the most-watched special on cable television in 1997, drawing 14.6 million television viewers. *Live from Central Park* also drew the largest audience of any program on CMT Canada since its inception. On April 22, 1998, Trisha Yearwood presented Garth with the Academy of Country Music's Special Achievement Award for *Live from Central Park*. Garth received a standing ovation when he walked to the stage to accept his award. The show was nominated for six Emmy awards at the September 13, 1998, show at Los Angeles's Shrine Auditorium.

BUT AS SUCCESSFUL AS Central Park was, as a promotional tool for Garth's new album, it was a wash. Prior to the Central

Park show, and unrelated to Garth Brooks, EMI fired Capitol's top management in New York, including Charles Koppelman and Terri Santisi, leaving the label in disarray. But a huge buzz already surrounded *Sevens,* with advance orders upwards of 6 million. Garth felt he had no option but to withhold the release until stability was restored.

But, as Bill Bell of the New York *Daily News* spoke with Garth from his home in Goodlettsville, Tennessee: "[Koppelman and Santisi] set up the album and the concert. And then thirty days before I'm supposed to deliver, this happens. I figure it's best to wait until things settle down, see where we all are."

Garth further explained to entertainment journalist Paul Lomartire, "The massive shifts and cuts and restructuring of our label from EMI has totally wiped out the branch that was handling the new album in conjunction with the HBO Central Park release. Timing is everything in music. This time it's worked against me."

Garth left New York for California, where he had a fifteen-show run scheduled in three cities. Garth had seen little in recent months to make him believe that, without New York, Capitol/Nashville could be counted on to promote *Sevens.* Despite the high he felt from Central Park, he was deeply troubled about his record label and his new recording.

Unbeknownst to Garth Brooks, the corporate changes had begun in 1996 when EMI made the decision to cut back on budgets and bodies. And because key Garth supporters Koppelman and Santisi were shown the door, anyone who thought Garth was secretly running his record label should have seen the error of their thinking.

The president and chief executive of EMI Records Group International and Virgin Music Group, Ken Berry, was named worldwide president of the newly formed EMI Recorded Music unit in a corporate restructuring. It would have been foolish to release a new album until things settled down.

Garth saw trends that were both encouraging and troubling in country music during 1997. One of the bright spots was the growing list of country record labels, under ten when he arrived in Nashville, now over thirty. But he wondered if the music was suffering from such rapid growth. He spoke at length with Ben Fong-Torres in the *Gavin Report* about some of his concerns.

"You gotta never forget that I'm a fan, and was a fan of country music before I was ever an artist. So I speak from the point of view of a guy listening to the radio. Narvel Blackstock, Reba's husband, said in an interview that in the first twenty weeks of this year, forty-four debut singles from forty-four new artists came out. I don't see how we can ask fans to keep up, to find something recognizable and distinguishable, and something to follow. And it's tough to ask that of me as a fan."

The effect of the federal Telecommunications Act of 1996, which allowed companies to buy up any number of stations in one market, was also a problem. When that law went into effect the money people moved quickly and over four thousand radio stations changed hands. Radio has long been accused of making music decisions with little concern for purity, diversity, or merit. As fewer companies owned more stations, the already short playlists were tightened even more. Fewer chances were taken with material because it might cause some listener to switch the dial. More than ever, music was seen as something to sandwich in between advertisements as opposed to something to entertain the audience. Disc jockeys often fought this trend, but it was a difficult battle.

Garth used an example from Nashville's WSIX as his kind of country radio programming. When the morning show producer Devon O'Day took charge one week she played exactly what she wanted, paying no attention to prescribed lists. "It was the best radio I'd heard in years. For me. She'd play one of those new people that you think you might know, but you're going to wait for two, three singles down the line and see what's going on, followed by Gene Watson's '14 Karat Mind,' followed by something like Deana Carter's 'Strawberry Wine' mixed in with John Anderson's 'Black Sheep.'

"It worked so well that I was glued to the station. [Nashville's] WSM-AM does old and new country together and it works for me. Maybe that's showing my age. But it's punks like me that need to be reminded of how country is done—like Merle Haggard and Gene Watson."

Garth had had a difficult time recording *Sevens*. He was solidly on the road, so writing was slow. He wasn't sure what was going on with his label and with his career. And yet this is the album Garth now listens to when he wants "to feel happy."

"*Sevens* is really Allen Reynolds's album," Garth told Steve Morse at the *Boston Globe*. "I think Allen saw me questioning myself and wondering if I still had a future and how long was it. So he just sort of took over and drove. Allen never gave the wheel back over. In a good way, he kept driving, even coming down to the sequencing and the number of songs. I wanted eleven and he wanted fourteen. I always get what I want, but no way this time! He just didn't let go."

Even though Garth had written only six of the songs, the album sounded very personal. "People thought I wrote most of the album," Garth said. "But it's because the songs were so perfect for me, songs like 'Longneck Bottle'—which Steve Wariner wrote. When some of the promotion guys heard it they said it was too much of a honky-tonker for radio. I said, 'Who'd have thought you'd hear *Garth Brooks* and *too country* in the same breath?'"

The potential for airplay wouldn't have been central to Garth's song selections anyway. Garth explained his thinking on songs, songwriting, and airplay to *Country Weekly*.

"You try to be emotional," he said. "If you want to laugh, you want to laugh your butt off. If you're going to cry, you just want to be so dang miserable you just can't stand it. But never, ever do you let it cross your mind, 'Will country radio play this?'

"Please don't ever do that when you're writing. If we had all thought, 'Will radio play this?' we would never have heard the Beatles. Their stuff was so new and out there.

"Our job is to surprise ourselves, surprise country radio and surprise the people. Country radio wants what fits their format— they know that. But if you surprise them and it's a good surprise, they're all of a sudden ten times further down the road than they would have been if they had got what they expected."

On the Jim Rushing/Carl Jackson bluegrass gospel song "Fit For A King," Garth combined two of his favorite musical touches: a fuzzed-out '70s electric guitar and a mournful country fiddle. And most would have thought that Garth wrote the opening lines in the Gordon Kennedy/Pierce Pettis song "You Move Me," lines comparing life to therapy that costs a lot but comes with no guarantees.

"Two Piña Coladas," by Sandy Mason, Benita Hill, and Shawn Camp, was a number 1 hit beach anthem written on a cold, dark day in Nashville. It was so dreary, in fact, that all the three could think about was how much they wished they were at the beach. Sandy Mason later laughed that even though she wasn't a drinker, she pictured herself dancing around a cabana with a drink in each hand. The writers planned to pitch the song to Jimmy Buffett until Reynolds said, "Not so fast. I hear this for Garth."

"Two Piña Coladas" was recorded with a drum, bass, keys, two acoustic guitars, and one electric. "At its best, music has space," Reynolds explains. "I love to hear musicians and writers who can say a lot, sparingly."

Benita Hill collaborated on another song included on *Sevens*, and the two cuts were life changing. Benita was forging a career that included singing backup for Conway Twitty, the Allman Brothers, and J. J. Cale. She was an accomplished songwriter and member of Nashville's Two Desperate Women. But she dreamed of making a recording, and it hadn't happened.

Finally she took matters into her own hands, maxed out her credit cards, and made her own CD, *Fan the Flame*. Working as a receptionist and worried sick over her financial situation, one day she handed Garth a copy of *Fan the Flame,* simply hoping for some encouragement. He loved her song "Take The Keys To My Heart" (written with Tommy Smith and Pam Wolfe) and called her with those magic words: "I want to cut 'Keys.'" When he also recorded "Two Piña Coladas," Benita paid off her credit cards.

The songs that Garth did contribute to *Sevens* were among the standouts. "Cowboy Cadillac" combined his love for tongue-in-cheek lyrics, all things western, and rapid-fire lines with internal rhyme schemes. Most of Garth's co-writers groan when he starts a song with this shotgun technique, coming at you "bam-bam-bam," because it is so difficult to sustain.

"How You Ever Gonna Know" returns to his love of "go-for-the-gold" optimism, and "She's Gonna Make It" finds a man hanging on and a woman moving on. "Belleau Wood" is yet another historical three-minute movie, in this case the inspirational story of German and American soldiers laying down their arms on Christmas.

"*Sevens* has become my favorite album," Garth said in 2005. "For a long time it was *The Chase,* but now I have to say it's *Sevens,* mainly because of two songs. When I wrote 'How You Ever Gonna Know' I hoped it would encourage someone to try even when the odds were against them. A few years after the album came out someone told me that the song had been life changing. I don't want to say what her circumstances were, because she told the story in confidence. But she made some decisions that turned her entire life around. In your dreams, you want music to do that for people."

Perhaps the finest performance on the album, and one that would win a Grammy the following year, was the Garth/Trisha Yearwood duet, "In Another's Eyes," penned by Bobby Wood, John Peppard, and Garth. "It was an inspired performance," says producer Reynolds. "They nailed the vocals on the first try."

This was a song that started out as something entirely different. Wood had taken some of Peppard's title ideas to Garth, including "Through Another Man's Eyes." Garth liked the general idea, but changed it to "In Another's Eyes," about two people in love who can't bear to leave their partners because of the resulting pain.

People speculated that the song was a description of Garth and Trisha's relationship, but that was not the case. They were not star-crossed lovers, but were trying very hard to hold on to their own marriages. Garth and Sandy had a new baby at home, and three daughters took up what little free time Garth had. And Trisha was still wed to the Mavericks' Robert Reynolds, although the relationship was said to be strained by the directions their two careers had taken.

Trisha remained one of country's most important superstars, lauded by critics, radio, and fans, while the Mavericks' time on the charts appeared to be over. The group remained critical darlings, able to book into nearly any hip venue they wanted, but their last *Billboard* showing had been 1996's "All You Ever Do Is Bring Me Down" from *Music for All Occasions* on MCA. The single hit number 13, the highest of their career. Writers who knew Reynolds said he was unhappy over being seen as "Trisha Yearwood's husband," and it bubbled to the surface from time to time. Once, at the L.A. House of Blues, Reynolds was visibly irritated when a fan shouted, "Say hi to Trisha!" Reynolds responded: "Make sure you ask about me when you go to her shows, okay?"

Garth made an interesting musical decision for "I Don't Have To Wonder." Although penned by Shawn Camp and Taylor Dunn, "I Don't Have To Wonder" is a bone-chilling finale to the scenario started by the team of Blazy, Williams, and Brooks on "She's Gonna Make It." With "I Don't Have To Wonder," the listener actually *is* left to wonder if a disheartened lover is not "gonna make it" and commits suicide. When guitarist Chris Leuzinger first listened to the demo, he assumed the song needed a big guitar part. Instead, Garth said he wanted sorrowful steel provided by Bruce Bouton. Chris Leuzinger shook his head: "Well, I'll be home by the phone if it doesn't work." It worked, as did the soaring choir: Trisha Yearwood, Susan Ashton, Vicki Hampton, Robert Bailey, Yvonne Hodges, and Kathy Chiavola.

Nowhere is the wisdom of those two decisions more obvious than on the song's video, where the musical drama sets up every scene. The piece opens with a forlorn man standing on a bridge during a hard rain. Does he kill himself? And what might the afterlife for a suicide be: reliving that final day for eternity?

Sevens was ready to go when EMI's 1997 summer shakeup happened. The album was not released until November, when EMI named Pat Quigley Capitol's executive vice president and general manager. It was later announced that Scott Hendricks would head another EMI label, Virgin Records. Two things, however, should be noted. Some insiders at EMI expected Quigley would go, along with Koppelman and Santisi. But EMI knew that firing Koppelman and Santisi would upset one of the company's biggest stars. So while Garth did not ask for it, Quigley's promotion was a kind of consolation prize offered to both executive and artist. Second, from the beginning EMI didn't see the Quigley transfer to Nashville as permanent.

CHAPTER NINETEEN

"Hopefully, we're starting to build a family"

Pat Quigley's promotion marked a bittersweet time for Garth. He hoped it meant that marketing for himself and others on the label would improve. But Music Row buzzed with speculations that he had again played power politics, and engineered Scott Hendricks's removal.

Yet even as he was under fire, he soon began to receive support from his contemporaries. Reba McEntire sent an encouraging personal letter, and other Capitol artists, including Steve Wariner, spoke out on his behalf. Then Garth had a phone call from one of Capitol's new superstars, a young woman who always spoke her mind: Deana Carter.

"I'm in agreement that we needed to change things around here," Deana said. "But I want to sit down and tell you my experience, and how I think we could revive the label. It starts with communication."

"I want to hear every word you have to say!" Garth replied.

Garth talked to Steve Morse at the *Boston Globe* about the conversation: "Deana Carter really keeps those people on their toes. She's sweet as she can be, but also tougher than a tank. You don't mess with her. I've really fallen in love with her attitude. She was very open and frank with me about what she thought.

We've also had meetings at the label since the restructuring. The artists are now coming to those meetings with the label people.

"Hopefully, we're starting to build a family."

FIVE HIT SINGLES WERE released from *Sevens,* starting with "Longneck Bottle" and "She's Gonna Make It." "Two Piña Coladas," the third single from *Sevens,* was a number 1 hit. ("Do What You Gotta Do" was an additional release, in the year 2000.)

The number 1 "To Make You Feel My Love" was sandwiched in between "Two Piña Coladas" and "You Move Me," but it was not from *Sevens.* The song was Garth's version of a Bob Dylan composition from the soundtrack of *Hope Floats* starring Sandra Bullock, Harry Connick Jr., and Gena Rowlands.

When *Hope Floats* director Forrest Whittaker and soundtrack producer Don Was first approached Garth about singing Bob Dylan's "To Make You Feel My Love," Garth turned them down. "I don't hear this as a Garth Brooks song," he said at first listen. But when he sat down and studied the lyrics, he was sold on the beauty and simplicity of the words. He ended up loving the recording so much that he made his first new solo video in two years. Visuals from the film are prominently featured. Garth is seen walking through a house as images from the movie are projected on the walls.

"Longneck Bottle" not only wasn't "too country" but made music history, thanks to the fans. Before its release, a Toronto station classified it as "western swing" and announced they'd not be playing it. Outraged fans responded with telephone calls and angry letters. Other stations in the region started using the slogan "We play 'Longneck Bottle.'"

"Longneck Bottle" became the only single to be added by every *Radio & Records* reporting station on the day of its release. The song debuted in the R&R chart at number 10, the highest single debut in its history.

Garth used the opportunity to challenge radio to play more records from country's legends: "The reason why I stand here is because of George Jones and Merle Haggard, and there's the era before them, Hank Williams Sr., and Jimmie Rodgers, and the other people who started this whole thing. Why can't we hear nine of the new things and every now and then throw in the reason we're all here? Throw in a Haggard tune, or Jones?"

IT WAS SENSIBLE OF Garth to postpone the release of his seventh album for Capitol until he believed the label to have some semblance of stability. And ultimately, the decision to replace Hendricks was made in New York. People speculated that Jim Fifield and Ken Berry got rid of Hendricks out of desperation for Garth's new album, and that Garth was behind the entire thing.

In fact, as had happened with Jimmy Bowen, there was another element to be factored in. Just as some of Bowen's executives had burned up the phone lines complaining about his time on the golf course, one of Scott's own team reportedly had been privately calling EMI complaining that Hendricks wasn't up to the job. One executive brought in by Hendricks lamented the situation: "At one point some of the so-called Scott team got together on Tuesday nights where you couldn't tell who they were trying to separate the rest of us from, Scott Hendricks or Garth Brooks—or both. It was ugly."

"I know people believe that I'm some kind of a puppet master behind the scenes," Garth confided. "I was unhappy with the way Scott handled *Fresh Horses,* but I didn't call for his head. Give credit where it's due—Scott did a good job with Trace Adkins and Deana Carter. I thought some kind of a co-presidency might work, with both Quigley and Hendricks in place. I've got influence at EMI, but I guarantee you, I don't tell people like Jim Fifield or Ken Berry what to do. And I mainly wanted Quigley in charge of marketing *Sevens.* As great as Joe

Mansfield is, I learned that you've got to have the marketing team *at the label* behind your records."

Indeed, one of Fifield's closest associates laughed at the idea that Garth Brooks was ordering around the CEO of EMI. "Jim made corporate decisions—EMI decisions," she said. "It was not that he didn't listen to people, but ultimately he always went his own way."

But rumors of an out-of-control star ego persisted, fed by Jimmy Bowen's newly published memoir, *Rough Mix*. The book prompted a flurry of press, including comments from Knight-Ridder's Howard Cohen, who neglected to mention the people who actually were responsible for Garth's record contract, Jim Foglesong and Lynn Shults. "Bowen, who was at the helm of the label when Brooks released his first album in 1989, portrays Brooks as a backstabbing '800-pound gorilla' with a runaway ego."

After ignoring the original Capitol bloodbath, Cohen continued to quote Bowen:

"When I refused to give Garth a new contract barely one year after renegotiating his original deal, he shook his cage. He went around me and won himself a rich, precedent-setting joint venture from EMI-America in New York. The deal had the potential to destroy Capitol Nashville."

Steve Popovich, the man who'd run PolyGram at the turn of the decade, laughed out loud when he heard that comment. "That's typical record label bullshit. Even the biggest, most powerful artists get screwed with their contracts. First there's the cross collateralization, where labels get paid per dollar and not per album. That means the label controls the making of an artist's early albums. Maybe wrong decisions are made, maybe the label pays too much for production or doesn't promote worth a damn. Down the road, the artist gets his groove and starts kicking ass. But he still owes for all that went before. And he doesn't even own the albums.

"Then there are all the recoupables nobody fully explains—tour support, press costs, promotion costs, those limo rides artists think the label is treating them to—it all comes out of the artists' hides. And you don't even want to talk about how the accounting is done. Irving Azoff once said that out of every 3,000 record company audits where errors are discovered, 2,998 of the discrepancies discovered are in favor of the labels. And that's just the tip of the iceberg. If artists don't take care of their own business, they'll be robbed blind."

Bowen liked to say that Garth insisted on a "rock 'n' roll" deal, meaning similar to contracts that pop stars like Michael Jackson and Madonna could demand. Bowen told his artist, "You're not Michael Jackson, Elvis, or the Beatles." But Garth had the same career momentum as those artists. Further, using that concept as an indictment was an excuse that labels often used to treat their icons shabbily. When Columbia Records let Johnny Cash go in the late 1980s, the "rock 'n' roll deal" defense surfaced, with Cash supposedly asking for too much signing money. It didn't hold water then, either, because Johnny Cash had brought so much money to his label that some called CBS headquarters in New York "The House That Cash Built." The people in charge of record companies are not paid those big bucks to protect the financial interests of their artists. Some try to, of course. Others don't.

Garth had been reticent about responding to the Bowen charges over the years, but when Bowen's book was published, he finally did.

"I made a better deal. These labels are charging an artist to make their albums and then they own it. My biggest problem with the label was this attitude of disposable music and its 'Let's move on to something new' mindset. Catalog is everything to me and music is timeless. I don't accept the fact that an album is over. Look at the Eagles' *Greatest Hits*. It's still going on."

Garth never did really speak out against Bowen, personally, however. In 2000 he told *Billboard*, "I still sing Bowen's praises, even though he didn't mine in his book. I'm convinced Bowen knows what it takes to sell a book and I don't think Bowen feels bad about me. I could be totally wrong, but Bowen was too sweet to me in the private times, and he was too concerned about my happiness in the private times—or convinced me of that."

GARTH'S CONCERN ABOUT THE Nashville's "let's move on" syndrome was justified and it was a problem endemic within the entire business. Throughout its history the industry has espoused the concept of disposability. Whether it involves a single that stalls out or an album whose sales slow, too often the answer is a shrug. For all his faults as a label head, faults that would surface soon enough, Pat Quigley understood what the label owed to its artists. When a record label took the blood, sweat, and tears of a creative person it involved a responsibility. He agreed with Garth's original key man, Joe Mansfield, on most sales philosophies. Neither saw each new album as simply the label's latest entry in a beauty contest, but believed in selling a body of work.

"We need to look at Garth differently," Quigley said. "His music will live forever. He is an entertainer, works harder than anyone, and is loyal to his fans. We can always find new customers for Garth. New customers will keep this business going."

Quigley said he was willing to spend millions to market *Sevens* and that led to further speculation. Could Bowen have been right about Capitol taking a bath on Garth's albums? No, according to a January 1998 analysis by *Rolling Stone,* which anticipated a substantial label profit. CDs cost pennies to produce, hence record companies' willingness to throw product against the wall and see what sticks.

Moreover, *Rolling Stone* pointed out, when the label brought substantial marketing dollars to the table, others joined the effort. "Kmart, in an effort to link its name with the country superstar, spent several millions pitching *Sevens* with its own TV spots, and HBO dropped more than $10 million producing Brooks' show at New York's Central Park last summer."

Sevens debuted at number 1 on both the *Billboard* 200 and country albums chart, the top-selling debut week of any album released in 1997. It topped the *Billboard* 200 chart for a total of seven weeks and the country chart for thirteen weeks. It has now been certified at 10 million sales. Additionally, by keeping Garth's entire catalog easily available, those albums also gained in sales. *Fresh Horses,* especially, received a healthy boost in visibility.

USA Today's critic David Zimmerman proclaimed *Sevens* Garth's best ever album. "The track that shows an (almost) understated Brooks at his best is 'She's Gonna Make It,' a story of a seventh-month crash of a former husband devastated by his ex-wife's ability to cope."

The urban markets were especially strong in 1997. The *Boston Globe* reported that Garth's number 1 U.S. market was New York City, number 2 was Chicago, and number 3 Los Angeles. New York was also now the top market for Faith Hill and Wynonna. This is a stunning disclosure, given that New York City's one country radio station, WYNY, was sold in 1996, changing its format to CHR (contemporary hit radio). The lone country voice was Y-107, broadcasting from Long Island, and often difficult to pick up in the city. Touring and television appearances were what kept country's major stars visible.

In December 1997, the Country Music Association worked with pollster Edison Media Research and learned that one in five Americans considered country their favorite genre. The Midwest was the region with the highest percentage of country radio listeners and tape or CD buyers. Garth was the favorite artist, followed by Reba McEntire, Alabama, George Strait, LeAnn Rimes, and Shania Twain.

The final year of the 1996–1998 tour became one of the biggest in Garth's career. In between tour dates, he squeezed in television appearances, awards shows, and work on a new project, assembling his first live album.

For that last year of the tour, reigning Country Music

Association Female Vocalist Trisha Yearwood often appeared as the opening act and duet partner. To have her out on the tour was a coup. Trisha was a platinum-selling superstar with a string of hit records and country music awards. In 1997 she had a greatest-hits package in the stores and in 1998 she released a new studio album, *Where Your Road Leads.* "In Another's Eyes," from *Sevens,* earned a Grammy for Best Country Collaboration with Vocals for Garth and Trisha in 1998.

It had surprised Garth when Trisha approached him about going on part of the '98 tour. Given her superstar status, Garth said, "Are you kidding? I can't afford you!"

But, as Garth told Tamara Saviano, "Trisha said, 'I'll trade the money for the chance to play for big crowds and promote my album.' My respect for her went through the roof. And I figure I'm going to look great bringing a woman of this caliber to town for this price!"

He also spoke of the long-term friendship and how much it meant to have Trisha out on the road with him.

"The things I value and cherish most are relationships and this one has lasted ten, eleven years. And it is one of the gifts I've had musically and professionally. People think we all hang out together, but none of us do. I never, ever get to see Vince or Alan or George or Reba or any one of those people. So it's neat to have someone at the end of the day that I can talk to about payroll, about dying onstage when it ain't going good. This is a great gift for me."

For Trisha's part, it was good business. She was in front of a big, friendly audience and it affected her performance: "The biggest challenge is to make your music fresh every night. I know when Garth gets onstage that's one of the things he thinks about. A lot of entertainers don't."

Writing in the Minneapolis *Star Tribune,* Jon Bream pointed to Garth's deferential treatment of his opening act: "Musical high-lights were Brooks' duets with opening act Trisha Yearwood on 'In Another's Eyes' and her 'Walkaway Joe,' on which he let her have the spotlight as he played guitar and merely sang harmonies. He came across as a true friend and fan of Yearwood's."

What came across onstage was a reflection of the truth: Garth and Trisha had remained very close friends through the years. He followed her career, cheered her on, and counted on her to add her vocals to his recordings.

GIVEN THE PRESSURES OF the tour that year, it was surprising that Garth had time to draw an easy breath between shows. But he squeezed in an impressive number of personal appearances and completed a significant recording project. However, the heavy schedule he kept would come back to haunt him in 1999.

On February 23, 1998, Garth appeared on *Saturday Night Live* as both musical guest and host. Garth said the producers of *SNL* had some serious work to do to make him funny to their audience. "Their humor is very dark. They're taking care of me, but I'm not hip so they're trying to fix that," he told CNN.

He had two requests of the producers. "I told them I didn't want to make fun of anybody. I said, 'If you guys are going to do a skit on the president or something, keep me out of it. And then, second, please don't make country music look ignorant, or the people that listen to it look ignorant."

As he said, "I guess I should have added a couple more stipulations, like no falling in love with male strippers named Mango and no cross dressing!" But in fact, Garth didn't mind making himself the butt of the gags. He appeared feigning a man-crush on the *SNL* character Mango and as an aging female prostitute.

The show earned overnight numbers of an 8.4 rating and a 22 share. It was the show's highest-rated episode since October 24, 1994.

He also played an exhibition game with the San Diego Padres, helped The Nashville Network celebrate its fifteenth anniversary with a two-hour televised special, and joined members of John Wayne's family in Washington, D.C., for a day-long

USO celebration of the late actor. *The Limited Series* (box set) was released, so named because only 2 million units were produced. The set contained Brooks's first six multiplatinum studio releases—*Garth Brooks, No Fences, Ropin' the Wind, The Chase, In Pieces,* and *Fresh Horses*—as well as a new bonus track on each CD, for a total of sixty-six cuts and over three hours of music.

In November 1998 Capitol released a collection of live music taken from concerts over the years. *Garth Brooks Double Live* contained twenty-six songs, recorded primarily at shows from his history-making 1996–1998 tour. What Garth hoped to do was recreate the spontaneity of the concerts. That would be tough.

Take the final night of a Canadian run in 1993. It had been a long, exhausting tour and the band was starting to wear down. They knew it. Garth knew it and decided to fix it. Prior to showtime he called the band together for a pregame huddle.

"I'll pay five hundred dollars in cash to anybody who can knock me down onstage tonight," Garth announced.

"Impress you with a guitar lick or what?" someone asked.

"No, I mean physically knock me flat on my butt," he said.

All through the night they took their best body slams much to the delight of the Canadians who witnessed it. When Garth was still standing by the final number, somebody gave the signal and they rushed to center stage, toppling him into a pile of laughing band members. They split the cash.

Stillwater was an important part of Garth's show and career, with each member playing a vital role.

Mike Palmer had started playing drums for the band in 1987. On the entire *Garth Double Live* package, Palmer never missed a beat. "He's always been a great drummer," Garth said. "But when we were in Ireland, I passed on some advice Allen Reynolds had given me and told Mike to try playing on the back side of the beat for that big fat sound. After a couple of shows he came over and said, 'Man, I wish you'd told me that *years* ago!'"

James Garver played lead electric guitar as well as percussion, banjo, and acoustic guitar. "I just loved it when James headed into one of his solos and all the guys out there in the audience were on their feet playing air guitar with him—'cause that's what his playing made me feel like doing, too," Garth said, laughing. James was one of Garth's original band, as was steel player Steve McClure. James and Steve started playing music together back in their native Kansas, and the two made the move to Nashville together.

Mark Greenwood provided most of the bass on *Double Live*. (Garth's sister, Betsy Smittle, played bass on "If Tomorrow Never Comes" and "Much Too Young," the two cuts gleaned from the Reunion Arena show.) "Listen to Mark playing that kickin' bass on 'Papa Loved Mama,'" Garth noted. "It's flawless. And the performance was all the more impressive when you saw us play the song, with Mark running around the stage like a wild man, all of us joking with each other.

"One of the things I'm proudest about on this album is the tight rhythm tracks. Dave Gant started out as our fiddle player. But when we added Jimmy Mattingly on fiddle, Dave settled in on the keys. So between his keys, Mark's bass, Mike's drums, and Debbie Nims's rhythm guitar, our rhythm section was locked up tight. Debbie is also a stand-up bass player, and her rhythm guitar is as good as anybody out there.

"Béla Fleck came in and added some banjo on 'Callin' Baton Rouge,' and he even mentioned how the live music swelled and surged with emotion. That's where the rhythm section made for a great, solid track."

One thing Garth listened for when he went through years of performances was audience reaction. "We went and found where people got pin-dropping quiet during the ballads, where they sang 'Unanswered Prayers' the loudest and where it was absolute chaos during the rowdy stuff," Garth told Glenn Gamboa. "Hopefully we got the best of all worlds." But, he added, listening to his onstage vocals wasn't always a pleasant experience. "You want a humbling experience? Listen to yourself on a recording straight off the board. You come off stage saying, 'We killed 'em, we killed 'em,' and you listen to it and think, 'My God, that's killing *me*.'"

Aside from the problem of somehow conveying the visual excitement, putting this double-album project together was difficult because the tracks came from tours dating back to 1991. Aside from the obvious, that the band got tighter and the audiences wilder over the years, some technical improvements had been made to the show. The system was upgraded from eighteen to thirty-six monitors because of the band's tendency to run all over the stage. And while the additions were made because of the live show, they certainly improved the recordings.

There remained one very important consideration, and Garth agonized over it: how "live" should they leave the project?

"There were some decisions to be made. After Allen and I talked it over, I decided that to reflect how the tours changed over the years, we should use some of the early performances. Allen convinced me to do some studio work, things like replacing an out-of-tune guitar here and there, and adding the choir to 'We Shall Be Free'—that sort of thing. We put the studio touches on when we felt to do otherwise compromised the music. We added Béla Fleck and a choir to the live performance of 'We Shall Be Free.'

"So I'm uneasy about saying this is a 'live' album. When I think of the live albums I've loved through the years several immediately come to mind—*Frampton Comes Alive, Bob Seger and the Silver Bullet Band, KISS Alive*. Those are the great *live* albums. I don't regret the few additions and changes we made, but I do want to acknowledge that they're there."

It was while they worked on the live album that Garth discovered a new song he wanted to add to the project. Benita Hill had written "It's Your Song" when her mother, Chicago big band singer Carmen Revelle, became ill. In the song, Benita gave credit to her singing mother for the things she'd accomplished in her own life.

The reason Benita questioned showing Garth this song was because she knew that Colleen Brooks was very sick and the prognosis was not good. But she also believed there was something in "It's Your Song" that Garth needed to hear.

As it turned out, Garth wanted to include something for his mother on his upcoming *Double Live* album. He'd been trying to write such a song for his mother ever since he started out in the music business, but the words never came, and were even more elusive once Colleen became ill. Tears began to fall as he listened to Benita's lyrics, which spoke of her mother's love giving her wings. "It's Your Song" did go on *Double Live,* and was a Top 10 single.

"My mother always told me I could fly," Garth said. "And I believed her."

CAPITOL RELEASED SIX DIFFERENT CD packages. One was a first edition marked with a silver foil label and accompanied by a booklet containing an overview of Garth's career. The remaining sets reflected five tour experiences: Central Park; Dublin, Ireland; Reunion Arena, 1991; Texas Stadium, 1993; and the 1996–1998 World Tour. Some critics decried the various sets as nothing more than a marketing ploy. And in fact, many fans did purchase a copy of each of the packages as collectibles. But releasing limited-edition recordings was nothing new. Just a month before *Double Live* went on sale, numbered editions of *The Best of U2: 1980–1990* hit Canadian stores and the Beatles' remastered White Album (*The Beatles*) had serial numbers like the original vinyl copies. Similar limited editions were released on Frank Sinatra and Queen, and acts including KISS had released CDs with a variety of covers.

Retailers were salivating over upcoming releases from major artists: Garth Brooks, Whitney Houston, Wu-Tang Clan, Jewel,

Seal. Some started calling November 17, the day *Double Live* was set to hit stores, Super Tuesday. Predictions varied but most agreed that sales could increase 20 to 30 percent over the previous year.

On the day of its release, Garth and the band played a concert in Los Angeles exclusively for Wal-Mart customers. The show was beamed via satellite into the electronics departments of 2,300 Wal-Mart stores throughout the United States. But even before the show started, fans had shown up. *Business Wire* reported:

> They lined the streets at dawn to be first at the counter. They created record-breaking sell-outs in record-setting time. They sang, they danced, they bonded with others in line with them. No, it wasn't another Garth Brooks live show. It was *Garth Brooks Double Live,* the CMA Entertainer of the Year's first live album, and the fans rushed to record stores all across the country. The buying frenzy began at midnight and continued throughout the day for *Garth Brooks Double Live.*
>
> In Rockford, Illinois, hundreds of music lovers arrived at Media Play at midnight, grabbing more than 300 copies of the album. The crowd started forming at 5:00 a.m. at Tower Records in Sacramento, where 400 albums were sold in two hours. A Sam Goody store in Ventura sold all their *Garth Brooks Double Live* supply in two hours, and made their usual full-day total in dollars in one hour.
>
> A Blockbuster Music in Dallas held a Mariah Carey/Whitney Houston promotion in connection with a local radio station. *Garth Brooks Double Live* outsold both of them. In Edwardsville, Pennsylvania, fans snapped up more than 1,000 copies of the album by 5 p.m. at Gallery of Sound. KFRG, a California radio station, asking for canned goods in connection with their Garth Brooks album promotional at the Wherehouse, collected more than 8,000 pounds of food in 2 hours, and sold out of their entire stock of *Garth Brooks Double Live* at the same time.

Double Live sold over a million copies during the first week, breaking a previous record set by Pearl Jam's *Vs* in 1993. Wu-Tang Clan's *Method Man* came in second with 410,000 sales. Despite *Double Live*'s performance, first-week pop releases fell short of sales expectations. Whitney Houston's *My Love Is Your Love* sold far less than Arista had hoped for, as did Mariah Carey's Columbia hits package. Seal's *Human Being* on Warner Bros. shocked retailers by finishing ahead of Houston. But the big surprise was Jewel's *Spirit* on Atlantic, which finished right behind *Double Live* in many markets. Many retailers had underestimated Jewel's potential on Super Tuesday because the audience for her folky music was deemed more mature, less likely to show up at record stores for a first-day purchase. But others speculated Garth's live set benefited her by bringing in the more country and folk-friendly masses. *Double Live* went on to sell 21 million albums.

The *Buffalo News* named *Double Live* one of the best albums released in 1998. Dan Herbeck put together an eclectic list of picks, including the Dixie Chicks' *Wide Open Spaces,* Travis Tritt's *No Looking Over My Shoulder,* Jim Lauderdale's *Whisper,* the Thompson Brothers Band's *Blame It on the Dog,* Faith Hill's *Faith,* Randy Scruggs's *Crown of Jewels,* Vince Gill's *The Key,* the Joey Miskulin Band's *Warner Western Instrumental Series Volume I,* Ray Charles's *Complete Country and Western Recordings,* and the soundtrack for *The Horse Whisperer,* which included songs by Emmylou Harris, Allison Moorer, Dwight Yoakam, and the Flatlanders. Herbeck also gave a hat tip to Buffalo's Steam Donkeys' *Little Honky Tonks,* writing, "This roadhouse band reminds me of old Commander Cody and His Lost Airmen."

Taken as a whole, the *Buffalo News* listing showed garage band, honky-tonk, and roadhouse running right alongside contemporary country. Those close to him would tell you that this list is a pretty good example of the wide assortment of country music Garth Brooks loves. There's the western side of the music

in Miskulin's work, the great vocals of Vince Gill, the singer/
songwriter tradition of Jim Lauderdale, and the sassy female attitude of the Dixie Chicks. Material ranges from classic compositions found on the Ray Charles recordings to works from new
writers appearing on Faith Hill's album.

Most important, every album represents an identifiable artist
and sound. And Garth was becoming more and more convinced
that too many artists that he heard on radio were starting to
sound alike. "I hope we don't see too many artists developed
just in the studios," he told a friend. "An artist's sound needs the
road, the clubs, and the live audiences to find its soul."

Bob Doyle agreed. "I sometimes worry that people think we
are just in the recording business, where too often it's about the
latest technology. We are in the *entertainment* business. To make
a lasting impact—like George Strait and Randy Travis—careers
need to be developed outside of Nashville, on the road. There's
a validity to these artists.

"I know that some people think it's just hits that sell records,
but I believe that's wrong. Tickets sell albums. It's the people who
come to these shows and have that experience who become solid
fans. And I think you learn things about your music on tour that
you never get in Nashville. Garth would hear one thing in the
offices of Nashville, then go out playing live and hear the truth
from the public. They'll tell you when something's working—
and when it's not."

The concerns were well founded. It had been a rough year for
country newcomers. Radio consolidation had drastically affected
the size of playlists, and few new acts made an impact. In fact,
only the Dixie Chicks could claim a move into superstar territory with their 1998 string of chart-topping hits: "There's Your
Trouble," "Wide Open Spaces," and "You Were Mine" from
Wide Open Spaces, which went on to become one of the biggest-
selling albums in country history. And with those three singles,
the Chicks stayed at number 1 for two months. The Chicks were
no studio creation. Founded in 1989 by multi-instrumentalist

sisters Martie and Emily Erwin, the band had several releases and played steadily on the road with some success. But it was in 1995, when Natalie Maines came on board as lead singer, that the group signed with Sony Records' Monument label and took off. Natalie was the daughter of steel player/producer Lloyd Maines, who'd often appeared on Chicks' recordings.

Their wide-ranging song choices were in many ways reminiscent of Garth's. They loved the ballads ("You Were Mine"), themes like murder and mayhem ("Goodbye Earl"), tongue-in-cheek truisms ("There's Your Trouble"), and sex ("Sin Wagon"). Like Garth, they took chances and, more often than not, benefited from the risks.

GARTH WOUND UP HIS historical three-year World Tour on November 19 through 21, 1998, with three sold-out shows at Reed Arena in College Station, Texas, with opening act Trisha Yearwood. *Pollstar* named it the Country Tour of the Year for 1997 and 1998. *Amusement Business*'s Ray Waddell provided the wrap-up to the record-breaking three-year tour (November 16, 1998): "The total gross tops $105 million, from 350 shows in 100 cities that drew close to 5.5 million people. It is easily the top country music tour of all time and likely the biggest arena tour ever."

Garth responded to *AB:* "I'm not going to say that we were the biggest tour ever, but we were hell-bent on making sure everybody who wanted a ticket got one."

Being on the road and away from Nashville had helped tremendously during Garth's label difficulties. As he told Waddell, "If [the controversy] showed up at all on the road, it was in a way that you would want, people holding up signs like 'Keep fighting for us.' That's a nice thing to say . . . [the road] is where all the bullshit stops and things become real. That's where the artist meets the people. No business gets in the way, no hype.

"In all fairness, I thrive in that environment because it's been good to me. The true test of character is when things don't go well. Everybody is always talking about paying dues. I don't remember that part. It's always been a blast, whether it was 20 people in a club, or 20,000 in an arena."

In December *Amusement Business* named Garth and George Strait as country's top 1998 touring acts: "In terms of numbers, Strait came out on top, with seventeen of his nineteen Country Music Festival dates finishing in the top twenty-five for the year. But in terms of sheer people and dollars pulled from one city, the honor goes to Garth, with his nine-night stand at Target Center in Minneapolis coming in as the top BOXSCORE of the year, or any other year." As Varnell Enterprises Ben Farrell said, "When you put these two men [George Strait and Garth Brooks] together they are the most phenomenal back-to-back story in the history of the country music business."

On the heels of his concert tour de force, Garth's sales hit 82 million. But Garth often downplayed the horse-race aspect of his numbers. When asked about his potential for passing the Beatles by the *San Francisco Examiner's* Gary Graff, Garth said, "[The Beatles] had some double albums that didn't count as double albums at the time, eight-tracks, stuff like that. We're not close. It's not a goal. If we do pass the Beatles, it'll be because they haven't reassessed them yet. When they do—forget it. With the numbers stuff, you just have to take it with a grain of salt. Yeah, you feel proud, but the true guy in me has to say, 'Come on—you're not on the level of the Beatles, Michael Jackson, Elvis Presley, James Taylor, Billy Joel and 100 more guys.'"

Garth found himself with some time on his hands after the final show of his three-year world tour. When the tour wrapped, he closed GB Management, giving his employees and musicians two years' salary and benefits. "They traded ten years of their lives to chase my dream," he explained to the *Daily Oklahoman*. "They're good people. Everybody is taken care of for the next two years whether they work or not." During his early years on the road, Garth had seen a consistent problem: musicians with no security. One of the first things he did when any money came in was to set up his operation so that in addition to being paid very well, everyone had health insurance. When he closed up shop, he didn't want to leave people hanging.

Garth was only too happy to be able to spend more time at home. The lengthy tour had again reminded him of the time he spent away from family, and he spoke about it often out on the road. Capitol's VP of national promotion, Terry Stevens, was often with Garth on the road, and believed him when the star started talking about retiring. "The deejays he met with didn't make an issue out of his statements, but Garth often mentioned a growing belief that he would not be able to do another tour of this magnitude while his children were small."

It was during this time that Kenny "Babyface" Edmonds approached Garth about an unusual film project. Finally, after years of being characterized as a marketing mastermind, Garth put together a blueprint combining music and film promotion. Ironically, no one would believe it was a marketing plan.

CHAPTER TWENTY

"Has Garth lost his freakin' mind?"

It was the second time that Kenny "Babyface" Edmonds had called Garth about the film project he and his wife, Tracey Edmonds, were passionate about. It was a movie they'd tentatively titled *The Lamb,* a thriller that focused on the life of an international pop/rock superstar named Chris Gaines. Babyface wanted Garth on board.

"We think you're the guy who can take on the role of Gaines and put together a soundtrack of greatest hits for this character," Babyface explained for the second time. "Look, we've got one of the best scriptwriters in the business working on this, Jeb Stuart. Think *Die Hard.* Think *The Fugitive.*"

"Man, I don't know," Garth said, weakening a little. "Don't you think you need a rocker to play a rocker? What about Prince? He'd be great. I might be lousy."

"No, no, no!" Babyface was adamant. "We think you could pull this off better than anybody in the business. We want you and Paramount wants you. Besides, Tracey and I will be right beside you. You can't fall that hard."

BETWEEN 1997 AND 1999 Garth received some of the music press's highest accolades. *Performance* magazine readers named him Country Act of the Year for the sixth time. *Newsweek* called him "the most-loved country singer in history." And *Playboy* named him the Male Country Vocalist of 1997. *People* magazine readers named Garth their Favorite Male Singer, with runners-up including Elton John, George Strait, Michael Bolton, and Elvis. He became the first artist to win four Entertainer of the Year awards from the CMA, besting the record three wins he had earlier tied with Alabama. And he received the 1998 Distinguished Artist Award from the Music Center of Los Angeles. Past winners included Gregory Peck, Jack Lemmon, and Shirley MacLaine.

In January 1999 the *Los Angeles Times* announced its 1998 Top Ten of Pop Music: "The King of Country had the Midas touch in 1998, both in record stores and at concert box offices. Nashville powerhouse Garth Brooks is the runaway #1 in the second annual Calendar Ultimate Top 10 of Pop Music, a tally that combines the year's album sales and concert grosses. Brooks finished 1998 with about $144 million in U.S. album sales, based on SoundScan reports, and $37.2 million from North American concert grosses, according to *Pollstar,* the concert industry trade publication. That adds up to $181.2 million, which blows away the 1997 winner of the Ultimate Top 10, the Rolling Stones, who amassed a mere $100 million."

You'd think those figures would buy a guy a lot of political capital within the industry.

But by then Garth should have known that life sometimes gives you an ice cream cone with one hand and smacks a pie in your face with the other.

The film Babyface proposed was a biopic wrapped in a mystery. The original idea was that a rock star name Chris Gaines has died under mysterious circumstances. One of his fans suspects foul play, and starts investigating the star's life, stage by stage. The Gaines character, played by Garth in his later years, would appear via interview and concert footage.

Garth had been interested in films since the early days of

his career, when he had opened a film production company, Red Strokes, with friend Lisa Sanderson. It was possible, Garth thought, that this idea Babyface had brought him was a perfect vehicle for Red Strokes' first major venture. Garth's interest in scriptwriting had intensified over the years. During the 1993–1994 tour he began working on script ideas at night on the tour bus. Despite the flap over his portrayal of an abusive husband in the video for "The Thunder Rolls," Garth still loved the idea of playing the heavy in a movie. "I thought Dwight Yoakam's role in *Sling Blade* was a great bad guy. That's the kind of role you look for."

Other movies inspired him. *To Kill a Mockingbird* was one, and he even thought that if he ever had a son, he might name the boy Atticus, after the protagonist, Atticus Finch. Two more favorites were *Field of Dreams* and *Forrest Gump*. Of Kevin Costner's *Field of Dreams* character, he said, "Thank God there are still crazy people in the world who believe in the impossible dream." And after seeing *Forrest Gump,* Garth said he wanted "to stand up and hug everybody in the theater." The *Los Angeles Times*' Robert Hillburn mused that in film, as in music, Garth tended to love the concept of the common man put in extraordinary circumstances. And the Chris Gaines story would certainly give Garth the opportunity to help create a character who was in extraordinary circumstances.

Once Garth decided to get involved with Babyface's project, he jumped in with both feet, dividing his time between the character and the concept of releasing a soundtrack first to promote the film. But while he usually saw marketing from the same perspective as Capitol's new chief, Pat Quigley, this time they differed. When talking with the *L.A. Times,* Quigley posed the question, "Can you put out an advance soundtrack and succeed without benefit of the movie being in theaters?"

One of the first things Garth thought about was how difficult playing a character would be in the audio format, something like an established artist who made a Broadway show album and tried to keep his or her own style out of it. And from the early stages of putting the album together, Garth worried that there might be more initial interest in the character than in the music, especially with his involvement. That this was simply a "role," he thought, would have to be carefully explained up front.

The writing team of Gordon Kennedy, Wayne Kilpatrick, and Tommy Sims penned "Change The World," which both Wynonna and Eric Clapton recorded. The Clapton cut resulted in three Grammy awards: Best Male Vocalist/Pop, Record of the Year (awarded to Clapton and his producer, Babyface) and Best Song (awarded to Kennedy, Kilpatrick, and Sims). The Grammy made the three writers Nashville celebs. It was only the second time Nashville writers had ever competed and won in the all-genre Grammy category. (The first was "Wind Beneath My Wings.") The three had a strong writing history, including cuts by Bonnie Raitt, Joe Cocker, Peter Frampton, Trisha Yearwood, Alison Krauss, Tim McGraw, and George Strait. But it was the Clapton/Babyface cut of "Change The World" that gave the writing team a connection to *The Lamb* from two directions, because Gordon Kennedy was the brother of one of Garth's closest friends, Bryan Kennedy. In fact, the history went back to 1991.

"Wayne and I were recording some of our songs, trying to get a pop music deal," Gordon said. "My brother gave Garth one of the demo CDs. One day Bryan called me and said, 'You aren't going to believe this, but Garth was into your music so much that he got a speeding ticket driving through Arkansas!'" Three songs from those sessions ended up on *Chris Gaines*—"White Flag," "My Love Tells Me So," and "Digging For Gold."

When Garth decided to get involved with *The Lamb*, he knew he needed a collection of pop songs that would work for a "greatest hits" package, dating back to the 1980s. One day, Gordon Kennedy was playing a Brooks session with a young guitarist Garth believed had a big future in Nashville, Keith Urban. After they finished Garth pulled Gordon aside.

"Babyface got me involved in this film project," he said. "It's about a singer, and the story will play out over a period of several decades of recordings. Can you send me some songs?"

"Country?" Gordon asked, puzzled.

"No, pop/rock," Garth said. "Beatles, Eagles—the guy's music will change over time."

Gordon went back to PolyGram Publishing and ran a CD of ten songs from the 1990s, spanning about eight years. Then he dropped it off for Garth and went to lunch thinking that "It Don't Matter To The Sun" might have a chance of making the soundtrack. By the time he got back he had a message from Garth asking him to put "Maybe" on hold.

"I was stunned at his pick," Gordon said. "But just a little while later he called back and said he also wanted 'It Don't Matter To The Sun.' Then I realized that he hadn't heard all the songs when he first called. But the most exciting thing was that after listening to that one CD, he asked to hear our entire catalog."

The result would be music primarily drawn from the Kennedy/Kilpatrick/Sims catalog, but also include material such as the socially conscious rap written by Cheryl Wheeler. Garth declined to write anything for the project because he wanted to keep it from being a "Garth-singing-pop-music" album.

"As we went through the material, Garth would use each song that he liked to help him create a backstory," Gordon explained. "These demos had been done over a long period of time, so there was a definite 'feel' to each of them. For Garth, that translated into the time period his fictional character was going through. Actually, Garth contributed to the writing on a couple of the newer songs, but we couldn't get him to take a writer credit for it."

But what Kennedy, Kilpatrick, and Sims didn't expect was to hear Garth say that he wanted to use the original demo tracks and build the recording around them in order to reflect the passage of time. "We thought we'd be doing completely new sessions," Gordon said. "One of the songs, 'Maybe,' was recorded in my garage! Garth loved that. He said that was perfect. Then he put a George Massenburg forty-piece orchestra around it."

Drum machines were replaced. Additional instruments were added. But the base remained those demos done over two decades. Gordon's "garage demo" took an unexpected turn. "While the final mix was being done, J.B., the engineer, asked me to come in and listen to something. He'd separated everything down and all of a sudden on this one track you hear a door open and a little voice—my two-year-old son Dylan—say 'Hi!' Then you hear my wife, Tracey, say, 'Dylan just made a stinky. And so did your daughter Caitlin. There's stinky everywhere in here!' The engineer was falling all over himself laughing. But don't listen for that little conversation on *Chris Gaines,* because we obviously took it out!"

There were several times when those in the studio believed a song wouldn't work, starting with the first song Garth put his voice on, "Lost In You." Tommy Sims had sung the original in falsetto. When Garth stepped up to the microphone, the falsetto was there. "Our jaws were on the floor," Gordon Kennedy recalls.

Even when something didn't work, it did. Garth had planned that "My Love Tells Me So" would be the song included from an early album when the Chris Gaines character was in a band named CRUSH with a now-dead lead singer, Tommy Levitz. That was the one song demo in a key Garth couldn't navigate. So they left the original vocals on the track—Gordon Kennedy, aka Tommy Levitz.

It was new territory for Garth. He was working with both music and with Paramount Pictures and his film production company, Red Strokes. Once Garth had the backstory down, a "bio" was prepared for *The Lamb*'s lead character, pointing to his childhood in Australia, the son of Olympic swimmers. As a writer on the project, Garth invented names and chart positions for five fictitious Gaines albums over a fourteen-year career—*Crush*, 1986; *Straight Jacket*, 1989; *Fornucopia*, 1991; *Apostle*, 1994; *Triangle*, 1996—the cover designs to be displayed inside the CD, *Garth Brooks in . . . the Life of Chris Gaines*.

The album's producer, Don Was, who had worked with Garth on "To Make You Feel My Love" for the film *Hope Floats*, said he was impressed by how serious Garth was in scripting the character for the film. Was told Reuters' Gary Graff, "When [Garth] wasn't doing stuff at the sessions, he sat there at the word processor, and his wife said he was up at night, shaping the character. He was never confused about it."

He was fascinated with the idea of creating a singing character away from his own musical style, and listened carefully to how Kennedy, Kilpatrick, and Sims performed their own songs. He was even more fascinated with how artists evolve, especially a rock performer, over a period of time. And as intrigued as he was with the musical evolution, he was equally absorbed with the development of the character.

"I love writing this so much that Don Was finally had to order me to get my nose out of my laptop and get back in front of the microphone," Garth told a friend. "Now I'm just praying that people 'get it.' "

As a fan of the songwriters involved in the project he tried to keep coming back to the music. But very quickly Garth noticed an unsettling tone entering into interviews. Reporters were more interested in Garth Brooks–as–Chris Gaines than in the character as a fictional entity. *R&R*'s Steve Wonstewicz, who conducted an even-handed interview the month prior to the album release, pointed to an emerging problem: "The dilemma seems epitomized in the Chris Gaines song, 'Right Now,' which features you rapping and a sample of the Youngbloods' classic 'Get Together.' Some people really love the song, yet they give each other puzzled looks because it's pretty removed from Garth."

Garth answered: "If this project does not succeed, it will be because we did not get past the stumbling block that it's from Garth Brooks. That's it."

He continued to explain that this was not an attempt to "go pop" and that he did not have an alter ego. "I'm just doing a character for a movie, and the character happens to be a pop-rock artist who has a catalog and a career."

For better and worse, Garth's whole career had played out in the press. But at no time did the media ever dictate public opinion as it did with *Chris Gaines*. In the beginning the press seemed to better understand that this was strictly a way to approach a film project and that Garth found the idea an interesting challenge.

On July 5, 1999, the *Los Angeles Times* said, "Garth Brooks will shed his twang and assume an alter ego that will have him singing pop songs for an upcoming movie, *The Lamb,* scheduled for release next year. Brooks will also release a collection of fictional artist Chris Gaines' greatest hits in September. [Brooks's] fans may not recognize his voice on the 14-track album. He reportedly hides his twang and sings in a higher pitch."

But just a few days later, on July 9, the *Times'* Geoff Boucher worried that there was a risk: "The 14 songs on the [Chris Gaines] 'greatest hits' package range wildly in style, a purposeful effort to depict the evolution of a career artist. One song has a calliope and horns that evoke the Beatles, another sounds like a Bruce Springsteen anthem, yet another has the distinct drum sound and rhythms of Fleetwood Mac. The most startling may be 'Lost In You,' a smoky R&B song and the first single.

"There is one constant among the songs: None of the vocals sounds anything like Brooks. Singing high and with unfamiliar cadences, Brooks deeply submerges his familiar baritone and twang. Will this new persona and voice bring Brooks to a whole new plateau or is he risking the foundation he's already standing on?"

Ironically, Garth's real-life foundation was already shaken at the time. After a long illness Colleen Brooks died in August 1999, just a month before her son's experimental album project was released. Colleen's final days were spent at Deaconess Hospital in Oklahoma City, where she was surrounded by her family: Raymond, Garth and Sandy, Betsy, Kelly, Mike, Jim, and Jerry. The family was desolate, drawn together missing the woman who had been such a bright light in their world. Colleen's death made any reaction to *Chris Gaines* pale by comparison.

On September 9 two singles were shipped to radio prior to the CD release: the pop/R&B "Lost In You" and country "It Don't Matter To The Sun." Videos, produced by Picture Vision and Jon Small, were made for both songs.

Garth had some initial worries when "Lost In You" started playing on some country stations, fearing that if it was played strictly because of his name value, it would be bad for the format. "I didn't want to bring 'Lost' to country radio," he said. "When you turn on country, you're hearing decades of music."

"It Don't Matter To The Sun," on the other hand, reminded him of "To Make You Feel My Love," and in his mind, did fit the format. "It's the best-written song on the album," he said. "And because of my allegiance to country radio, it's the only one I'd take to them. I don't want them *not* to have this project, but at the same time, I don't want to bring country radio something that makes their format even more unidentifiable."

With the singles' releases, it was obvious that some *would* listen to the music without bringing a Garth-the-country-star bias to the experience. A third single also received airplay: "That's The Way I Remember It."

The *Record* reported: "Lost" became the #1 most added song on Top-40 and adult contemporary stations and "It Don't Matter To Me" was the most-added track on country stations. After previewing a Brooks-as-Gaines industry showcase, Stan Atkinson, program director for Milwaukee's WLTQ-FM, where "Lost" was featured along with the Backstreet Boys and Eric Clapton, said: "I was blown away. He just did Chris Gaines songs, and he had some dance songs like Prince, some rock, some softer songs. It's top-notch music."

On September 28 *Garth Brooks in . . . the Life of Chris Gaines* was released, and on September 29 NBC aired the Chris Gaines special, *Behind the Music.* This was a fictional look at Gaines's life, introducing a costumed Garth as Chris to the potential audience for *The Lamb.* It was an interesting experiment in advance marketing, and cross-promoting music and film. Extremely experimental, in fact, given that the film was not yet in production. And Garth was crucified by many for donning a wig and playing the role of Chris Gaines in this promotional film and on a variety of television appearances.

When he had first started on the Chris Gaines project, Garth said, "I think it's gonna be a lot of fun." He couldn't have been more wrong. It only took a few weeks after the television special and the CD release for the idea that this was an identity crisis to catch on. Then the fun died fast. Even though many early reviews of the music were glowing, and pop radio played singles from the CD, the mood turned. The *L.A. Times* went from embracing the idea to worrying that it was a risk, to calling it a huge mistake.

One critic asked, "Has Garth lost his freakin' mind?"

Another couldn't get around the fact that Garth often referred to himself as GB. "Some music fans continue to insist that Chris Gaines is make-believe and Garth Brooks is real. But this is preposterous when you look at the evidence. In interviews Mr. Brooks always refers to himself in the third person as if he has just created a character. Mr. Gaines speaks of himself in the first person."

This "evidential" theory is what was preposterous. Garth had long separated himself and his music from the career phenomenon that included sales numbers, press coverage, management decisions, label operations, fanfare, and folderol. Almost as absurd was the accusation that Chris Gaines was more important to Capitol than Garth's *Magic of Christmas* album because it received more marketing and promotion, selling 1 million. Christmas albums almost never receive the same intense marketing as other albums. Moreover, *Chris Gaines* was approached as a soundtrack setting up a movie, which in turn would set up another album. A lot was potentially at stake.

It was also speculated that the entire Chris Gaines project was Garth's payback because the Backstreet Boys had beat out his record for single-week sales of the previous year's *Double Live*. "What's next? Master P transforming into a patchouli-loving Lilith Fair performer, or Andrea Bocelli switching it up to go ghetto fabulous?"

In a *New York Times* article titled "Split Personalities Can Be Better Than One," Frank DeCaro questioned all this questioning and wrote, "[Brooks] got more grief from critics than the Village People got when they put on face paint and poet shirts for their 1981 New Wave album, *Renaissance*."

DeCaro went on: "The intensity of the criticism of role-playing is surprising. Alter egos, after all, are not exactly an unprecedented career move. Two decades ago, David Bowie unveiled his most famous alter ego, Ziggy Stardust—which also was initially derided as too strange for words."

Perhaps it *was* due to the fact that Garth appeared in "character" before there was a film, but the identity questions started to overwhelm the conversation. In October 1999, *Rolling Stone's* David Wild, while giving the CD an uneven review, said Garth should be given credit for trying something different, but suggests that he is "confronting some serious identity issues." And some press began to report industry insiders claimed that the real reason for "Chris Gaines" was to remove Garth from the isolated world of country music. Yet no one said who these industry insiders were.

Some couldn't separate the Chris Gaines sales figures from Garth's. The *Daily News* called the Gaines first-week sales "feeble by Brooks' usual standards, selling 262,067 copies and opening on *Billboard*'s Top 200 at #2. Brooks' last album, *Double Live,* moved 1,085,000 copies in its first week." (*Garth Brooks in . . . the Life of Chris Gaines* has since been certified with over 2 million in sales.)

Others tried to compare the song selections in Chris Gaines to Garth's own releases. In January 2000, the *L.A. Times* called *Chris Gaines* a bad idea, because it contained no "character-filled songs" such as "The Dance" and "Unanswered Prayers."

Some, when referring to the Chris Gaines biographical material and character-development copy that Garth had taken such pains to compose, refused to consider it an exercise in fiction writing. "He's even handing out a bio recreating himself as a brilliant rock icon." Thank God this crowd wasn't as wild about critiquing music as storytelling when Willie Nelson released *Red Headed Stranger* as a concept album and later as a western movie.

Not everyone in the media discounted Chris Gaines as a case of multiple personalities. David Sokol wrote this first-person account in *Stereophile:*

> I recently played various cuts from this album for a half-dozen unsuspecting friends—not a scientific sampling, to be sure, but these cronies know their music. None had a clue that they were listening to the biggest-selling solo artist of all time.
>
> "Sounds like the Doobie Brothers," said one female thirty-something know-it-all on hearing "Snow In July." A slightly older newspaper sales rep (it says 'account executive' on his business card) insisted that "Way Of The Girl" had to be Bad Company singer Paul Rogers. And there was heated debate when "Unsigned Letter" came on. "Rick Springfield! The Wallflowers! Donovan . . . ?"
>
> And on and on. "It Don't Matter To The Sun" reminded some of David Gates and Bread. And the last track, "My Love

Tells Me So," elicited cries of Badfinger, Paul McCartney, Emitt Rhodes, and The Rutles. Other songs invoked Kenny Loggins, the Youngbloods, and "Knockin' On Heaven's Door."

How can one guy be singing all these songs? And how come they sound so good?

Sokol concluded: "Give Brooks some credit . . . he's invented a character whose character will never be confused with his creator, and whose record will surely stump your friends."

Garth continued to promote the project, which sold 2 million. He kept up a positive attitude in public, but in private, he was upset that the project was being misrepresented. He was proud of the album, believed in it. When *The Lamb* was put on hold, press accounts left the impression that it was because of the negative publicity. In truth, the reason *The Lamb* had not gotten to production stages was that the film's writer, Jeb Stuart, faced a lengthy family medical crisis when his wife, Anne, fell ill. Garth didn't feel it was right to replace him under the circumstances.

And while he was let down by the experience, he could fall back on a life philosophy he'd long acknowledged: "Sometimes you win and sometimes you don't. When it's all over you just hope the wins outnumber the losses."

In the end, given the reactions from pals of *Stereophile*'s Sokol, one must consider what would have happened if the advance soundtrack had been released anonymously. It might very well have had the same outcome as Charley Pride's welcoming launch. Concerned that country radio would reject a black artist out-of-hand, RCA sent his first records out with no photo. By the time people figured it out, the music was already accepted.

SOME MUSIC ROW EXECUTIVES took great delight in the Chris Gaines commotion, less because of Garth than as a reaction to Pat Quigley. It was strangely reminiscent of the Music Row party Bowen had thrown when *Ropin' the Wind* topped the pop and country charts. When some declined the invitation, it had been more about the label head than about the artist.

After moving to Nashville, Quigley had made few friends in his peer group. His brash personality and cutting the price of CDs having made him a pariah in most executive circles. But the real problem lay not with Row-felt opinion, but the feelings of his employees. Garth had been right when he said he wanted a co-presidency at Capitol, because Quigley turned out to be a marketing marvel but ill equipped to lead the Nashville staff. The problems had started soon after he came on board.

One of the qualities Garth had most appreciated in Pat Quigley had been his willingness to take a project and run with it. He was a self-starter, willing to play a lone hand if warranted and single-mindedly dedicated to his job: marketing and selling records. But at Capitol he seemed unable to delegate or utilize the team. Quigley loved dealing directly with artists, gave them his personal phone numbers and encouraged them to deal with him, not others on the staff. Individual duties were usurped, and many started to wonder why they were even there.

Pat Quigley was also disdainful of many country traditions, vastly preferring pop country to any hint of traditionalism. He even trademarked the term "Town and Country" supposedly as country music's new name. Citing artists like Shania Twain and Faith Hill, Quigley insisted that it was the concept of country music that needed to change, suggesting that people were more intelligent than the music being offered them. "Country for me in Manhattan was the Hamptons," he told the *New York Times*. "Why does country have to be some backwoods place in *Deliverance*?"

Going for a name change wasn't a new idea. After country dropped the "western" part of its name, some at the Grand Ole Opry went so far as to suggest changing it to "American" music, but it didn't take. Country listeners were better educated than, say, in the 1950s, and the numbers of artists with college degrees was growing. But the listeners couldn't have cared less about a change in I.D. In fact, many fans were reportedly miffed at the idea, whether they preferred pop or traditionalist trends.

Then there was the joke that spread through Nashville to the point that it became a tiresome story. When talking about a potential John Berry duet with the late Patsy Cline, a Capitol employee said it was doubtful that Cline's Decca masters were available from MCA. Quigley brushed that aside and asked why they couldn't just get Patsy to record with John.

"Uh, because she's dead?" The employee answered.

Reports from Capitol staffers didn't help Quigley's profile on the Row. He often called employees "hillbillies" and his favorite joke was

Question: "What do you call a New Yorker in Nashville?"
Answer: "*Boss!*"

Curiously, Capitol employees reported that they never heard him tell that joke or mention *Deliverance* when Garth Brooks was at the label.

Quigley had his defenders within the label. Both John Berry and Steve Wariner saw him as an astute marketer who was genuinely concerned with their careers and their music. Berry believed he received enormously important input from Quigley. Wariner, surely a gem in the business, tried to warn Quigley that he wasn't always showing his best side. "I seem to spend a lot of time defending him to friends around town," Steve laughed. And some employees claimed Quigley was misunderstood.

"I never saw the rude side of Pat," said one staffer who had been with the label since the Bowen days. "And I think he genuinely tried his best on behalf of the artists. I remember one time he called me into his office worried about an artist's latest recording. He said he'd been up all night worrying that it wasn't up to par. He didn't want to have to turn it down, but didn't know what else to do. I had the feeling that his anguish was real."

In May 1998, music journalist Beverly Keel wrote a lengthy article for the popular weekly alternative publication, the

Nashville Scene. The piece was titled "Will Pat Quigley Destroy Music Row?" Keel wrote,

> Quigley usually remains easygoing. But when he defends himself against his critics, he reveals a side his employees regularly see. Quigley has already won a reputation as a screamer and an intimidator. "There's a support group for people who worked for me," he told one employee. "They might not have liked me but they all learned something. Shut up, listen and learn."
>
> The attitude apparently hasn't played well with Capitol's rank and file. Many staffers say they are looking for other jobs; others say morale is at an all-time low. "He says we're like a family, but he hasn't bothered to learn everyone's name," says one employee. "I hate coming in here every day."

Keel's article pointed out that Pat Quigley was under fire from some in the business for "jumping on the bandwagon of paying radio stations to back announce songs [naming artist and title], dedicating $500,000 to a campaign to make it easier for listeners to identify songs on the radio." In Quigley's defense, this action was taken after the Country Music Association had conducted a groundbreaking nationwide survey that showed a whopping 92 percent of country listeners resented the fact that artists were not identified by deejays spinning their tunes.

Other criticisms coming from the Row included Quigley's pricing of Garth's *Limited Series,* released the same month the article was published. The set sold for around twenty-eight dollars, compared to box sets selling for fifty to a hundred dollars.

But Keel made an astute summation of Quigley and his critics, a stinging conclusion that unfortunately went right over a lot of heads: "Then again, for Music Row, the only thing more dangerous than Pat Quigley failing would be Pat Quigley succeeding. What if other barbarians were to follow him through the gate? Imagine a spate of multiple-CD box sets at affordable prices. Imagine major artists having a say in every facet of their labels' operations. Imagine the country music industry—shudder—controlled by *Yankees*. Nashville resists nothing so vigorously as new ideas."

And you couldn't argue with success. In 1998 one in every ten country records sold was a Garth Brooks record and Capitol was the most profitable label in town.

Despite comments made by some staff members for the 1998 *Nashville Scene* article, when talking to Garth the employees who disliked Quigley downplayed their growing dissatisfaction. Even when Garth specifically asked how things were going internally, his friends at the label denied any real problems. Most employees had intense loyalties to Garth. He stood on their side on many occasions: saved their jobs, backed up decisions, and in one instance, sent a car every day for nearly a year to pick up an employee whose surgery had left her unable to drive. They believed that Garth's music hadn't been adequately promoted under the previous regime. So in a strange way, many of the rank and file saw themselves as protecting him by staying quiet.

That changed in 1999. When a Capitol employee quit suddenly and unexpectedly, Garth phoned a close contact at the label and asked her what was going on. The young woman broke down and told Garth exactly what had been happening, including the lack of respect, the rude comments, and the indignity of being made the butt of bad jokes. It was true, she said, morale was in the toilet. Garth told her to do one thing for him.

"Don't mention this conversation. I'm going to call a staff meeting and I don't want anyone—not the other employees and not Pat—to know you had anything to do with this. I don't want any fallout coming at you."

Garth was at the label within the hour to meet with the staff alone. He explained that no one should fear for his or her job or the way they'd be treated in the future. He wanted people to tell him how they felt and how he could make things better. It took some urging but they had their say. Garth listened as one by one people came forward and spoke of being discounted at best and insulted at worst.

Before Garth left he promised that things would change. People close to the label head believed that this meeting convinced Quigley he had lost credibility with the man who'd gotten him the gig. Quigley had other concerns, because EMI was once again going through reorganization. Jim Fifield was gone. Sir Colin Southgate had retired under harsh criticisms. *Fortune*'s Frank Rose addressed the Chairman's exit:

"Not three years ago, Sir Colin Southgate was the toast of British industry. As chairman of EMI, the $5.4 billion music giant, he'd saved a national institution, transforming the sickly, grab-bag conglomerate that was Thorn EMI into a global music powerhouse. Today his company is in free fall. EMI's stock has dropped from a high of about $13 a share to a recent price of below $8. Little wonder that in a poll of London fund managers, Sir Colin was voted Britain's Most Disappointing CEO, with 40% of the vote."

In May 1999, Eric Nicoli, the former CEO of United Biscuits, took over as interim chairman. Ken Berry remained as head of EMI Recorded Music. But the company remained in upheaval. As *Fortune* described it, "The company has lurched from crisis to crisis: Southgate's designated heir, Jim Fifield, making his exit after a sudden boardroom putsch; press reports about Ken Berry's wife cavorting with rock stars; the stock showing a pulse mainly when a new takeover rumor surfaces. 'It reads like a crappy novel,' says one high-level victim. 'Intrigue, jealousy—all that stuff.'

"'You do know what EMI stands for, don't you?' retorts one embittered refugee. 'Every Mistake Imaginable.'"

It was an environment that left everyone at top corporate levels about as nervous as Nashville label employees had been back in the old days, when Jimmy Bowen was thought to be considering taking over their company.

Garth played no active role when Pat Quigley was removed

the following year. Far more important in that particular corporate shuffle was the fact that EMI was involved in yet another
quest to sell the company, creating cutbacks and maneuvering
at every level of the business. When *Billboard* asked Garth about
that meeting he'd called with the label's staff, he downplayed it.
"I just offered to step in and listen," he said.

CHAPTER TWENTY-ONE

"Say it ain't so, Garth"

"My mother could always see the positive side of things," Garth told a friend. "She called it 'Seeing sunshine in the middle of a storm.'" He stared at the floor for a few minutes, then shook his head.

"I had such good parents," he went on. "And I worry about how I'm doing in the job. Mom was always so supportive of anything we wanted to try. And Dad was there to help us develop at sports. You know, I think Taylor's capable of being a first-class soccer player," he said. "I've been on tour and doing a million other things while Taylor could have used a dad there helping her develop into a soccer champ. That makes me feel like hell."

REACTION TO CHRIS GAINES hit Garth hard, but it wasn't what knocked him to his knees in 1999. That was his mother's death, an event that not only hurt him to the core, but also caused him to take a hard look at his own life.

Colleen's death brought Garth face to face with how a parent so completely affects children's lives, and caused him to again question the time he was spending with his daughters. So he slowed down. He had finished a Christmas album, and owed Capitol one more, but that could wait. He had been talking about his need for family time for years, and he had longed for some kind of normalcy in his relationship with his girls.

"I want them to dare to fly, to make stupid mistakes and learn from them," he said. "I want them to be foolish—and I want them to be responsible. Life only goes by once—let's rip it up!"

Over the next months, while Garth spent time with Sandy and the children, he began to realize just what his time on tour had done. It had separated him from his wife—they had grown apart at an alarming rate—and he worried that he had lost touch with his daughters' lives and progress. He saw something that unnerved him: his daughters had talents that he hadn't been around to encourage adequately.

So in December 1999, when Garth dropped the retirement bomb on The Nashville Network's *Crook & Chase,* many of those close to him were not surprised. When he said he was thinking about hanging it up sometime in the next year to spend more time with his wife and daughters, ages three, five, and seven, it seemed a natural outcome.

"Throughout Garth's career he had told me that when his children got to the age that they couldn't be out on the road with him, he would retire," says producer Allen Reynolds. "This was no big secret. Everyone around him knew it. I can't even say how many times I heard him tell me or others that his parents had been there for him, and he planned to be there for his own children."

The long 1996–1998 tour and other issues firmed up his decision. "The announcement certainly didn't come as a surprise to me," says national promotion VP Terry Stevens. "Between the touring, his mother's death, and wanting to save his marriage and be a good father, it was almost a given that he would retire on some level. In my mind, anybody even half listening to what Garth had been saying knew that he was knocking on retirement's door, and ready to walk inside."

After his first daughter, Taylor, was born in 1992, Garth said he would have to see if his career had gotten so big and pressure-filled that he couldn't function as a dad. If it became impossible he'd consider quitting. In April 1994, when his second child, August, was due during his two-year world tour, he again speculated about leaving the business. And as he told journalist Michael McCall, when in 1995 he dressed as Mickey Mouse and took Taylor and August trick-or-treating on Halloween, "I've never been happier than that night. I was just another big mouse with a bag full of candy."

But in recent years Garth had spoken less about retiring. Many times when he publicly worried about his home life and possible retirement, it was perceived as some sort of Machiavellian marketing maneuver, an effort to sell albums or concert tickets. He'd been burned enough by those charges to make the effort to stay silent when speaking on the record. Instead, he waited until the 1999 *Crook & Chase* moment.

As Garth explained on the show, "I never, ever thought in my life I'd say this, but music is not the first thing in my life anymore. Those girls somehow come along and all of a sudden, all you want to do is make them smile."

When host Lorianne Crook tried to pin him down, he said he would probably just "lay low" for the next nine or ten months and announce a retirement sometime in the year 2000. But, he said, retirement for him primarily meant that after the grueling three-year tour that had taken him away from his daughters for too long, he would not go on the road.

"I was talking to my dad the other day on the phone, and I said, 'Dad, Taylor is seven years old. When I was four years old I could run circles around her playing baseball.' And I said, 'That's because I have the dad I've got and she's got the dad she's got.' And you just look at it and go, man, it's time to step up and take care of the responsibility that I took on seven years ago when we had our baby."

Lorianne was aghast, asking him if he felt like he'd been a bad father. "I feel like I've been a good dad all the times I've been home. But, you know, if you do something, if you put your name on something, then you give everything you've got to it. Well, I put my name on that baby seven years ago, and August *and* Allie, but somehow I've been able to justify it by saying I was out making a living for the family. I think it's time to sit in and focus."

Clearly befuddled, both Charlie Chase and Lorianne Crook attempted to get Garth to really define this "retirement." Finally Charlie said, "I don't think it's to the point where the only time we see you is at the drive-through of Taco Bell."

Garth laughed at the mention of his famously favorite fast-food establishment. "You can see me a lot there right now."

He would, he explained, continue to write songs and, he hoped, work on some film scripts for his production company, Red Strokes. No matter how people viewed the *Chris Gaines* album as a soundtrack for *The Lamb,* Garth's enthusiasm for scriptwriting had not dimmed. "Writing seems to be what my bag is," he said.

Some were skeptical. ASCAP's Connie Bradley said she wouldn't believe it until she saw it happen. And some of Garth's friends and fellow songwriters wondered if he was just tired, and after a few months might change his mind. Pat Quigley told the *Tennessean*'s Tom Roland that he wasn't 100 percent sure that Garth would really walk away.

Garth spokesman Scott Stem put it in perspective: "He's saying that for right now fatherhood needs to be his priority and that's where he's putting his attention."

Media response was immediate. The following day the Nashville *Tennessean* headline read, "Life After Garth? Music Row Faces Impossible Challenge If Brooks Bows Out."

A follow-up article lamented, "Say It Ain't So, Garth."

Ed Benson, executive director of the Country Music Association, told the *Tennessean,* "Somebody's got to wake up in the morning on Music Row and figure out: who do we put in that spot, and how quickly do we get them selling multi-platinum records? Over the last decade Garth's the artist who had the most sales impact in our business, and maybe in music." The AP's Jim Patterson wrote (December 17), "It's hard to overestimate Brooks' impact on country music. In 1998 he accounted for more than 10 percent of the industry's total sales of 73 million albums. This year his US sales stand at 3.1 million with a week left in the holiday season, according to SoundScan."

Lon Helton, country music editor for trade magazine *Radio & Records,* weighed in with the AP's Jim Patterson on Garth's tour impact: "When he went through a market, he helped country radio stations gain a couple of shares. You could feel Garth in the marketplace. You could feel Garth at the record stores. Half of selling records is getting people into the store. He brought them in and maybe they'd buy something else."

Ben Farrell, president of Lon Varnell Enterprises, one of the promoters Garth worked with on his 1996–1998 tour, said that Garth and Elvis were "the two strongest touring acts to ever set foot on the North American concert stage, without question." And Buddy Lee president Tony Conway called Garth "the most significant country touring artist that ever existed."

R&R's Helton worried that the intensity of criticism *Garth Brooks in . . . the Life of Chris Gaines* had received was playing into his decision. "I hope he doesn't view it as a failure. He tried to do something new and different. It's always the pioneers who come back with arrows in the butt."

Garth understood slings and arrows. As far back as 1993, when pop and rock critics had turned their ire in his direction, a close industry friend talked with Garth about a conversation with Asleep at the Wheel's Ray Benson. "This had to happen," Benson had said. "Everybody's always gonna try to tackle the guy carrying the ball."

Garth had laughed at the sports analogy. "Yeah. I guess that's why it's good to have some people out there blocking for you!"

Frequent collaborator Victoria Shaw ("The River" and "She's Every Woman") lamented the genre's loss of Garth as a writer and performer of great songs. "Garth is one of the people cutting the most interesting songs, and that's what makes me sad. It's one down for people with guts to say something interesting and push the envelope."

Several currents were at work in the industry during that time, and some of them spelled potential trouble for the business of country music. Consolidation was the motto of the business world, and radio, record stores, and labels were being sucked into conglomerates that intensified pressure on bottom-line thinking. Major labels were laying off staff members and rumors floated of a shutting down of newer companies, where executives were seldom given time to develop a substantial roster. Publishers worried that singers were leaning toward writing much of their own material rather than drawing from Nashville's rich song pool.

However, there were positives when it came to country artists and durability. Looking back on the artists signed in the late 1980s and early 1990s, we see a large number of them exhibited considerable staying power. The singers who were just trying to make it into a recording studio about a decade earlier—Trisha Yearwood, Faith Hill, Shania Twain, Alan Jackson, Travis Tritt, Tim McGraw—had become a very successful establishment.

The females, especially, were a diverse lot: glamorous pop-flavored figures like Shania Twain and Faith Hill; the lasting appeal of a Trisha Yearwood, Martina McBride, or Reba McEntire; and the edgy traditional-weds-rock sound of the Dixie Chicks. New and tougher-imaged women like Terri Clark and Jo Dee Messina made chart news. Sara Evans made a splash that year with her first number 1 single, "No Place That Far," from the RCA album of the same name. But those successes were dwarfed by the men: Brooks & Dunn, Alan Jackson,

George Strait, Toby Keith, Kenny Chesney, Tim McGraw, Trace Adkins, Mark Chesnutt, and Lonestar. Brooks & Dunn and Tim McGraw, in particular, had utilized tours that effectively translated to sales.

Brad Paisley was an act with staying power, first charting in 1999. His "He Didn't Have To Be" was the second single, and first number 1, from his platinum-selling Arista debut, *Who Needs Pictures*. Just a year later, he won the CMA's Horizon Award. The West Virginia native brought strong country credentials with him to Nashville, having started opening shows for artists including Ricky Skaggs and George Jones when he was only thirteen. He signed a publishing deal with EMI prior to obtaining a record deal, and wrote hits including David Kersh's "Another You." Like Keith Urban, Paisley brought both songwriting and formidable guitar skills to the Nashville table.

Keith Urban's solo debut, "It's A Love Thing," only reached the Top 20 in 1999, but the following year he started a string of hits that included "But For The Grace Of God," "Where The Blacktop Ends," and "Somebody Like You," which stayed at number 1 for six weeks. Interestingly, given the singer's impending chart dominance, in 2000, Capitol had difficulties rounding up New York media figures who were interested enough to attend a reception in his honor. That lack of interest quickly vanished and, at long last, Capitol Records in Nashville had produced another superstar.

The top-charting singles in 1999 were Alan Jackson's "Right On The Money," Martina McBride's "Wrong Again," Jo Dee Messina's "Stand Beside Me," Mark Chesnutt's "I Don't Want To Miss A Thing," Sara Evans's "No Place That Far," the Dixie Chicks's "You Were Mine," and Kenny Chesney's "How Forever Feels." Nashville had by now welcomed Clint Black's "movie star" wife, Lisa Hartman, into the fold, and the two performed their duet, "When I Said I Do," on the CMA awards show. The song was another of the year's top singles.

The striking thing about 1999's top singles (devised by mon-
itored airplay time) is how the list had grown steadily shorter
over the years. Shrinking playlists had been a trend for a while
and consolidation exacerbated it. In 1999, for example, the list
included eighteen releases. Through the 1980s the same year-
end lists usually contained around fifty singles. Radio not only
had continued to shorten playlists, but to keep songs in the top
spots longer, which kept many records off the airwaves. For example, in 1999, Kenny Chesney's "How Forever Feels" stayed at
number 1 for six weeks; Tim McGraw's "Something Like That"
and "Please Remember Me," five weeks each; George Strait's
"Write This Down," four weeks; Martina McBride's "I Love
You," five weeks; and Lonestar's "Amazed," eighteen weeks.
So during a fifty-two-week period of time, five artists dominated the top of the charts for thirty-three weeks. And between
the end of 1998 and early 2000, the Dixie Chicks spent twelve
weeks at number 1 with five releases.

Lonestar was the biggest news of the year. One of the group's
two lead vocalists, John Rich, had been fired from the band in
1998, so after the overwhelming success of "Amazed," a good
many people in Nashville thought he'd missed the Big Time
Bus. But Rich took his energy and talents in another direction.
With "Big" Kenny Alphin, Jon Nicholson, and Corey Gierman,
Rich founded the MuzikMafia, a loosely organized jam session
headquartered at Nashville's Pub of Love. The Mafia encouraged
and supported people who might not otherwise have gotten a
shot, most notably Gretchen Wilson. Among his biggest songwriting hits are, "Like We Never Loved At All" (Faith Hill and
Tim McGraw) and "Redneck Woman," "When I Think About
Cheatin'," and "All Jacked Up" (Gretchen Wilson). As an artist
(Big & Rich), a writer, producer, and new talent proponent,
Rich has given far more to the industry than he would have
swapping Lonestar vocals with Richie McDonald. John Rich's
kind of innovation was just what Nashville needed.

It was becoming painfully obvious that new talent had to have room to grow in Nashville, because far fewer were breaking through. With too much targeting of the youth market, a smaller number of singles making it to number 1, and fewer breakout artists, it's not surprising that country music found itself with a shrinking number of big-selling acts. George Strait, Garth Brooks, the Chicks, Shania Twain, Tim and Faith, Reba, Martina, and Trisha, among others, could sell multiples of platinum, but of the next in line, only a few, such as Kenny Chesney, Keith Urban, and Rascal Flatts, would sustain multiple platinum sales.

By 1999 most executives understood that Garth Brooks was a phenomenon that was not likely to happen again, especially by design. "Find me the next Garth Brooks" had been replaced by "Find me a few acts that can together sell on those levels." And they had quit trying to predict who was going to even come close. One of Nashville's most respected producers, Paul Worley (Dixie Chicks, Martina McBride), told the *Tennessean's* Jay Orr and Tom Roland that the thought process had changed: "No one would have predicted Garth's huge success when he was developing as an artist. Nobody predicted the Dixie Chicks' success when they were developing as artists. I love their music the way I love most of the music I work on. Why does it translate into something larger than life? It has a lot to do with the qualities of the artists as human beings."

DETERMINED TO SAVE THEIR marriage, in early 2000 Garth and Sandy bought a farm near Sandy's parents' home in Oklahoma, and a short trip away from Raymond Brooks's house. The new property had several hundred acres, barns, and a small house. "Nobody ever tried to stay married more than Garth did," Allen Reynolds says. "I've never seen anyone work as hard to put things back together."

In addition to working on the marriage, Garth was also very serious about being a better father and son.

"I wanted to stay close to Dad, because Mom's death hit him *very* hard," he said. "Years back, when this whole career got so big, my dad told me that I better remember that I was no longer living in the real world. And he was right. But after Mom died, I realized that both my dad and I needed to get back to the world. For me, a big part of it was taking care of the girls. I started hanging out in the kitchen, learning to cook, making the girls' lunches. I found out that I really liked doing it, too."

Although Garth spent a great deal of time at home, he was no recluse. He continued to work on his lifelong dream of playing with a professional baseball team, joining the Padres and the Mets whenever possible to raise money for his Teammates for Kids Foundation (originally named the Touch 'Em All Foundation) incorporated in 1999 in Colorado. Teammates for Kids, still located in the Denver suburb of Littleton, Colorado, is run day-to-day by co-founder/president Bo Mitchell, formerly a chaplain with the Denver Nuggets. It is a nonprofit that contributes financial resources to selected nonprofit organizations that effectively serve and benefit children with an emphasis on health, education, and inner-city needs. The foundation enlists sports figures who will contribute a predetermined sum based on selected categories of on-field performance.

Private donors and corporate sponsorships then match the athletes' contributions. Funds are distributed to various organizations that serve children, especially in the areas of health and education.

Garth and Mitchell developed an operating system with every precaution taken against the criticisms celebrity-connected foundations sometimes receive. Merrill Lynch oversees donations, and an accounting firm provides an audit available to any ballplayer who has contributed. Garth had seen one too many charities lose credibility because of misused funds and excessive overhead. To ensure the foundation remain, in Garth's terms, "squeaky clean," all donations go directly to charitable gifts while expenses and overhead funds are raised privately and through special events. The Teammates for Kids Foundation has raised over $17 million for child-related charities throughout the world.

Baseball was both invigorating and humbling for Garth. He was up to bat twenty-two times with the Padres and only got one base hit, off Mike Sirotka of the White Sox. And he realized that age was catching up with him. When asked why he hadn't been at the workout room as much as he might have, Garth's answer was, "I don't need to stretch. I'm so slow I can't possibly get hurt." By the time he got to the Mets, Garth said he'd decided to take George Brett's advice to heart: "Swing hard. You might hit it."

IN APRIL 2000 HE brought the audience of 45,000 to its feet singing "Freedom" with George Michael at Equality Rocks, a concert benefiting the Human Rights Campaign Foundation at RFK Stadium in Washington, D.C. It was an all-star affair turning the spotlight on gay rights, with performances by artists including Melissa Etheridge, Chaka Khan, and the Pet Shop Boys. And in case anyone thought the blond woman playing drums on several songs looked familiar at first glance, a second look showed her to be Tipper Gore.

Garth got involved with Equality Rocks through his friend and Red Strokes partner, Lisa Sanderson, who was co-executive producer, and learned early in the booking process that some straight performers were uncomfortable at the thought of playing Equality Rocks. Lisa spoke to *Entertainment Weekly*'s Chris Willman: "There was some resistance felt even in the entertainment industry, which is the most liberal of all."

Sanderson told Willman that part of Garth's interest involved Equality Rocks' heavy concentration on hate crimes and how they affect the children in our society. "Garth's gonna stand on that stage to try to make people hear that the violence with our children in *all* communities has gone way too far."

Willman "got it" and wrote about it, but some reporters didn't receive the memo. Given Garth's advocacy for human rights, and the lyrics of his hard-fought-for song "We Shall Be Free," it was surprising that anyone questioned his solid support for the event.

"Does anyone in my family think it's odd that a non-homosexual is at what some refer to as a 'homosexual event'?" Garth responded at one news conference. "I'm here because it's Equality Rocks for human rights. I'm not here for gay, straight, white, or black. I'm here hoping that our intelligence will rise a step forward, get beyond the fences that we've put up ourselves. That someday we will look and say that we are all human—and *that* is true equality."

The gay community never forgot Garth's support. In 2002 the *Washington Blade,* a prominent gay publication, listed "We Shall Be Free" as one of the all-time most important songs inspiring pride in gays, saying, "Every movement talks about support both from within and from 'outside.' For gays, this means 'straights.' The struggle for equality can't work without them. That's why Garth Brooks' song about personal rights and freedoms is so important. He's straight, hugely famous, and asks his hordes of country fans to love one another and let everyone else love whom they choose."

In October 2000, he was a surprise performer when Allen Reynolds was inducted into the Songwriters Hall of Fame for writing songs including "Five O'Clock World," "I Saw Linda Yesterday," "Ready For The Times To Get Better," and "I Recall A Gypsy Woman." Garth sang a medley including "Five O'Clock World" and "I Saw Linda Yesterday."

When a friend pointed out that in recent years Reynolds had primarily been known as a producer, he answered, "Songwriting brought me to the music industry in the first place, and a love of great songs is what brought Garth and I together. I can't explain how much it meant to me that he came out for the induction. And, speaking of inductions, there's not a doubt in my mind that Garth Brooks should be in the Songwriters Hall of Fame—as well, I might add, as the Country Music Hall of Fame."

Garth also co-produced a film project with Whoopi Goldberg, *Call Me Claus*. The film was a Columbia Tri-Star production, in association with Red Strokes Entertainment and Whoopi's One Ho Productions. *Call Me Claus* starred Whoopi and featured new music by Garth, who said he learned a great deal during the filming. In the recording studio, as on tour, he could be in complete charge. But he soon found that in the making of a film, he had to rely on others.

"Whoopi takes orders from no one," Garth laughed to AP Radio. "And there's a good reason for that. She's smart. She's very smart. When it comes to TV, and when it comes to Whoopi, nobody knows Whoopi more than her!"

The year 2000 was filled with special appearances. In January, he was one of the artists who sang a medley of Burt Bacharach songs in tribute to the composer at the seventy-second annual Academy Awards at the Los Angeles Shrine Auditorium. With Nanci Griffith in March, he guest starred in Don McLean's first-ever television special, *Starry Starry Night,* on PBS. Also in 2000, Garth was the featured artist on *Austin City Limits'* twenty-fifth anniversary show on PBS. The pilot episode of *Austin City Limits* had been taped on October 17, 1974, in a University of Texas TV studio and starred Willie Nelson and Family. Garth first taped *Austin City Limits* in 1990, when he told the show's producer, Terry Lickona, that the experience felt like being a ballplayer and making it to the World Series. Then there was the hat tip that made Garth laugh: *Playgirl* named him one of the eight hottest celebrity cowboys, along with actors Matthew McConaughey and Johnny Depp.

But a private drama cast a pall over that entire summer and fall. The inconclusive tests that Garth's friend Chris LeDoux had ignored almost a decade earlier came back to haunt him in

2000. He began to feel fatigued, in his words, "out-of-kilter." It wasn't anything specific, but Chris knew that something was wrong. When he went to a doctor that summer, he heard bad news. The diagnosis was primary sclerosing cholangitis, a serious liver ailment that requires a transplant. But, the doctors told Chris, everything depended on finding a match.

When Garth got the news he was devastated. It would have been one thing if his stepping in with financial help could have made a difference. He had done that for various people through the years, always very quietly. But money couldn't help Chris LeDoux. Only a transplant match could do that.

Finally in October, Chris did find a match, and underwent successful surgery. At first Chris kept the news quiet, but speculation heightened about shows canceled and hospital stays. At that time, he released a letter to his fans. This is a portion of what Chris wrote: "I was in pretty bad shape when I checked into the University of Nebraska Medical Center in October. Garth Brooks had already been there taking tests to see if he could donate part of his own liver, willing to risk his own life to save mine. But it was not to be. His liver wasn't compatible. Garth was determined to keep his action secret, but I thought people ought to know."

Chris finished his letter with a short piece of advice for his fans: "Life is a miraculous and mysterious thing. It can be beautiful, and it can turn downright ugly. Enjoy the good parts."

THE AVERAGE LENGTH OF a first marriage prior to a divorce is eight years. Garth and Sandy had been married for fourteen. They had gone the extra mile time and again to save their marriage, even renewing their vows in 1996. But Garth had been solidly on the road, in the studio, or traveling to one personal appearance or another for years. Their lives had become so separate that at one point Sandy even had her own fan club.

When they went back to Oklahoma it was soon obvious that their children were what they had left in common. At that point, as in so many marriages, a decision has to be made. Do you stay married "for the children" or do you divorce in time to retain a good relationship with each other as parents. Garth and Sandy opted for the latter solution, determining that the best option.

Garth knew an announcement would have to be made, especially since Sandy did not plan to attend the biggest party of his career. In October 2000, Capitol Records planned to throw a black-tie party at the Nashville Arena celebrating Garth's passing the 100 million sales mark, a feat unmatched by any other solo artist in history.

The week prior to the celebration, *Billboard*'s Melinda Newman interviewed Garth and he spoke about the divorce, saying, "Right now, we're focusing on the impact it will have on the children and how to handle that. We want to remain parents, even if we don't remain husband and wife."

The primary focus of the interview was Garth as an artist. In answer to what sorts of events had affected him more than the 100 million sales, he answered, "Truthfully, there are so many other things in my career that have affected me more. Like the first No. 1, "If Tomorrow Never Comes." Getting to play Central Park. Getting my very first platinum and gold record, getting to play Fan Fair, getting to play the Opry. This wasn't one of those 'stand on the mountain' things, going, 'I made it to here' kind of feelings. Which I thought it would be."

He took the opportunity to make an additional point about his sales. "The Recording Industry Association was sweet to give us the largest-selling solo act in history, but I think we all know it's Elvis. It's just the method of counting wasn't as certifiable then as it is now. It's cool and everything, but at the same time please know that I'm seeing it with a very real look."

Newman also asked Garth to address the misunderstandings about his career. "Well, I don't think I'm misunderstood by the public. I think the public sees me as a guy who will fight for his music, will die for his music, and has been tough about that. I think the industry, as a majority, feels I do things for numbers. And the people that think that about Garth Brooks don't have a clue who I am."

In the days approaching the celebration, Garth thought about what his achievement really meant, and about the challenges he had faced over the years. The conclusions he came to about why he'd been able to succeed to this remarkable extent appeared complicated, yet in reality were stunningly simple. Among other things, he recalled some advice a friend had given him years earlier: "It was something that most of us could take to heart," he confided. "She said, 'Be sure you know who's willing to ride shotgun and who's just along for the ride.'"

At a news conference just prior to the event, Garth reiterated that he was no longer touring and that his career was not his top priority. "I've done my career with the old saying, 'Burn bright, burn fast.'"

He went on to talk about possible new projects—an album still owed Capitol, a duet project with Trisha Yearwood, and another soundtrack album. But for the time being, fatherhood took precedence: "My children and I are together every day. And every night I tuck those children in, and I'm responsible for their safety. I feel good about that."

On the night of his gala, when he listened to words of praise sent from luminaries ranging from President Bill Clinton to Whitney Houston, he discovered that the high didn't compare to hearing his first record on the radio, or to being inducted into the Grand Ole Opry. And on the night of his 100 million party he was not surprised that, as thrills went, cheering for a soccer-playing daughter had replaced receiving the applause of the past ten years.

CHAPTER TWENTY-TWO

If you ever wonder what happened to me

G arth sat alone in a back room at Bob Doyle's office, listening to songs for the final album he owed Capitol. He was incredibly frustrated and suffering from writer's block. He was still depressed because of his mother's death, and worried that his father was in even worse emotional shape.

As he opened yet another box of tapes Allen Reynolds had recommended, he was reminded of a piece of advice Jerry Kennedy had given him during his first year in Nashville: "The song you're looking for is on the tape you haven't listened to yet."

EVEN THOUGH CAPITOL'S PARENT company, EMI, reported pretax earnings up 8 percent in 1999, the market share had tumbled. EMI believed it was due in great part to the lack of a big seller from Garth Brooks. That knowledge alone would not have brought Garth back to Nashville. The truth was, while he loved his time at home, he missed making music.

Former Arista record executive Mike Dungan had taken over at Capitol. Dungan kept Garth's team at the label, including longtime press agent Karen Byrd, who was vice president, public relations. In making the announcement, Capitol Group president/CEO Roy Lott (also formerly with Arista) said that Pat Quigley had never been considered a permanent label head, but one hired for the interim. Dungan, said Lott, was chosen for his ability to spot and develop talent.

Dungan had practically grown up in the music business. Born and raised in Cincinnati, Mike started working part-time in a record store as a young teenager, a job he kept through college. After graduating with a degree in biology, he took a job with RCA's pop promotion division, working his way up to a regional manager position before moving to sales with RCA's parent company, BMG. In 1990 Arista's Tim DuBois hired Dungan to head the Nashville label's sales and marketing. In 1998 he was named general manager of the label, and in 2000 he came to Capitol as its new president.

Mike and Garth got along from the beginning, sharing a mutual respect. Dungan also treated the staff very well, and that went a long way with Garth. Moreover, the new label head understood the most important thing there was to know about Garth Brooks: his music wasn't negotiable. Dungan had no interest in strong-arming him about specific cuts or recording techniques. What Garth had been doing had connected with millions of fans and Dungan felt no need to try and get in charge of it. Perhaps if Mike had come along in 1995, Garth would have stayed at Capitol. But by the year 2000 he was burnt out on major labels. His attitude could best be illustrated with his two favorite Ricky Skaggs quotes:

1: "Life's too short to live like this."
2: "Life's too long to live like this."

But one last album loomed. Dungan wasn't surprised when Garth finally came to him and said he was ready to record. Each time the two spoke, Garth got more enthusiastic as he talked about making music. "It was just a matter of time," Dungan later said with a laugh.

"I honestly didn't know if I was up to making a record yet," Garth told a friend. "But both Allen [Reynolds] and Bob [Doyle] convinced me that I needed to get back in the studio. I felt like I'd been out of the loop for so long that I didn't even know if I could still write a decent song."

Garth was also worried about the state of country music. Nashville labels were actively promoting singles to pop radio, pop stations were playing more country records, and there was a decline in the numbers of country stations across the nation. The biggest problem, as he saw it, was that pop deejays would never admit that the records they were spinning were country. "A whole new group of fans will grow up not realizing that this music is coming out of Nashville."

Given Garth's writing worries, Reynolds put the word out: bring on the tapes. In the end, the two listened to over ten thousand songs. "Everyone in Nashville knew I'd had a hard time with Mom's death," Garth said. "And we didn't want people thinking they should pitch me a bunch of 'downer' material because of it. So Allen told publishers not to try and second-guess the album. In the end, the songs did have a lot to do with my personal life. But it happened in an organic way, not contrived."

One thing both artist and producer agreed on was that Nashville writers were better than ever. They found hundreds of extraordinary songs, many of them from new writers they'd not previously been aware of. It portended well for the industry but, too often, not for Garth's sessions. "I heard songs I thought would be smashes for half the artists in town," Garth laughed. "I'd be suggesting that the writers get that song to Tim McGraw and this one to Deana Carter and another one to Reba. But I didn't hear so many that were right for me. It makes you wonder if time has passed you by."

Approaching his return to the studio with great trepidation, Garth admitted that he felt his hands tightening up and his throat getting dry at first. He continued to have a hard time writing, and considered scrapping the entire album several times. "Allen Reynolds told me, 'I'd tell you if I thought it was time to quit, and it isn't,'" Garth said.

In the end, Garth decided to title the new album *Scarecrow* because, "In Oz, the Scarecrow led with his heart. But remember, he was brainless," he laughed. "That pretty much sums me up."

In fact, Allen Reynolds insisted that Garth stay true to his heart through the entire process, from writing his own material, to listening to outside songs, to the recording itself. "I've always advised Garth to stay close to his emotions when he records. This time those emotions ran the gamut, and they all ended up on the record," says Allen Reynolds. "It is very difficult, this far into a career, to stay fresh, but Garth accomplished it by staying honest with himself about everything he was feeling."

And so, once again, Garth's album was a reflection of a time in his life, one that combines extreme lows and highs. Many of the songs on *Scarecrow* address family, with one speaking directly to his devastated father. "I had trouble after Mom's death, but I knew I had to pull myself back. Dad wasn't even trying. My sister and my brothers and I kept attempting to bring him out of his shell, but nothing seemed to work. Then I heard a song by Kevin Welch, who was one of the first artists I met when I moved to Nashville in 1987. The song was titled 'Pushing Up Daisies.'"

Kevin allowed Garth to modify the lyrics somewhat to fit what he wanted to say to his dad, that he must break the cycle of wishing he, too, had died, that he couldn't go on without Colleen by his side.

"Dad responded to 'Pushing Up Daisies' in that it drove home how much we all wanted him back," Garth told a friend. "But it wasn't any cure."

"Thicker Than Blood," written with Jenny Yates, was another song aimed at family. "This song was also for my dad, to show him what a wonderful life he and Mom made for us kids," Garth confided. "Our family was the old 'yours, mine, and ours' story. This song paid tribute to how my parents made it work."

One self-penned song on the album raised eyebrows, "The Storm," which addresses surviving a breakup. Of course, that was a topic Garth had written of many times, but this time was different because he was getting a divorce. "The Storm" is about those times in life when the storm finally catches up to you, and you realize that you can survive it.

"Yes, the song is autobiographical in a way," he said. "It could have been written about a man or a woman. And I've found that the personal songs on this album have been healing, not depressing."

Garth explained to a friend: "I needed to open up. The two albums I probably revealed the most on have been *The Chase* and *Scarecrow*. There's some dark moments on *Scarecrow*, but there's also laughter. It was like that scene in *Steel Magnolias*, where the woman buries her daughter, and standing at the cemetery, she shouts, 'I want to hit somebody!' One of her friends pushes another woman toward her and says, 'Here, hit her!' And even though it's the saddest situation you can imagine, you break up laughing.

"I know it's a cliché, but you really do laugh to keep from crying. That's what I felt while we made *Scarecrow*. I'd find myself with the worst blues, then turn around and find something so lighthearted, so funny. Eventually those emotions smooth out, and you get back on some kind of an even keel. It's a process you go through trying to remember that *you* are still alive."

When Garth talks about *Scarecrow,* he often brings up the musical side of it. He points to the accordion playing by Joey Miskulin on "Pushing Up Daisies" and the string arrangements by Dennis Burnside on "When You Come Back To Me Again."

"One of my favorite things about this album is the instrumentation on 'Don't Cross The River.' It's an old America cut, but strangely, I hadn't heard it. The version I heard was done by Doyle Lawson and Quicksilver, with Jerry Douglas playing Dobro. I got Jerry to come in and play on the song, and he told me that the Lawson cut was his very first session."

Another favorite musical moment came on "Wrapped Up In You," when Terry McMillian traded harmonica licks with fiddle player Jimmy Mattingly. "The best part of that whole song happened when I stopped singing," Garth laughed.

The video for "Wrapped Up In You" took Garth back to something he told Bob Doyle when the two first met. When Bob asked him if he could summarize one thing he'd like to do with his music, Garth thought a moment, then said, "Bring it out to the front porch." What he visualized was music that reflected family, close-knit ties, and laid-back living. Main street. And in the "Wrapped Up In You" video, he took that concept to a general store in small-town America, with townspeople and tradesmen using brooms, checkers, and wooden blocks to set a percussive mood.

There was a duet with George Jones, one of his idols, called "Beer Run," which George also included on his 2001 album, *The Rock: Stone Cold Country.* George released it as a single in October 2001, and it hit number 24, his highest-charting single since 1997. Garth laughed about being on record with the Possum: "He lapped my ass one hundred times while he was singing. I thought, 'Shit, I can't compete with this.' So I just did the best I could."

Of course, he'd long said he couldn't keep up with Trisha Yearwood in the studio. "I just hang on and hope," he once quipped. Their duet on *Scarecrow,* "Squeeze Me In," written by Nashville blues-rockers Gary Nicholson and Delbert McClinton, was nominated for a Grammy the following year.

Over the months it took to record *Scarecrow* Trisha was often in the studio both singing harmony and performing on duet material. As time went by, the friendship she and Garth had had for the past decade began to change. Trisha was divorced from Robert Reynolds in 1999 and knew what Garth was going through. The two had always had an upfront relationship when talking about music, the industry, touring, careers, and their own personal value systems. Now the conversations took on a more personal tone: marriages, the pain of divorce, and trying to put lives back together. The more time they spent together, the more Garth became convinced that his longtime friend represented the beginning of the rest of his life.

This was not a situation where they started to "date" as such. Nor did Trisha spend more time at the studio than usual. She came in to sing when she was needed, no more. But they did spend more time talking, at Trisha's home and on long drives. Trisha also faced some career decisions. Her MCA label deal was almost up, and she was considering making a move. She had problems deciding on the direction of her next album. And so everything that made the two trusted friends, platonic soul mates, came into play on an intensified level.

But while Garth did talk about the relationship to friends, the couple did not go public for over a year. The event that brought them out was the March 19, 2002, memorial service for Harlan Howard. Both artists had loved Harlan and been deeply affected by his March 3 death. Trisha, in fact, sang one of Harlan's songs on her last demo session after signing with MCA Records in 1990. Garth and Trisha arrived at the Ryman Auditorium for Harlan's service arm in arm, making no attempt to hide the fact that they were, indeed, a couple.

As soon as the couple went public, singer/songwriter Gary Nicholson told a friend, "Delbert and I are planning to take full credit for this." He laughed. "Garth and Trisha went into the studio and sang 'Squeeze Me In' and realized they couldn't live without each other."

There was a flashback to earlier days on *Scarecrow*. When

Garth heard the demo for "Big Money," written by Shawn
Camp, Randy Hardison, and Wynn Varble, he immediately recalled his first album. "That song would have fit in perfectly on
Garth Brooks," he said. "It's country and it has a message that
will put a grin on your face."

Scarecrow was released in 2001. What happened just a year
later to one of the songwriters on the album was one of Nashville's great tragedies, with all the drama of a country song. In
June 2002 a neighbor found Randy Hardison lying outside his
apartment building in a pool of blood, still alive. The neighbor
immediately called an ambulance, and friends began gathering
at his hospital bedside. It was first thought that he had fallen
off a ladder, but that theory was soon replaced by suspicions of
foul play.

In the end two men were charged with criminally negligent
homicide. They served seven months and were released for good
behavior.

Shawn Camp, who wrote "Big Money" with Randy, was
devastated over the murder. "It was one of those times when you
come up against something so terrible that you are numbed," he
reflected. "Randy was a funny, funny guy. That's why he was so
perfect for a tongue-in-cheek song like 'Big Money.' He hadn't
even had a chance to get his first royalty check from the song,
and it kills me to think how much that financial security would
have meant to him."

Many of the artists and writers who were deeply affected by
Randy's death mentioned him in their shows, hoping to keep
his spirit alive. Ironically, that is exactly what another song on
Scarecrow, "When You Come Back To Me Again," is about.

In 1999 when asked to write a song for the ending of the
movie *Frequency,* Garth phoned his frequent writing partner
Jenny Yates and asked her to accompany him to a screening
at New Line Cinema in Los Angeles. Garth loved the story.
After the initial twists and turns in the mystery/drama, what

might appear to be a happy ending only sets in motion a series of changed events that must be put right. The final scenes, for which Garth was to write a song, show three generations of a family reunited and playing baseball.

When the film wrapped, Garth turned to Jenny Yates and asked, "Are you ready to get to work?" The two went to his hotel room in L.A. and started talking about life, family, touchstones. Garth's late mother Colleen was very much on his mind. And the image that came to him was that of the family as a lighthouse.

And so, from beginning to end, Colleen Brooks was a force in *Scarecrow*. Garth believes that her positive spirit pulled him to safety, much like the lighthouse in the harbor in "When You Come Back To Me Again."

Frequency did not have a soundtrack album, so in 2000 Garth put together clips from the film and released "When You Come Back To Me Again" as a video. Almost immediately, radio began pulling the audio off the video and played the song right up the charts to number 21. That "When You Come Back To Me Again" was a tribute to family, and Colleen in particular, meant a great deal to Garth. That the public loved it so much that they made it an unreleased hit caused him to include the cut as the final song on *Scarecrow*. It received a Golden Globe nomination in the category of Best Original Song.

Under Mike Dungan's direction *Scarecrow* was released on November 13, 2001. Since he wasn't touring, Garth hosted three CBS-TV specials to promote the album. *Garth Brooks: Coast to Coast Live* aired on November 14, 2001, from the Los Angeles Forum with special guests Keb' Mo' and Trisha Yearwood. Guests at the Forum show included Kenneth "Babyface" Edmonds, Woody Harrelson, Marlee Matlin, and John Travolta. The second aired on November 21 with special guest Jewel from the flight deck of the USS *Enterprise* just as it was returning from an extended deployment. The series ended on November 28 with a concert on the beach in South Padre Island, Texas, with special guests Steve Wariner and Jerry Jeff Walker.

Together with Joe Mansfield and Capitol marketing VP Fletcher Foster, Dungan put together a massive effort that included commercials involving Dr Pepper and Kmart, talk show appearances, and a limited-edition version of the album.

"There won't be a person in the world that doesn't know there's a new Garth Brooks out," Dungan said. But, he added, the label was not promoting *Scarecrow* as "Garth's final album." The *Chicago Sun-Times* pointed to a *final album* pitfall Garth wisely avoided: "Garth Brooks has resisted the urge to make a Grand Statement. Instead, he opted for a solid, exquisitely produced, no-strings-attached contemporary country disc."

Noted music journalist Jack Hurst, writing in the *Nashville Scene,* called *Scarecrow* "a mainstream masterpiece offering touches of everything from hard-core country and bluegrass to big ballads to delicious swing, soul, and Celtic music, infused throughout with a mix of sexy humor and altar-call seriousness. Sometimes employing strings and other times stark sparseness, he delivers it all with a winning, backing-off-self-assurance born (one suspects) of the fact that he finally has nothing left to prove . . . undeniable artistic genius."

The *Daily Oklahoman* said, "Just when you thought country music was set to be taken over by young punks, here comes Garth Brooks to show you how real country sounds." *Time* noted that *Scarecrow* is "a reminder that Brooks is a man with a significant gift. Like Elvis and Sinatra, Brooks isn't just a singer, but an interpreter." *People* called it "his best work to date."

Scarecrow debuted at number 1 on the *Billboard* Top 200 and country albums charts with first-week sales of 465,523. Shakira's English language debut sold 202,000 and Madonna's third hits collection, *GHVD,* sold 105,000. Even Paul McCartney had a bad sales week with *Driving Rain:* 66,000.

This marked the seventh time Garth debuted at number 1

on the Top 200 chart (more times than any other artist) and the ninth time atop the country albums chart. It was the highest-selling debut week for a country album since the release of *Garth Brooks Double Live* in 1998. The album was also among the ten best-selling country albums of 2001.

The critical reception to *Scarecrow* led to questions about Garth's retirement. Was he still serious about it? Would he really be able to keep himself from booking another big tour? Was this his final album for Capitol? Was he turning his back on music? The answers were yes, yes, yes, and no.

Garth was philosophical in a lengthy interview with *Billboard*'s Melinda Newman. He admitted to being torn between examples like Elton John, who had said that he didn't want to be a forty-year-old guy still out there rocking, yet he was still out there rocking. Garth didn't want to announce a retirement, then run out and tour again. Yet, as Newman pointed out, James Taylor and others had said that despite age, giving up music was impossible.

"Have you gotten everything you wanted from it [the music]?" Newman asked.

"No," Garth said. "Music is such a wonderful partner and mate. It's like every time you go there, the love you make is better than the first time, but it always *feels* like the first time . . . but because of choices I've made I am now a father that sings, whereas I used to be a singer that was a father."

Garth settled into life as a divorced dad in Oklahoma. He and Sandy had farms close to each other. They both saw the girls every day, were in constant communication about their upbringing, and in absolute agreement that their children were the priority. As divorces go, this one was as cordial as you could find.

He explained the differences between life in Oklahoma versus Nashville: "I have a new love for Nashville. Where I live in Oklahoma, the creative energy has a lot to do with agriculture, with just blue-collar muscle. In Nashville, the energy pool has a lot to do with dreaming, a lot to do with expressing yourself in an artistic way. When I would come to town, the first thing I noticed was this massive ball suddenly churning inside of me again, and it made me feel like I wanted to record. In Oklahoma, the energy you feel makes you feel very American. You get up and take your kids to school and it's a wonderful rush and joy and it's solid as a rock. So what's weird about Oklahoma and Nashville is, it's like my life has been with my mom and dad. One is a very realistic, grounded foundation and the other is, 'Let's see how high we can fly and see how dangerous we can get up there.' And I found out that they are both what I need."

In a phone call to Nashville to discuss his final Capitol album, Garth did an unusual thing. He put talking about his music on the back burner. "This has been a strange year," he began. "For a long time after my mom died I was living in a funk. Something was growing inside me and I couldn't seem to stop it. It was growing inside my dad, too. Neither one of us were moving on and I couldn't help but think my mom would tell us both to snap out of it. Because of my girls, it was so important for me to get completely back to myself. You don't get a second chance when you're raising children.

"I started thinking about how I had been changing, and realized that I had been so passionate about my music, my career—that a lot of the time I was out of touch. I never knew what day it was, let alone the hour. I was passionate about the moment, always trying to go new places. But I didn't have a clue about what was going on in the world in general, and sometimes not even in my own world. Somebody would ask me if I'd heard about this or that event, and I'd have to admit I hadn't. But I had started watching the television news on a daily basis, started paying attention to my surroundings.

"Finally, I decided to tell my mother about what was going on with me. I started writing a poem to her. It started out, 'If you ever wonder what happened to me, I've become the man that I feared I would be. Politically conscious, a payer of dues, aware of the hour and the hourly news.' I really wanted to try and explain this crossroads I was at. I was making changes that both scared and excited me. And in the end, I wanted her to know that she was still with me, still guiding me."

In the poem, Garth wrote of being in a room and blending in, rather than being the pivotal point. Garth put the poem up on his wall and stopped to read it every time he walked by.

"What I started learning is that you can be passionate about many, many things. Obviously I'm passionate about my kids— but I've even become passionate about learning to cook, learning to take care of myself on very basic levels."

"Do you want to talk about the music?" he was asked.

"I'm gonna have to call you back later to talk about *Scarecrow*," he said. "Because I want to talk about Miss Yearwood—how insanely happy I am right now."

Well, all right.

"When I started making this record at that low point, I had my best friend by my side at every step. Trisha would not let me sink any further down. You remember that I always said I could never get into too much of an ego trip because my family would beat me up? Well, Trisha was that fierce about pulling me out of the hole I was in. I've always loved Trisha Yearwood as a friend. But then I realized I was *falling in love* with her. I want to tell you that when I saw how our whole relationship was changing, I was so happy that I worried it was a dream and I might wake up."

How does this story end, he was asked. "I'd rather tell you how it starts," he laughed. "I'm beginning this next stage of my life with my best friend beside me. My new goal is to be known as Mr. Trisha Yearwood."

Time is not your enemy

Giants of the industry would be turning out on that Sunday night in May 2005 to honor two towering figures: Gentleman Jim Foglesong and Kris Kristofferson. The Country Music Foundation had issued the invitations, and if the crowd turned out as expected, it would be the largest number of Hall of Fame members gathered at the HOF Museum in the foundation's history. It was being billed as a Family Reunion. Among those asked to take part in the musical tribute were Ray Price, Vince Gill, the Oak Ridge Boys, and Garth Brooks.

Garth was scheduled to sing his first number 1 song, "If Tomorrow Never Comes." He'd been away from Nashville doings for several years by then, so he thought long and hard about what to say to these two legends. Neither man had stepped back from their lives or careers. In the years since Jim Foglesong left Capitol he had devoted himself to his family and to music education. Kris Kristofferson was still a prolific writer and performer, living in Hawaii with his wife and children. Finally, on the night of the event, after reflecting on the men and their longevity, he said, "It's funny how if you take care of what you do, time's not your enemy."

★   ★   ★

NOR HAS TIME BEEN Garth's enemy. In the eight years since
he announced his retirement, between his 100 Million event in
2000 and 2008, Garth has sold an additional 28 million records.
And he is still making history. When a new single, "More Than
A Memory," was released in 2007, it became the first to ever
enter the *Billboard* charts at number 1. He has spent his time since
retiring being a father to three daughters, working on charitable
efforts, and, as of 2005, a husband to Trisha Yearwood. He
is also making music at a pace that doesn't interfere with his
family life.

At the time his final Capitol album, *Scarecrow,* was released,
the industry still looked to Garth to bolster overall sales. Country
music had not seen an upward swing since 1998, according to the
CMA's year-end wrap-up. Moreover, the entire music industry
had been in a slump, with a 2.8 percent loss in album sales.

Then, in 2001 country sold 67.2 million albums, up 1.3
million from 2000. Two albums led that charge. Just as *Urban
Cowboy* brought renewed excitement for honky-tonks back in
1980, a film and soundtrack helped revive country and bluegrass
sales and influence two decades later. *O Brother, Where Art Thou?*
was the ninth best-selling album in all genres during 2001, at
3.5 million, and spent twenty-four weeks at number 1 in *Billboard*'s
Top Country Albums chart. *O Brother* took home CMA awards
for Album and Single of the Year ("I Am A Man Of Constant
Sorrow" performed by Dan Tyminski). Garth's *Scarecrow* entered the top country and pop album charts at number 1, the
seventh time one of his albums had done so. *Scarecrow* sold 2.3
million during the same time period.

Tim McGraw had the next highest sales with 2.7 million
in sales from two offerings: *Set This Circus Down* and *Greatest
Hits.* Other artists selling over a million that year included Toby
Keith, Lee Ann Womack, Kenny Chesney, Faith Hill, and the

Dixie Chicks. *Amusement Business* named Tim McGraw the top touring artist of the year, bringing in $23.5 million, followed by Brooks & Dunn's Neon Circus tour at $17.6 million.

Following the release of *Scarecrow* speculation again ran high: would Garth Brooks tolerate being out of the spotlight? Given his years on the road, could he live up to his decision to be a stay-at-home dad? Moreover, would he be capable of staying away from the recording studio?

"After *Scarecrow* was released, I had a long talk with Garth," recalls Allen Reynolds. "I understood his wanting to give up the time-demanding tours, but I thought he might still record new albums. But he told me that with the passion that goes into making an album of new material, he believed he'd *have* to tour to support it. He said he'd consider other creative outlets in music, just not the emotional investment involved in the writing, song search, and recording of something brand-new. Not until he felt he could take it to his fans on the road.

"What struck me during that conversation, and in others since that time, is that Garth is not sacrificing anything to be with his children. He does not see this as him *giving up* anything, but rather, *receiving* something far more important."

In fact, rather than longing for another big tour of his own, Garth applauded the acts carrying his torch. He was especially proud of Girls Night Out, the biggest all-female tour in country history, headlined by his close friends Reba McEntire and Martina McBride, and featuring Jamie O'Neal, Sara Evans, and Carolyn Dawn Johnson. And the following year, Garth did do a short—albeit nonmusical—tour. After being named honorary chairman of the National Education's Read Across America 2002 celebration, he participated in a six-school reading tour. He kicked off the events by appearing on *Good Morning America,* where he read from Dr. Suess's *I Can Read with My Eyes Shut.* Steve Wariner joined him for a Nashville reading, and Trisha Yearwood accompanied him to Los Angeles, where the couple read Suess's *Horton Hears a Who.*

Garth built a second house on his Oklahoma property, across the road from Sandy. He and his former wife easily shared custody of Taylor, August, and Allie. Both parents remained dedicated to making the new arrangement work, and it did. One of the decisions both Garth and Sandy had made when they returned to Oklahoma in the first place was to hire no nannies. Garth was especially concerned about other people basically raising his family, and took the "daddy duties" seriously.

He continued to cook for the girls, to take them to school and pick them up, and, as many fathers do, to monitor where they were, whom they were with, and what they were doing. He was every bit as hands-on as his own parents had been. And he wanted desperately to fit back into a lifestyle he remembered and cherished. The first time he attended a game where he was just another soccer dad, it brought tears to his eyes.

One thing Garth wasn't doing was writing songs. "I'd give anything to hear Garth say he was consumed with songwriting again," Allen Reynolds reflected. "For one thing, I can't think of many people who have a better grasp of a story song."

Garth's storytelling instincts were not going to waste, though. In his new life, he had time to think about scriptwriting, films, and the events that make compelling tales. Songwriters often grab lines from each other: "Man, that's a great hook! I'm gonna write it if you don't!" In Garth's case he started saying things like, "That's a funny line! I bet I could use that in a script!"

His inspiration in great part came from being in Oklahoma, in watching real life unfold every day. He said it was there that he saw the complex character of the country, the struggles and successes people have each day. It's just that instead of hearing the stories in audio, he saw them in video.

Trisha and Garth spent as much time as possible together in both Tennessee and Oklahoma. Trisha was determined that her new role within the group not be considered threatening to the children. She had been a good friend of Sandy's and Garth's for many years, and that did not change. But before she and Garth made any permanent plans, she wanted the three girls to view her as a friend—one that in no way wanted to replace their mother.

Trisha was still evaluating her recording process and career direction, having had concerns for several years. In 2000, the same year she was inducted into the Georgia Music Hall of Fame, she released a new album. *Real Live Woman* was one of her most critically acclaimed: it was nominated for two Grammy awards, Best Album and Best Female Country Performance, and named in the top-ten lists of many publications, including the *Los Angeles Times* and *USA Today*. But it had only had one top-twenty single. She changed producers for 2001's *Inside Out,* but that album didn't make waves at radio either. For some months, Trisha considered taking time off from her career. But she eventually reunited with producer Garth Fundis and went back in the studio. Finally, dissatisfied with the results, Trisha shelved the material she'd cut and began to move toward her next project at a slower pace.

For this decision, she could have had no greater ally than Garth Brooks. It was not because of his very real desire to spend more time with her, though. He believed that Trisha could and would find the right songs if she put aside any immediate pressure to record. Her decision proved the right one, because although her next album would not be ready for three more years, 2005's *Jasper County* (which included a new duet with Garth, "Love Will Always Win") would reflect the time and focus it had received. Unfortunately, the MCA promotion team she'd worked with was gone. When Scott Borchetta moved to DreamWorks, MCA lost a promotion powerhouse, and Trisha's chart showings were not what they should have been.

In fact, between 2002 and 2005, country music was in a state of flux. Despite lackluster overall industry performance, Nashville's sales continued on 2001's uphill swing through 2002. While music sales overall were down 8.7 percent, 2002 showed country moving up by 12.28 percent, garnering 11.84 percent of the market. The CMA reported that for the first time in history, country had seven albums go to number 1 on the Top 200 chart, including releases by Alan Jackson, Toby Keith, the Dixie Chicks, and Faith Hill. Shania Twain's *Up!* held the top spot for five straight weeks.

Sales of catalog albums spiked in numbers that took them to gold, platinum, and multiplatinum status. Included in this group were recordings by artists such as Merle Haggard, Roy Orbison, Marty Robbins, David Allan Coe, Johnny Cash, Hank Williams Jr., Mary Chapin Carpenter, George Jones, Charlie Rich, and Willie Nelson. There was no doubt that country's continued visibility was affecting sales of new and established artists alike.

The roller coaster ride continued. Country experienced a downward slide in 2003 before picking back up in 2004. Industry watchers were encouraged by the upswing, the strongest in the past five years. Artists whose new albums helped drive the success were Kenny Chesney, Gretchen Wilson, Tim McGraw, Toby Keith, Big & Rich, and Brad Paisley. But despite Gretchen's success, and Shania Twain's *Up!* reaching 10 million in 2004, it was not an impressive year for female artists. Sales continued to trend up into 2005, but chart statistics still showed male artists dominating, while many established female artists faced the same struggle Trisha Yearwood had with *Jasper County.*

Garth could have made a career during that time frame just showing up at awards shows and industry galas. On January 9, 2002, he was presented with the Award of Merit at the twenty-ninth Annual American Music Awards in Los Angeles. Previous award winners include Paul McCartney, Frank Sinatra, Stevie Wonder, Irving Berlin, and Willie Nelson. That March he traveled to Washington, D.C., to receive ASCAP's Golden Note Award for outstanding contributions to American music as a performer and songwriter. In June 2002 he received a Hitmaker Award in New York from the Songwriters Hall of Fame. Garth and Trisha both participated in Loretta Lynn's ceremony at the twenty-sixth annual Kennedy Center Honors in January 2003, performing the classic Loretta Lynn/Conway Twitty duet "Louisiana Woman, Mississippi Man."

Without the pressures of big tours, Garth could spend more time on the foundation he'd founded in 1999, Teammates for Kids. He had long been reluctant to participate in charitable occasions that involved a flurry of publicity, often agreeing to meet sick children with the strict agreement that there be no publicists or flashbulbs involved. But Garth made an exception when it came to Teammates for Kids. His dedication to this organization was so well known that in February 2002 the major website devoted to the artist's news and history, PlanetGarth.com (founded by Brandon Wiesner in 1995), opted to raise money to donate on the occasion of Garth's fortieth birthday. It sent a message to Garth's fans about how to pay tribute to their artist.

Teammates for Kids also gave Garth the opportunity to continue playing baseball. After staying relatively low key through 2003, Garth came back to play with the Kansas City Royals in 2004, the result of a chance meeting with right-hander Jason Grimsley, who suggested that the team could raise money for Teammates for Kids. "He blends right in, moving from field to field," the Royals' David Witty told the *Kansas City Star*. "You wouldn't even know there's anything special about him."

Even though his teammates razzed him about being a part-timer because he left every weekend to be with his daughters, the players respected Garth's commitment. He was lauded for hard work, his positive energy, and for taking every drill, every batting practice seriously. There was never a time when it seemed that he was a dilettante interested in a diversion.

One of his biggest thrills occurred in March 2004 when Charley Pride showed up at Surprise Stadium in Arizona, shared by the Royals and the Rangers. A former ballplayer himself, he was there for the Rangers' spring training. Charley, who has a photo of Garth on his wall at home, remembered predicting that Garth would be a big star from the first time he heard him sing. Garth shook his head and reminded the crowd that it was Charley Pride who was the country legend, an icon and inspiration to generations of singers.

While interviewing Brooks and Pride, the *Fort Worth Star Telegram*'s Jim Reeves asked Garth to describe the difference he saw between making music and playing baseball. Garth laughed.

"Music is like breathing in and out. It's fun, and easy, easy, easy. This? I'm sweatin' my butt off just to look like the least worst guy on the field."

He thought about it for a moment, then added, "If it wasn't for the hitting and the fielding part, and the running, I'd be good at this game."

That same month, however, baseball fans gave him a standing ovation when he singled for the Royals against the Seattle Mariners. "I was more surprised than the pitcher," Garth laughed.

Garth continued to participate in Teammates for Kids with a hands-on approach. From the beginning, he has been determined that the charity be his in more than name. It has his attention, his time, and his resources. But that same year life stepped in and slowed him down when it came to fund-raising efforts.

Chris LeDoux, who had hit the concert trail just six months after his life-saving transplant in 2000, was diagnosed with bile duct cancer in 2004. He immediately began radiation treatment, but in the end, it was not enough. Chris died in March 2005. Mike Dungan, who had loved getting to know Chris since coming to Capitol, said, "In a world of egos and soundalikes, he was a unique artist and a wonderful man." And Chuck Yarborough, writing in the *Cleveland Plain Dealer*, said that because of Chris's being such an inspiration to Garth, he should be remembered as being "directly responsible for the current popularity of country music." Yarborough went on to cite Chris's influence on Garth's fever-pitched road show, and concluded with this poignant reminiscence:

"In the course of my career, I've done three or four interviews with LeDoux. Every conversation felt like two old friends sitting at my grandma's kitchen table at our family ranch in East Texas, swapping lies, sipping sweet tea and listening to an impatient bull call for his supper. It's memories like these that make me want to echo Brooks in his live version of 'Much Too Young (To Feel This Damn Old).' *The worn out tape of Chris LeDoux, lonely women and bad booze, seem to be the only friends I've left at all.* And at the close of this stanza, Brooks yells out, 'God Bless Chris LeDoux.' Say it again for me, Garth. Say it again."

Garth later reflected: "You get up in the morning and in your mind you hoist up your flag—whether it's the flag of your dreams or the flag of a hero. Let me tell you, I'm always proud to hoist up a flag with Chris LeDoux's name on it."

Garth had the opportunity to run that flag up a tall mast sooner than he thought. A tribute song to Chris was already in the works, and there was no doubt that Garth would want to record it. But since he was unwilling to make an entire new album, it was uncertain how that might happen.

Then, in June 2005, Garth ended his association with Capitol Records. Because his label, Pearl, owned his masters and leased them to Capitol, the deal was basically a license termination with no money changing hands. Because he was no longer touring or actively recording, there was no need to remain on the label. It also took him a step closer to his ultimate goal: recording a duet album with Trisha Yearwood. Through the years, although the two wanted to make such a record, Capitol and MCA stood in the way. Both wanted to be in the driver's seat on a project of that magnitude. It has worked in the past, but as Waylon Jennings once quipped, "Every time Willie and I recorded a duet album, two or three executives lost their jobs."

After news of Garth's leaving Capitol was made public, Wal-

Mart approached him with a novel idea: putting together an album of songs he'd recorded that never made it to any of his earlier albums. This would not be a situation where Garth had to write, to listen to thousands of new songs, and to begin the process from scratch. Rather, it would be a way to bring songs he loved and had already recorded to life. In the forefront of Garth's mind, however, was one new song, "Good Ride Cowboy," the Chris LeDoux tribute.

After he started thinking about it, Garth realized that there was one period of time especially that he'd recorded a wealth of material, between the making of 1997's *Sevens* and 2001's *Scarecrow.* During this time period, Allen Reynolds had encouraged him to record anything and everything he loved, not thinking about whether it would fit on an album. The more Garth thought about those songs, the more he wanted to go back in and listen to them again.

The Lost Sessions was filled with gems that otherwise would have languished in the stacks at Jack's Tracks. But the very first song placed on the album, and the collection's number 1 debut single, was "Good Ride Cowboy." Bob Doyle had come up with the idea after reading Chris's biography, *Gold Buckle Dreams* by David G. Brown. In Brown's book, he talks about the time-honored hat tip given to rodeo cowboys after a successful ride: "Good ride, cowboy. Good ride." Doyle turned the song over to Bryan Kennedy, Jerrod Lee Niemann, and Richie Brown. Bryan Kennedy credits most of the final lyrics of the song to Garth, though he wouldn't take a writer's credit.

To reflect the spirit and energy of Chris's concerts, Garth assembled a cast of his and Chris's friends, band members, and family, including the three Brooks girls, Taylor, August, and Allie. They joined in first on a rousing chorus, and then in a kind of wake held in rooms throughout the studio. Friends told Chris LeDoux stories, talked about his love of family, ranching, rodeo, music, touring, and songwriting. It was a celebration of a life well lived.

Garth talked about the recording with Hazel Smith, the woman who, while working with Waylon and Tompall Glaser, coined the term "the Outlaw Movement." Asked about "Good Ride Cowboy," Garth answered, "I knew if I ever recorded any kind of tribute to Chris, it would have to be up-tempo, happy. A song like him, not some slow, mournful song. Chris was exactly what our heroes are supposed to be. He was a man's man. A good friend."

Another impact song on the album, the one Garth called "the Big Hoss," was the Garth and Trisha duet "Love Will Always Win." Written by Gordon Kennedy and Wayne Kirkpatrick, the song had spent months on hold for the soundtrack of *Armageddon*, and later for a variety of artists. It became a situation of music imitating life, about a couple coming together against all odds.

"That Girl Is A Cowboy" was a tribute Garth wrote about a female friend who once phoned to tell him his horse, Cracker Jack, had died. Garth tried to make it home that night to bury his horse, but couldn't get there until morning. When he drove his pickup into the pasture, there sat his friend holding a 30–30. She'd built a fire and spent the night beside Cracker Jack to keep away the coyotes.

Mike McClure, an old friend from Oklahoma, wrote "I'd Rather Have Nothing." Mike had been the lead singer in one of Garth's favorite Stillwater bands, the Great Divide. The strong rhythm track on this song is a good indication of the importance of the music that was added to these songs by Garth's old studio team, as well as some favorite guest artists.

Jerry Douglas was on Dobro and Sam Bush on mandolin for "Allison Miranda." Dennis Burnside wrote and arranged the prelude on "The American Dream," and the tracks for "Meet Me In Love" were built around the original piano demo of the song's co-writer, Bobby Wood. The Nitty Gritty Dirt Band's "Fishin' In The Dark" was a natural for the studio band, who followed the Dirt Band's lead, just played a little louder and faster. Chris Leuzinger's guitar on the Steve Wariner/Marcus

Hummon–penned "You Can't Help The One You Love" is almost another vocal. In addition to Trisha Yearwood, two of Garth's friends also sang on the record: Alison Krauss on "For A Minute There" and Martina McBride on "I'll Be The Wind."

"She Don't Care About Me" was originally on a 2000 album Garth produced for Ty England, *Highways and Dance Halls*. Garth had loved the song so much, he cut a version of it at the time. Another song from Ty's album made Garth's *Lost Sessions*, "My Baby No Está Aquí," penned by David Stephenson and Shane Brooks. Garth teamed with Bryan Kennedy on a song filled with tricky internal rhyme schemes, "Cowgirl's Saddle," and with Randy Taylor on the honky-tonker "Under The Table." Yet another honky-tonk, potential jukebox classic included was DeWayne Blackwell's hard-drinking "Please Operator."

The final and favorite cut on *Lost Sessions* was Ed McCurdy's "Last Night I Had The Strangest Dream," a plea for peace recorded over the years by Pete Seeger, Simon & Garfunkel, and Arlo Guthrie, among others. Garth had first rolled the song out on his 1993–1994 World Tour, but had held it back because he knew if it was ever included on an album, it would have to be in that final spot.

The *Los Angeles Times* called the collection reflective of "the fresh spirit of *No Fences* and *Ropin' the Wind*."

In November 2005, Wal-Mart released *The Lost Sessions* in a box set, *Limited Series,* which included *Sevens, Double Live,* and *Scarecrow* in addition to a ninety-minute DVD with interviews, videos, and live performances. At the time of its release, Garth said, "One of the greatest gifts of the Wal-Mart deal is that it allows me to bring something to the people and still stay at home with my children."

The retail giant reported that Garth's release quickly became the largest-selling music item in its history. "Good Ride Cowboy" was a hit at radio, and Garth was asked to perform the song with Chris's band for the CMA awards show held that year in New York City. As they had for the Central Park show,

Big Apple fans turned out in droves for Garth's Times Square performance.

GARTH STAYED ACTIVE IN his charitable work during 2005. That February he joined with Steve Wariner, Stephanie Davis, and Dan Roberts for a fund-raiser in Fort Worth, Texas. Dan organized the event after UCLA's advanced MRI equipment helped his daughter during a serious illness. Recognizing the need for such equipment at Cook's Medical Center in Fort Worth, Dan contacted some of his friends and co-writers. The group raised over two million dollars. In November the National Hockey League and the NHL Player's Association announced Teammates for Kids as their chosen charity. One of the first joint efforts was relief for victims of Hurricane Katrina. The NHL raised $530,470 in December, which was then matched by Teammates for Kids. Then, in March 2006, Garth and Trisha performed at the JW Marriott Desert Ridge Resort in Arizona to raise money for Parkinson's disease research.

Meanwhile, Garth and Trisha had settled into a comfortable relationship, where Garth's daughters loved and trusted her, felt she was a part of the family. It was a mutual admiration society. Garth believed the time was right.

And so, during the spring of 2005, while he was driving with his three girls, he asked them how they would feel about his proposing to Trisha. "What took you so long, Dad?" Taylor said, laughing. In May, Garth got on one knee and proposed to Trisha onstage. The occasion was the unveiling at Buck Owens's Crystal Palace in Bakersfield, California, of the Legends in Bronze, a sculpture garden honoring Garth and eight other country artists. Garth was in good company. The other statues included were likenesses of Johnny Cash, Elvis Presley, Hank Williams, Willie Nelson, Buck Owens, Merle Haggard, George Jones, and George Strait. A visibly flustered Trisha happily and tearfully accepted his proposal.

"I'm definitely getting the best of this deal." Garth laughed.

But just four months after the proposal another tragedy occurred. Trisha had just arrived in New York for a *Redbook* magazine Mothers and Shakers Award luncheon, when her manager, Ken Levitan, gave her the news that her father had passed away. Jack Yearwood died suddenly of a heart attack on September 20, 2005, at age seventy-two. Shattered, Trisha rushed home to Georgia. Like the Brooks family, the Yearwoods were incredibly close. Second only to his concern for Trisha, Garth's consideration turned to Trisha's mother, Gwen Yearwood.

"I told Trisha that the loss of her father would only be a part of what she'd miss," Garth said. "She'd miss something in her mother. When two people are as close as my parents were, as Trisha's parents were, the death of one leaves a hole in the other. You have to take care of your own grief, but you also have to be aware of what your living parent is going through and try to help with as much support as you can give."

Garth and Trisha married on Saturday, December 10, 2005, in a ceremony at Garth's Oklahoma farm that included Taylor, August, and Allie also exchanging rings with Trisha. "This was a family wedding," Garth explained. "The girls were a part of everything all along the way."

Garth and Trisha keep their life with Taylor, August, and Allie private. They allow no photographers at the farm, and try to keep the girls lives very normal. They love to go tubing on the lake and ride four-wheelers around the farm. They spend much time together, taking meals together, playing games, and simply having conversations, finding out what's on everyone's mind. They have an honesty night, where everyone can speak their mind on anything they wish. One child psychologist who read about that family event called it perhaps the most important thing a parent can do, to allow children the freedom to be honest.

One thing Garth worries about is how schools have changed. As he told Hazel Smith, "We're taking the kid out of our kids. They've got so much homework. They've got so much responsibility. My thing is, 'Hey, let's not try to keep these kids up with the rest of the kids in competition. Let's see that these kids have some common sense, some fun, and let them be kids."

While both Garth and Trisha are comfortable with their stardom, they share an affection for everyday life, away from the red-carpet, microphone-in-your-face world of the glitterati. They love comfort foods, sweat suits, card games, dominoes, watching sports events on television, and kicking back on lazy Sunday afternoons. They like the fact that they can attend events where the three Brooks girls are participating and remain just another family. Some of the other parents they've met through the girls' activities have become backyard barbecue friends.

Trisha says the three girls are a continual joy to be around, that their humor keeps her laughing and their intelligence keeps her on her toes. For his part, Garth looks ahead with trepidation to the time his daughters start wanting to date. "That's because I remember being a teenage boy," he says, shaking his head.

Garth finds he's come full circle as far as listening to a wide variety of music. When he was a child, the music played in his house ranged from Hank Williams to KISS. Now, with three girls at home, he might walk through the house at any given moment and hear KJ-52, Avril Lavigne, Keith Whitley, or the Disney radio network playing. Daughter Allie, who now likes to be called by her middle name, Colleen, loves to sing. Would Garth encourage it? He wouldn't discourage it. Although he'd like each of his daughters to have what he calls "a real job," he knows that if the music pull is there, it can be unstoppable. "If any of them want to be entertainers, I'd probably tell them that they were crazy, but that I wanted them to do the best they can at whatever they choose.

"I've said that someday I want my girls' friends to say, 'Didn't your dad used to sing?'"

Garth has continued to release music and play some special-event concerts for charity. On November 28, 2006, he released *The Entertainer,* a five-DVD box set that was available at Wal-

Mart. The collection included never-before-seen footage from four of his television specials as well as fifteen video hits. His next release was *The Ultimate Hits,* three discs, thirty-six fan favorites, with the new history-making single, "More Than A Memory." Garth added a special "pink" album to the offering, with proceeds raising funds for the Susan G. Komen for the Cure foundation for breast cancer research. Trisha encouraged Garth to get involved after participating in a three-day walk for the charity. Inspired by the fact that Trisha and a group of her friends did over six hundred miles of training for the event, Garth decided to donate a portion of the proceeds of *The Ultimate Hits* to the foundation.

He had also been thinking about a way to thank Wal-Mart for its continued support. He wanted to play a show in appreciation, but remained unsure how and where that might take place. Then in 2006, he was approached about playing a show to help launch the new Sprint Center in Kansas City. Once he realized that his daughters could accompany him on the short flight to Kansas City without too much disruption, he agreed to combine the Sprint extravaganza and his Wal-Mart thank-you. As had always happened, once the concert was announced, more dates had to be added to accommodate the fans. He played nine sold-out shows in November 2007. Cable channel Great American Country filmed one show and aired it as *One Man, One City, One Night.*

In January 2008 he played a series of concerts at Staples Center in Los Angeles for the McCormick Tribune Foundation to benefit firefighters victims of the California wildfires. The *Orange County Register* described one of the shows as starting out at fever pitch and gathering momentum. The article concluded that with respect to entertainment, "There's Garth Brooks. And then there's everybody else." As she had for the Kansas City shows, Trisha Yearwood also performed, bringing the house down. There is no doubt that this duo, a fan favorite since 1990, still has the magic nearly two decades later.

Despite her marriage and new life, Trisha spent as much time as possible with family after her father's death. And during conversations about Jack Yearwood, and especially his love of cooking and neighborhood gatherings, the Yearwood family ultimately collaborated on a cookbook in his honor. In 2008, Trisha, together with her mother, Gwen, and sister, Beth, wrote *Georgia Cooking in an Oklahoma Kitchen* (Clarkson Potter), a combination cookbook and family memoir. The stories are all-American reminiscences of a Georgia childhood that involved both family and many friends. The food is primarily in the down-home category: fried chicken, breakfast casseroles, chicken pie, brownies, fruit cobbler, Jack Yearwood's famous Brunswick Stew—and a staple in both the Brooks and Yearwood histories, hamburger gravy. It's a fun read and points to something that Garth and Trisha have always had in common: a lack of pretense. When, for example, making biscuits, Trisha shrugs and says to just go for the Bisquick. Excellent advice.

In 2006 Trisha was reunited with longtime friend and former MCA Records executive Scott Borchetta. When Scott formed Big Machine Records that year, Trisha became his flagship artist. Her first album for the label was *Heaven, Heartache and the Power of Love*, a stellar collection of songs that caused *USA Today* critic Brian Mansfield to compare Trisha's soulful vocal prowess to a latter day Tammy Wynette. One song in particular had great meaning to Trisha: "Sing You Back To Me," which was for her father. When she first recorded the song, she did it strictly for her mother and sister. But as producer Garth Fundis listened to her performance, he knew it had to be included on her new record. Trisha followed her husband's advice: "Just go in there and let the horses run." The new affiliation leaves the duet album door wide open, for the first time in Garth's and Trisha's careers.

WHEN IN NASHVILLE, GARTH spends a lot of time at Jack's Tracks or visiting with close friends like Steve and Caryn

Wariner. He sees his old co-writers and musician friends. He is interested in producing records and there is no doubt that he will be back in Nashville as a power, albeit a behind-the-scenes player, very soon. He loves the music too much. Because it would involve too much time away from family, touring might have to wait a bit longer, but the music has pulled him back in. Look for a duet album. It's no secret that Garth has been looking for duets among Nashville's writing community throughout his career. The time is ripe for those songs and new ones to make an appearance. Once again, he has a cardboard box of songs, like the one he brought to Allen Reynolds in 1989. Look for a major business move. And expect Nashville to once again have the benefit of Garth's passion.

It is that passion, the fire behind Garth's love of music, that sold nearly 130 million records. First and foremost, it was his love of performing, and his ability to connect to masses of people on a one-to-one level. Fans attending his arena shows felt as close to the artist as the people sitting around at the Bluebird when this man played an acoustic set. He was able to bridge that gap. He brought country music concerts to new energy standards, seen now in so many concert tours, Tim McGraw, Kenny Chesney, and Keith Urban, to name but a few. And he did it while keeping his ticket prices affordable.

He also pumped up Nashville's writing community, bringing so many great songwriters to the attention of the industry: Kent Blazy, Kim Williams, Pat Alger, Stephanie Davis, Victoria Shaw, Jenny Yates, Benita Hill, Larry Bastian, Bryan Kennedy, Dan Roberts, Tony Arata, and others. Garth loves songs and songwriters. Even when it worked against him, as it did during the used CD controversy, Garth stood on the side of "the boys who make the noise on Sixteenth Avenue." He also greatly broadened the scope of song subjects. The material he writes ranges from western themes to tongue-in-cheek to powerful message songs no one else would touch. As a writer, few in the 1990s surpassed him.

As Edward Morris, former *Billboard* country editor and the
author of Garth's 1993 biography, *Platinum Cowboy,* reflected in
2008, "Brooks gave country music the ambition and presence
to strive for universality, to move beyond its obsession with personal relationships and to achieve instead something approaching
a practical philosophy. His songs and attitude implored people
to embrace the world because it is a place filled with small but
urgent wonders."

Garth's contribution to country music videos is equally vital.
It would have been very easy for country to slip into the pattern
of ho-hum clips with no purpose other than to remind viewers
of a single release. "The Thunder Rolls" changed all that. Garth
despised the fact that it became a huge boondoggle, but the conflict ended up opening creative doors. One need only watch the
videos included on *The Entertainer* to see just what a difference
he made.

Garth's refusal to rely on studio tricks and his insistence on
keeping things real are also important to the industry as a whole.
Time and again he kept a track even when he'd missed a note
because the emotion was right. Too often these days we hear
fans complain about the difference between an artist's live performance and what was heard on CD. In a genre where authenticity is everything, that matters.

One of the best things Garth did for Nashville is that for
which he is most often criticized. He continued in the Outlaw
tradition, and when he believed he had to, he held his record
label's feet to the fire. By paying attention to the business side
of music, he often faced reproof. He was called power hungry,
a Machiavellian marketer, and an eight-hundred-pound gorilla.
One of the charges leveled at him was that he was the "anti-
Hank," referring, of course, to the legendary Hank Williams.
And that comparison deserves some dissection.

Appropriating Hank Williams as the example of an all-
music-no-business stance is as ill informed as it is disingenuous.
For one thing, that theory makes Hank Williams sound like a

bit of a dim bulb. He was anything but. Hank Williams was competitive, a voracious reader of *Billboard* who paid close attention to what records were ahead and behind of his own. He spent hours sitting in the stands at the Louisiana Hayride, checking out other acts while they rehearsed. He paid attention to what worked for the act, and what didn't. Moreover, Williams also often spoke of himself in the third person, Ole Hank.

Crossing over? Commercialism? Hank allowed Fred Rose to doctor melodies on his songs in hopes of getting pop cuts. And let's not forget that Ole Hank sold tickets to his own wedding—at several locations. The truth of the matter is that Hank Williams tried hard to keep track of his career. He just had this drinking problem that kept distracting him. It should go without saying that not one of these factors takes anything away from Hank's musical genius. And, in fact, speaks well of his intentions.

Anti-Hank talk about any artist is insidious. Beyond the spin, it leaves the impression that taking care of business is anti-art. The numbers of musicians who have awakened to face the taxman or the bankruptcy court is legend. Johnny Cash turned around one day and found a million dollars missing. Willie Nelson learned too late about bogus tax shelters. Wynonna Judd was pulled back from financial disaster in the nick of time. Johnny Paycheck was robbed blind, and there were years that George Jones had to rely on Waylon Jennings for pocket money. Dottie West lost everything and died trying to make a few bucks for rent. Tammy Wynette faced bankruptcy. Every one of them wished they'd paid closer attention.

And make no mistake about it—Garth Brooks is a *country* artist. He has proved it in a myriad of ways, beginning with his songwriting. Unfortunately, his admission of affection for acts including Queen and KISS cost him dearly. His critics seldom remembered that country artists including Hall of Famer Faron Young leaned toward Frank Sinatra before they leapt into Webb Pierce territory. The bogus charge, *that ain't country,* has done more damage to the genre than a trainload of synthesizers.

When all is said and done, Garth proved that country music is not only a big tent, but that expansion does not necessarily mean dilution. From "The Dance" to "More Than A Memory," the music involves great songs performed with great power. There's an old theory that some people have such overwhelming personalities that when they enter a room they suck the air out of it. Most who have been involved with Garth Brooks and his career will tell you that Garth does just the opposite, he breathes energy into the room. And in a creative industry, that's a good thing.

Garth Brooks Discography

Audio

Garth Brooks, produced by Allen Reynolds, released April 12, 1989, Capitol
C2–90897

No Fences, produced by Allen Reynolds, released August 27, 1990, Capitol/
Liberty C2–93866

Ropin' the Wind, produced by Allen Reynolds, released September 2, 1991,
Capitol/Liberty 96330

Beyond the Season, produced by Allen Reynolds, released August 17, 1992,
Capitol/Liberty C2–98742

The Chase, produced by Allen Reynolds, released September 14, 1992,
Capitol/Liberty C2–98743

In Pieces, produced by Allen Reynolds, released August 31, 1993, Capitol/
Liberty C2–80857

The Garth Brooks Collection, produced by Allen Reynolds, released
September 2, 1994, Capitol/Liberty (not sold at retail)

The Hits, produced by Allen Reynolds, released December 13, 1994,
Capitol/Liberty [29689]

Fresh Horses, produced by Allen Reynolds, released November 21, 1995,
Capitol 32080

Sevens, produced by Allen Reynolds, released November 25, 1997, Capitol
56599

The Limited Series (Box set: *Garth Brooks, No Fences, Ropin' the Wind, The
Chase, In Pieces,* and *Fresh Horses* with a new bonus track on each CD),
produced by Allen Reynolds, Released May 5, 1998, Capitol [Special
edition BC 724349457225]

Garth Brooks Double Live (Available in five 1-million-copy limited-edition
two-CD sets: *The First Edition, Central Park, Dublin, Ireland, World Tour
II (96–98), Texas Stadium 1993, Reunion Arena 1991,* and *World Tour I
(93–94)*), produced by Allen Reynolds, released November 17, 1998,
Capitol 97424

Garth Brooks in . . . the Life of Chris Gaines, produced by Don Was, released
September 28, 1999, Capitol 20051

Garth Brooks & the Magic of Christmas, produced by Allen Reynolds, released
November 23, 1999, Capitol 23550

Scarecrow, produced by Allen Reynolds, released November 13, 2001, Capitol
31330

Garth Brooks: The Limited Series (Box set: *Sevens, Scarecrow, Double Live,* and
The Lost Sessions), produced by Allen Reynolds, released November 22,
2005, Wal-Mart#005541737, UPC: 0085420600101

Video

Garth Brooks: Ultimate Hits, produced by Allen Reynolds, released August 21,
2007, Pearl Records

The Entertainer (Five-DVD box set: *This Is Garth Brooks 1992, This Is Garth
Brooks, Too! 1994, Garth Live from Central Park 1997, Ireland and Back
1998*), Wal-Mart #00000000, UPC: 0085420600120

Music Videos

"If Tomorrow Never Comes"
"The Dance"
"The Thunder Rolls"
"We Shall Be Free"
"Standing Outside The Fire"
"Callin' Baton Rouge"
"The Red Strokes"
"Ain't Going Down (Til The Sun Comes Up)"
"The Change"
"I Don't Have To Wonder"
"Anonymous"
"Tearin' It Up (And Burnin' It Down)"
"When You Come Back To Me Again"
"Wrapped Up In You"
"Good Ride Cowboy"

Sources

Chapter One

[Garth heard several other public figures admit that fear was an incentive.] *San Antonio-Express News,* April 14, 1998.

["If that guy's playing for twenty people I don't have any business being here."] Peter Cooper, *The Tennessean,* November 13, 2001.

[When they married they had one immediate mission] Colleen Brooks interview with David Huff, *In Country,* September 1993.

["You know, my mother didn't want] Author conversation with Colleen Brooks. May 1996. Additional early family information from Colleen Brooks interview with David Huff, *In Country,* September 1993.

[Garth remembers Colleen being the biggest kid in the family when it came to Christmas] Margy Holland, Launch.com, November 11, 2001.

["Dad's always been one of those your-word-is-your-bond men. I took that to heart."] Author conversation with the artist.

[My mother is the best female singer] Author conversation with the artist.

["It's a song I lived indirectly,"] Author conversation with the artist.

["After school he'd bring special children home with him,"] David Huff, *In Country,* September 1993.

[Garth never got over this early love of sports.] KNIX newscast, 1992.

["One of the greatest things I got from my dad was an appreciation of the importance of team work,"] Author conversation with the artist.

[Raymond Brooks once told a story about Kelly and Garth.] Interview with the *Believer*'s Tami Rose, 1993. (The *Believer* was Garth's official fan publication, founded and edited by Tami Rose.)

["She was probably one of my greatest friends"] Author conversation with the artist.

["The country lyric is everyday life"] *Country Fever,* August 1992.

[England disputes that Garth learned anything from him] Author conversation with Ty England.

["If I'd been a female country singer, I would have wanted to sound like Tammy Wynette."] MJI Broadcasting/Country Today, April 10, 1998.

["That's pretty good," his friend Randy Taylor said during the break] Author conversation with the artist.

[Garth stayed with an Oklahoma songwriter named Bob Childers] Edward Morris, *Garth Brooks: Platinum Cowboy* (New York: St. Martin's Press, 1993).

[Garth later admitted that he had a similar reaction as when in 1985 he sat in Merlin Littlefield's office and heard a well-known songwriter say he was broke] *The Tennessean,* Peter Cooper, November 13, 2001.

Chapter Two

["I don't pay that much attention to the tracks," Harlen mused.] Author conversation with Harlan Howard, 1987.

["It was five guys with five different] Lisa Smith, *Gavin Report,* July 27, 1990.

[The *Houston Post*'s venerable pop music critic Bob Claypool] Bob Claypool, *Saturday Night at Gilleys* (New York, Delilah/Grove Press, 1980).

[Nashville didn't learn] Author conversation with Chet Atkins, 1988.

[As Bowen often laughed] Jimmy Bowen and Jim Jerome. *Rough Mix* (New York: Simon & Schuster, 1997).

Chapter Three

["What's the secret"] Author conversation with the artist, 2000.

[When Garth sang the line, "Uncle Joe, you know we owe it to you," it was in tribute to Joe Harris] Author conversation with the artist, 1995.

["I was lucky that the people I found in those first couple of years were on the side of writers, artists, and musicians,"] Author conversation with the artist, 2000.

["What makes that song great is that it's universal," Doyle says.] Author conversation with Bob Doyle, 2008. Includes additional comments regarding Garth's early career.

["Bob's one of the town's honest brokers."] Author conversation with publisher Noel Fox, 1995.

[California writer Larry Bastian was among the first to co-write with Garth] Author conversation with Larry Bastian, 2005.

[One song plugger at MCA Music tried unsuccessfully to interest his biggest writers in scheduling a co-write] Author conversation, 2008.

[Kent Blazy was the first writer who'd had a top-10 cut who agreed to collaborate with Garth] Author conversation with Kent Blazy, 2005.

[That idea was "If Tomorrow Never Comes," a song involving a concept
    Garth's mother often spoke about.] Author conversation with the artist,
    1990.
["Listening to Trisha sing those first few times was a blessing and a curse,"
    Garth laughed.] Author conversation with the artist, 2000.
["That's where you hear the best songs," Garth says.] Author conversation
    with the artist, 1990.
[Bryan Kennedy was scouting for songs at the Bluebird one night when he
    heard a voice that he said knocked him on his rear.] Author conversation
    with Bryan Kennedy, 2005.
["Everything changed for me," Lynn later said.] Author conversation with
    Lynn Shults, 1991.
["The genius of Allen Reynolds is that his records have a timeless quality to
    them," Bob said.] Author conversation with Bob Doyle, 2008.
["I finally said to myself, 'I'm gonna stay right here on this corner and make
    the best music I can,] Author conversation with Allen Reynolds, 2008.
["There's an angel missing in heaven and his name is Allen Reynolds," Garth
    confided] Author conversation with the artist, 1990.
["Garth likes his music to kick] *Country Guitar,* April 1995.

Chapter Four

["I think every song on an album should be a song of consequence,"] Author
    conversation with Allen Reynolds, 2008.
["I'd been writing as much as possible, but didn't want to overload the
    album with my own material. No more than five songs, for sure,"
    Garth explained] Author conversation with the artist, 1990.
[Mark Casstevens talked about the importance of being] *Country Guitar,*
    April 1995.
["I watched his hands to"] *Country Guitar,* April 1995.
["Allen told me he wanted Bobby Woods, a writer and keyboard player, to
    be heavily featured on the song," Garth recalled.] Author conversation
    with the artist, 1990.
[What Garth insisted on, according to Ty] Author conversation with
    Ty England, 2000.
["I was over at Bob Doyle's when Larry Bastian played me that song,"]
    Conversations with the artist include all comments on the songs included
    on *Garth Brooks,* 1990.
[In 1995, *Billboard* editor Edward Morris wrote: "History lesson:] Also
    included in Edward Morris, *Garth Brooks: Platinum Cowboy* (New York:
    St. Martin's Press, 1993).
["I'm laying there in a fetal position saying,"] *Orange County Register,*
    December 13, 1994.

["I was driving my truck from Kaycee to Casper," recalled Chris LeDoux]
    Author conversation with Chris LeDoux, 1993.

["It's a lot like the West itself. It's wide-open spaces and big skies] Author
    conversation with Chris LeDoux, 1993, included in LeDoux box set
    liner notes.

["I had cold feet. I had faith in Garth, but I never had faith in myself.]
    Ty England interview with the *Believer*'s Tami Rose.

["The guys need to work, they need to eat," Garth said.] Joe Harris
    conversations are from interviews with the *Believer*'s Tami Rose.

[A good example of how the relationship between divisions ought to work
    involves Nashville executive Randy Goodman] Author conversation
    with Randy Goodman, 1997.

["Class of '89," Hat Acts. Garth Brooks, for one, hated the term, thinking it
    stereotyped] Author conversation with the artist, 1990.

["Kenny treated his opening acts with great respect," reflects Bob Doyle.]
    Author conversation with Bob Doyle, 2008.

[If Garth thought his mother would stay out of this fray, he was wrong.]
    Colleen Brooks interview with David Huff, *In Country,* September 1993.

Chapter Five

[Lynn Shults pulled into a parking space] All Lynn Shults comments from
    author conversations with Shults, 1990–1993.

[Bowen had moved from L.A. to Nashville in the late 1970s] Bowen's early
    days in Nashville are chronicled by Jimmy Bowen and Jim Jerome in
    Rough Mix (New York: Simon & Schuster, 1997).

[As a label head Bowen had been accused of everything from kickbacks and
    double billing to publishing conflicts of interest.] Bob Allen, "Jimmy
    Bowen Is the Most Respected/Reviled Man on Music Row," *Country
    Music Journal,* vol. 13, no. 3.

[Bowen approached Allen Reynolds at a party hosted by Waylon Jennings.]
    Author conversation with Allen Reynolds, 2008.

[When word reached Garth, he was shaken] Author conversation with the
    artist, 1990.

[Two days after the takeover Bowen phoned Reynolds and asked for a meet-
    ing.] Author conversation with Allen Reynolds, 2008.

[On one elevator ride, he stood next to Muhammad Ali and confessed that
    he could barely catch his breath.] Interview with Robert K. Oermann,
    Capitol electronic press kit (EPK), 1990.

["Pam and I did everything we could to get Garth known," Bob Doyle
    laughs.] Author conversation with Bob Doyle, 2008.

["I give Jimmy Bowen a lot of credit for the free hand he gave me when it

came to marketing Garth," Mansfield said.] Author conversation with
Joe Mansfield, 2008.

["So much great music has been forgotten because labels either didn't give
them the attention they needed or shelved them for the *next thing*," Garth
explained.] Author conversation with the artist, 1995.

[Nobody was happier about Bowen hiring Mansfield than Bob Doyle.]
Author conversation with Bob Doyle, 2008.

["I decided very early that I wanted to make videos with a third dimension,"
Garth said.] Artist promotional materials, 1990.

["I'd never compare myself to these people," Garth said.] Video content and
promotion EPK, 1990.

[In fact, when Jim died in 1982, there was a period of about six months that
I don't even recall happening] Interview with Robert K. Oermann,
Capitol EPK, 1990.

[Bowen described the meeting, where, he explains he gave him some straight
advice.] Jimmy Bowen and Jim Jerome, *Rough Mix* (New York: Simon &
Schuster, 1997).

Chapter Six

[In the summer of 1990, the *Winston Cup Illustrated*'s Tom Higgins]
NASCAR Winston Cup Illustrated, November 1998.

[Stephanie Davis was already sick of hearing about Garth Brooks when she
first met him.] Stephanie Davis interview with the *Believer*'s Tami Rose.

[When Willie didn't cut "Wolves," fellow outlaw Waylon Jennings decided
he wanted to record it, only to learn about Garth's cut.] Author conversation with Waylon Jennings, 1991.

["It's true," Ty says. "Garth anticipated what was going to happen.] Author
conversation with Ty England, 2000.

["DeWayne always needed money," Larry laughed.] Author conversation
with Larry Bastian, 2005.

["Don't worry about it," Lee laughed. "I've got friends in low places."]
Author conversation with Bud Lee, 1992.

[Chris Leuzinger played the second part, although it wasn't credited on the
album, Mark Casstevens said.] *Country Guitar,* April 1995.

["One of the things I'm most proud of in my writing career is Garth's cut of
'Two Of A Kind,'" he told a Nashville journalist.] Author conversation
with Warren Haynes, 1994.

["I was in the studio that day and had my 1979 Martin M-36,"] *Country
Guitar,* April 1995.

[Bowen described a scene of Joe Mansfield analyzing the sales trends] Jimmy
Bowen and Jim Jerome, *Rough Mix* (New York: Simon & Schuster,
1997).

Chapter Seven

[It was May 1, and Capitol's head of public relations, Cathy Gurley, was thrilled with the media cards she'd been dealt.] Author conversation with Cathy Gurley, 2008.
[Later that day TNN issued a statement] *USA Today,* May 2, 1991.
["He felt the script they gave him was in effect, pandering] Author conversation with Cathy Gurley, 2008.
[Garth and Cathy went to TNN] Author conversation with Cathy Gurley, 2008.
[WSIX in Nashville ran the video at the Wrangler] Sandy Neese and Robert K. Oermann, *The Tennessean,* May 7, 1991.
[". . . country music has a real shot to delve into some social commentary] Loretta Macias, *San Angelo Standard Times,* May 10, 1991.
["Even a cursory examination of Brooks' phenomenal output of monster songs] Paul Johnson, *Arkansas Gazette,* May 4, 1991.
[By Thursday, May 7, when VH-1 announced that the pop channel] Sandy Neese and Robert K. Oermann, *The Tennessean,* May 7, 1991.
[For example, the Genesis Shelter in Dallas] Letter from Jan Langbein, executive director, Genesis Shelter, May 22, 1991.
[Manager Pam Lewis agreed, saying] The Associated Press, May 2, 1991.

Chapter Eight

[Garth felt that the most important promise he had made was to open shows for Naomi and Wynonna Judd for what would be their Farewell Tour through 1991.] Author conversation with the artist, 1991.
[Throughout early 1990 Naomi had felt sick, to the point that she could barely get to the studio to sing her harmony parts for the album *Love Can Build a Bridge.*] Author conversations with Wynonna Judd, for her memoir, *Coming Home to Myself.*
[Trisha talked about making the tabloids with *Country Fever* editor Linda Cauthen] *Country Fever,* August 1992.
[The tour got across-the-board raves.] Michael McCall, *Country Music,* January/February, 1992.
["We invited representatives from every organization, publishing company and record label,"] Author conversation with Cathy Gurley, 2008.
[Publisher Ross and journalist Brian Mansfield interviewed Joe Mansfield] David Ross and Brian Mansfield, "The Six Million Pieces Man," *Music Row,* July 1991.
["Hell Frank," one said. "Randy *Travis* is too country for me these days."] Author conversation with Frank Leffell, 1989.
[the memory of how "Friends In Low Places" had threatened to overshadow "Unanswered Prayers," kept Garth up at night over one of his favorite

songs on the album, "What She's Doing Now."] Author conversation
with the artist, 2005.

[Garth's co-writer, Kim Williams, laughed when he thought back to the
"Papa Loved Mama" writing sessions:] Kim Williams interview with the
Believer's Tami Rose.

["Papa Loves Mama" features a blistering lap steel solo] *Country Guitar,* April
1995.

[In late 1990, Bowen had offered him a bump in royalties] Jimmy Bowen
and Jim Jerome, *Rough Mix* (New York, Simon & Schuster, 1997).

[*Fortune*'s analysis of his business style] *Fortune* magazine, May 24, 1999.
[Ultimately, EMI offered Bowen an astonishing five-year deal.] Jimmy
Bowen and Jim Jerome, *Rough Mix* (New York: Simon & Schuster,
1997).

["I did that simply because I couldn't expect somebody to stand up and
ask for what I thought was right," he said.] Ed Ochs, *Music Business
International,* June 1994.

Chapter Nine

[Garth sat there for a moment, laughing. He knew just how they felt.]
Author conversation with the artist, 1992.

["I loved the idea," he said later. "*Loved it!* I mean, to get the chance to put
our show on TV? Who wouldn't? But, and it was a very *big* 'but,' it was a
scary idea to think people would tune in."] Author conversation with the
artist, 1992.

[In hindsight, Garth said his biggest regret was that he hadn't secured the
flawed guitars well in advance.] Author conversation with the artist,
1992.

[Garth explained his feelings to *Country Fever*'s Frank Barron: "I've gotta be
honest. I'm] *Country Fever,* August 1992.

[gauntlet that *Forbes* inadvertently threw down] *Forbes,* March 2, 1992.

[*USA Today*'s country critic, David Zimmerman] Zimmerman and Edward
Morris responses are from Morris's *Garth Brooks: Platinum Cowboy* (New
York: St. Martin's Press, 1993).

Chapter Ten

[As a high school and college student] Author conversation with the artist,
1993.

[The concert season of 1992 was a "big bucks summer,"] Buddy Lee
Attractions president Tony Conway, *Nashville Business Journal,*
June 29, 1992.

["It was a year of records for New York State Fair] Brian Bourke, *The Post-
Standard,* September 8, 1992.

[205,000 attempted calls were logged through Boise Idaho's call switching center.] *Idaho Statesman,* April 23, 1992.

[The December 4 show at Thompson-Boling Arena in Knoxville, Tennessee sold 25,501 tickets. When Lynyrd Skynyrd played a free concert at Thompson-Boling in 2002, it brought out 17,400 to the show, still not breaking Garth's record.] Wayne Bledsoe, *Knoxville News-Sentinel,* May 29, 2002.

[After reports of $100-plus scalped tickets being offered at the New York State Fairgrounds, the State's Attorney General's office began looking into the problem.] Jacqueline Arnold, *The Post-Standard,* July 1, 1992.

["The country singer is the hottest commodity in creation, and his success was part of the Forum ceremony, which was less a concert than a community celebration."] Richard Cromelin, *Los Angeles Times,* July 20, 1992.

[While other artists made far more money per sale, Garth moved more merchandise.] Author conversation with Rondal Richardson, 2005.

[Garth had been thinking about a second NBC show even before his debut special first aired in January 1992.] Author conversation with Joe Mansfield, 2008.

[On June 12, Texas Stadium sold out in 92 minutes, selling over 65,000 tickets and breaking the previous sales record held by Paul McCartney. Dallas fans demanded and got more shows: a second show sold 65,000 tickets in 92 minutes, as did a third.] Capitol Records archives, *This Is Garth Brooks, Too!*

["Every time I worked with Garth he first sat down and told me his basic idea.] Author conversation with Jon Small, 2006.

[*This Is Garth Brooks Too!* took 40,000-plus man hours to produce, with 60 semitractor-trailers bringing in the equipment.] Author conversation with Jon Small, 2006.

["[Garth] has already studied all 450,000 feet of film shot from the 14 cameras.] Skip Hollandsworth, *TV Guide,* April 30, 1994.

Chapter Eleven

[Billy Ray Cyrus intro story] From an author conversation with a Mercury VP, 2000.

[Between 1989 and 1992 country radio went from 1,800 to 2,400 stations, with more people with incomes of over $40,000 listening to country than any other format. Country was generating over a billion in annual revenue.] CMA year wrap-up.

[Once the two saw him live, they were sold.] Author conversation with Harold Shedd, 1992.

[Tritt then spouted off on country radio about "ass wiggling," leading his
friend Marty Stuart to quip, "Travis, you couldn't have opened a bigger
can of worms if you'd said Roy Acuff was gay."] Author conversation
with Marty Stuart, 1992.

[Of course, the truth was that Jonie was herself a good old Texas girl from
Houston, and just happened to help Clint with media advice.] Author
conversation with Lisa's Hartman's sister, Terri Hartman, 1993.

[Critic Karen Schumer called it, ". . . nothing less than a concept
album about the meaning of country music."] Karen Schumer, "Marty
Stuart," *Country on Compact Disc: The Essential Guide to Country Music,*
edited by Paul Kingsbury, Country Music Foundation (New York:
Grove Press, 1993).

[Critic and music historian Robert K. Oermann called the record
". . . as close to perfect a country album as anything released during
1992."] Robert K. Oermann, "Mark Chesnutt," *Country on Compact
Disc: The Essential Guide to Country Music,* edited by Paul Kingsbury,
Country Music Foundation (New York: Grove Press, 1993).

[it took the band's management borrowing a page from Doyle/Lewis's
play book when they hired an independent team to rescue the record.]
Author conversation with Sawyer Brown manager TK Kimbrell, 1991.

[When presenter Roy Rogers announced the CMA win, journalists
sitting in the press room at the Grand Ole Opry House leapt to their
feet and applauded.] Author conversation with Robert K. Oermann,
1991.

[Once Garth introduced Joe Mansfield to Chris's music, the marketing VP
became a big fan and made Jimmy Bowen aware of the $4 million in
tapes sold from the back of the LeDoux truck.] Author conversation with
Joe Mansfield, 2008.

[It was perfect timing for Chris, who was experiencing tough financial
times.] Author conversation with Chris LeDoux, 1993.

["Might just be a touch of hepatitis," he was told. Probably nothing to worry
about.] Author interview with Chris LeDoux, 2000.

Chapter Twelve

[Stephanie Davis sat on a grassy hill on Garth's farm outside Nashville.]
Author conversation with the artist, 1993.

["It is impossible now to underestimate the impact of *Stranger*] Chet Flippo,
"Willie Nelson," *Country on Compact Disc: The Essential Guide to Country
Music,* edited by Paul Kingsbury, Country Music Foundation (New
York: Grove Press, 1993).

[Comments beginning with: Garth says his way of looking at albums] Author
conversation with the artist regarding the making of *The Chase,* 1992.

["I wrote 'Face To Face' in 1987 or 1988," Tony recalls.] Conversation with the *Believer*'s Tami Rose.

[Co-writer Kent Blazy didn't think it stood a chance in hell of getting airplay.] Author conversation with Kent Blazy, 2006.

[Stephanie wasn't so sure.] Conversation with the *Believer*'s Tami Rose.

["I embarrassed myself," he told a friend soon after the appearance.] Author conversation with the artist, 1992.

[Several years later, Gary Graff asked Garth if he regretted speaking out] *Country Song Roundup,* April 1996.

[Bowen blamed Garth for making a somber record and for being too candid on television shows] Jimmy Bowen and Jim Jerome, *Rough Mix* (New York: Simon & Schuster, 1997).

[But at a Gus Hardin concert in Nashville, Betsy told a table of journalists that the whole furor was a joke] Author conversation with Betsy Smittle, 1993.

["I told him that when he was talking to the press he shouldn't *offer* anybody anything,"] Colleen Brooks talking to David Huff, *In Country,* September 1993.

[The label head had developed an intense dislike for some of Garth's representatives] Jimmy Bowen and Jim Jerome, *Rough Mix* (New York: Simon & Schuster, 1997).

["There's bound to be issues between artists and the people who run the record labels," Doyle reflects.] Author conversation with Bob Doyle, 2008.

["I'm afraid that all these sales and awards are getting in the way of the music," he said.] Author conversation with the artist, 2003.

Chapter Thirteen

[Kim Williams asked Garth what it felt like to be on top of the mountain.] Conversation with the *Believer*'s Tami Rose.

["I loved the thought of heading back to one of those honky tonks," Garth later said.] Author conversation with the artist, 1994.

[He even started using what he called the "Shorty's bar" test] Author conversation with the artist, 1993.

[One worry Sandy had was that her "rocking schedule" with Taylor would by necessity change with an infant in the house.] Conversation with the *Believer*'s Tami Rose.

[She found co-writing somewhat difficult until she started collaborating with Garth.] Conversation with the *Believer*'s Tami Rose.

["That experience may be one of the biggest things that ever happened throughout my career," he later confided.] Author conversation with the artist, 1993.

[Since starting his career Garth's business sense had sharpened, and
    Raymond credited that to using the tools from his college years.]
    Conversations with the *Believer*'s Tami Rose.
[Garth confessed that much of his time during the world tour was spent in
    search of food] Garth report to the Country Music Association, 1993.
["Having a second child is an eye opener," he later told friends at Jack's
    Tracks] Author conversation with the artist, 1994.
[One leg of the tour lost money, but it was not unexpected] KNIX,
    May 1996.
["I couldn't believe it when Garth called and said he wanted Dan Roberts
    and me to open a show that important!"] Author conversation with
    Bryan Kennedy, 2006.

Chapter Fourteen
["Well," he thought, "this attention-grabber is going to kill me."] Author
    conversation with the artist, 2005.
["We titled this album *In Pieces* because that's pretty much how it came
    together," Garth said at the time.] Author conversations with the artist
    regarding *In Pieces,* 1994.
[writing at Kent Blazy's new house, which Blazy laughingly referred to as "a
    real fixer-upper."] Author conversation with Kent Blazy, 2006.
[One of the reasons Kim Williams loved working with Garth was
    because of his melodies] Conversation with the *Believer*'s Tami Rose.
["Every so often, Garth would call and talk about video, and say, 'We'll
    work together one of these days,' " Small said.] Author conversation with
    Jon Small, 2006.
[*In Pieces* shipped fewer than expected] Jimmy Bowen and Jim Jerome, *Rough
    Mix* (New York: Simon & Schuster, 1997).
["I don't understand this idea of, *just throw it against the wall and see if it sticks,"*
    Garth confided.] Author conversation with the artist, 1995.
[And during one encounter with Garth, Bowen said, "Just go fix the damned
    music."] Jimmy Bowen and Jim Jerome, *Rough Mix* (New York: Simon
    & Schuster, 1997).
[Bowen respected Koppelman's love of music, but remained skeptical of his
    relationship with Jim Fifield] Jimmy Bowen and Jim Jerome, *Rough Mix*
    (New York: Simon & Schuster, 1997).
["For me, sales mean people are hearing your music, that somebody is being
    affected by it."] Author conversation with the artist, 1994.
["To say I carried a grudge because Bowen turned me down in 1988 makes no
    sense," Garth said to a friend.] Author conversation with the artist, 1994.
[To the end Garth continued to give Bowen credit when he spoke publicly.]
    Interview given before Bowen left Capitol, *Country Song Roundup,* April 1996.

Chapter Fifteen

["This is insane," Reynolds said.] Author conversation with Allen Reynolds, 1995.

[On March 10, he officially became the fastest-selling artist of all-time] RIAA certified.

["It's fun to see numbers and all that," he confided. "I'd be lying if I said anything else.] Author conversation with the artist, 1995.

[This album was moving full circle, back to the more straightforward country of Garth's debut.] Author conversations with the artist about songs on *Fresh Horses,* 1995.

["There's a lot of rodeo and cowboy culture in *Fresh Horses,*"] Author conversations with Allen Reynolds regarding *Fresh Horses,* 1995.

[When asked about the title, Garth explained: "It's all about giving] Andrew Vaghn, *Country Music International,* January 1996.

Chapter Sixteen

["I guess we can work with it."] Comment made to author, 1995.

[During their first meeting, Scott Hendricks told Garth two things] Author conversation with Joe Mansfield, 2008.

[The only song in the collection that Hendricks perceived as having radio potential was "Beaches Of Cheyenne."] Author conversation with Joe Mansfield, 2008.

[A few years down the line "Fever" would gain two very passionate fans: Garth's daughters, Taylor and August.] *Country Song Roundup,* December 1996.

[One artist who offered insight into Garth's dilemma was Gary Morris] Author conversation with Gary Morris, 1995.

[In an effort to pull the new and old staff together Hendricks decided to hold an all-employee weekend at Tims Ford Lake near Winchester, Tennessee.] Author was in attendance.

[In some meetings it became obvious that the record label was counting on her best-selling memoir, *Nickel Dreams,* and the marketing prowess of its publisher Hyperion, to pick up Capitol's slack.] Author was in attendance.

[From the time the new team came on board there was a split between the old and the new.] Author conversation with Capitol promotion VP, 2008.

Chapter Seventeen

["Who the shit is paying for all this?"] Story told by the artist in several instances, including conversation with the author in 1996.

["Did you ever see Rod Stewart's show when he was having a three piece
bagpipe group open for him?" Garth asked a friend] Author conversation
with the artist, 1996.

["Debbie came in and whipped the hell out of all the boys"] *Country Song
Roundup,* December 1996.

["I thought I was dreaming when they called my name,"] Author conversation with the artist, 1996.

["Like, when Taylor leaves half a sandwich on the plate, I start thinking]
Lorrie Lynch, *USA Weekend,* December 20, 1995.

[Just a year later Garth and Sandy were with the girls] *Linedancer,* June 1997.

[Garth said, "People are telling me that if we have two more, I'll have a basketball team!"] Author conversation with the artist, 1996.

Chapter Eighteen

["Central Park is under the jurisdiction of four or five various police and fire
departments, each one dealing with separate areas—that's even before
you get to the various divisions of the Parks Department," Small ruefully
reported.] Author conversation with Jon Small, 2006.

["How do you repay a guy like that? You work hard for him."] *Press
Enterprise,* November 17, 1998, Riverside, Calif.

[The corporate changes had begun in 1996] *Fortune,* May 24, 1999.

[He spoke at length with Ben Fong-Torres] *Gavin Report,* July 4, 1997.

["People thought I wrote most of the album," Garth said.] Author
conversation with the artist covering the songs on *Sevens,* 1997.

[Garth talked to *Country Weekly* about the subject] *Country Weekly,*
November 18, 1997.

["Not so fast. I hear this for Garth."] Author conversation with Sandy
Mason, 1997.

[Benita paid off her credit cards.] Author conversation with Benita Hill, 1997.

["*Sevens* has become my favorite album," Garth said] Author conversation
with the artist, 2005.

Chapter Nineteen

["I know people believe that I'm some kind of a puppet master behind the
scenes," Garth confided.] Author conversation with the artist, 1997.

["Jim made corporate decisions—EMI decisions,"] Author conversation with
Fifield associate, 2008.

[That's typical record label bullshit.] Author conversation with Steve
Popovich, 2008.

[But, as Garth told Tamara Saviano: "Trisha said, 'I'll trade the money for
the] *Country Weekly,* November 17, 1998.

["I'll pay five hundred dollars in cash to anybody who can knock me down
on stage tonight," Garth announced.] Author conversation with the
artist, 1994.

["He's always been a great drummer,"] Author conversations about the band
and *Double Live,* 1999.

["We went and found where people got pin-dropping quiet during the ballads, where they sang 'Unanswered Prayers' the loudest and where it was
absolute chaos during the rowdy stuff,"] Glenn Gamboa, *Akron Beacon
Journal,* November 15, 1998.

[The *Buffalo News* named *Double Live* one of the best albums released in
1998] Dan Herbeck, *The Buffalo News,* December 31, 1998.

[The reason Benita questioned showing Garth this song was because she
knew that Colleen Brooks was very sick] Author conversation with
Benita Hill, 1999.

["My mother always told me I could fly," Garth said. "And I believed her."]
Country Grapevine, December 1998.

["I sometimes worry that people think we are just in the recording business,
where too often it's about the latest technology.] Author conversation
with Bob Doyle, 2008.

[Ray Waddell provided the wrap-up to the unprecedented three-year tour]
Amusement Business, November 16, 1998.

["They traded ten years of their lives to chase my dream," he explained]
Sandi Davis, *Daily Oklahoman,* November 13, 1998.

["The deejays he met with didn't make an issue out of his statements] Author
conversation with Terry Stevens, 2008.

["Thank God there are still crazy people] *Los Angeles Times,* Sunday,
March 3, 1996.

Chapter Twenty

["Wayne and I were recording some of our songs, trying to get a pop music
deal,"] Author conversation with Gordon Kennedy, 2008.

["Now I'm just praying that people 'get it.'"] Author conversation with the
artist, 1999.

[Neil Strauss couldn't get around the fact that Garth often referred to himself
as GB.] *The New York Times,* December 2, 1999.

[Still another speculated that the entire Chris Gaines project was Garth's
payback because the Backstreet Boys had beat out his record for single-
week sales of the previous year's *Double Live.*] Renee Graham, *The Boston
Globe,* August 14, 1999.

["He's even handing out a bio re-creating himself as a brilliant rock icon."]
Miriam Longino, *The Atlanta Constitution,* July 28, 1999.

["For the album cover, Mr. Brooks, the balding country superstar, put on a tousled] Frank DeCaro, "Split Personalities Can Be Better Than One," *The New York Times,* October 17, 1999.

["Country for me in Manhattan was the Hamptons,"] Neil Strauss, *The New York Times,* October 30, 1999.

[And you couldn't argue with success] Neil Strauss, *The New York Times,* October 30, 1999.

[When Pat Quigley left Capitol the following year, *Billboard* asked Garth about that meeting he'd called with the label's staff.] Melinda Newman, *Billboard,* October 14, 2000.

Chapter Twenty-one

["I had such good parents," he went on. "And I worry about how I'm doing in the job."] Author conversation with the artist, 2000.

["I want them to dare to fly, to make stupid mistakes and learn from them. I want them to be foolish, and I want them to be responsible. Life only goes by once. Let's rip it up!"] *Country Grapevine,* December 1998.

["The announcement certainly didn't come as a surprise to me,"] Author conversation with Terry Stevens, 2008.

[Ed Benson, executive director of the Country Music Association, told the *Tennessean:* "Somebody's got to wake up in the morning on Music Row and] *The Tennessean,* December 20, 1999.

["This had to happen," Benson had said] Author conversation with Ray Benson, 1993.

[Frequent collaborator Victoria Shaw] Tom Roland, *The Tennessean,* December 16, 1999.

["No one would have predicted Garth's huge success] Jay Orr and Tom Rowland, *The Tennessean,* December 26, 1999.

["Nobody ever tried to stay married more than Garth did,"] Author conversation with Allen Reynolds, 2008.

[Teammates for Kids, still located in the Denver suburb] For up-to-date information about Teammates for Kids, visit www.Teammates4Kids.com.

[Lisa spoke to *Entertainment Weekly*'s Chris Willman] Chris Willman, *Entertainment Weekly,* April 14, 2000.

["Songwriting brought me to the music industry in the first place] Author conversation with Allen Reynolds, 2000.

["Right now, we're focusing on the impact it will have on the children, and how to handle that.] Melinda Newman, *Billboard,* October 14, 2000.

["She said, 'Be sure you know who's willing to ride shotgun and who's just along for the ride.' "] Author conversation with the artist, 2000.

Chapter Twenty-two

["The song you're looking for is on the tape you haven't listened to yet."]
Author conversation with the artist, 2001.

["I heard songs I thought would be smashes for half the artists in town,"
Garth laughed.] Author conversation with the artist about the music and
songs on *Scarecrow,* 2001.

[This time those emotions ran the gamut,] Author conversation with Allen
Reynolds, 2001.

[Shawn Camp, who wrote "Big Money" with Randy] Author conversation
with Shawn Camp, 2006.

["There won't be a person in the world that doesn't know there's a new
Garth Brooks out,"] Mike Dungan interview with *Billboard,*
November 3, 2001.

[He put talking about his music on the back burner.] Author conversation
with the artist, 2001.

Epilogue

[Garth has sold an additional 28 million records.] RIAA figures.

["After Scarecrow was released, I had a long talk with Garth,"] Author conversation with Allen Reynolds, 2008.

[He was especially proud of Girls Night Out] Author conversation with the
artist, 2002.

["I'd give anything to hear Garth say he was consumed with songwriting
again,"] Author conversation with Allen Reynolds, 2008.

[In fact, between 2002 and 2005, country music was in a state of flux.] CMA
wrap-up.

[that in February 2002 the major website devoted to the artist's news and
history] PlanetGarth.com.

["He blends right in, moving from field to field," Royals VO David Witty]
The Kansas City Star, February 27, 2004.

[After he started thinking about it, Garth realized that there was one period
of time especially, that he'd recorded a wealth of material] Author conversation with the artist about assembling the songs for *The Lost Sessions,*
2005.

[Bob Doyle had come up with the idea after reading Chris's biography]
David G. Brown, *Gold Buckle Dreams: The Rodeo Life of Chris LeDoux*
(Wolverine, 1989).

[At the time of its release, Garth said] Jonathon Cohen, *Billboard,*
November 11, 2005.

[Hazel Smith, the woman who, while working with Waylon and Tompall
Glaser, coined the term The Outlaw Movement.] Hazel Smith,
CMT.com, November 2005.

[And so, during the spring of 2005, while he was driving with his three girls, he asked them how they would feel about his proposing to Trisha.] Author conversation with the artist, 2005.

["I told Trisha that the loss of her father would only be a part of what she'd miss,"] Author conversation with the artist, 2005.

[One child psychologist who read about that family event called it perhaps the most important thing a parent can do, to allow children the freedom to be honest.] Dr. Mari Jo Renick, The Gow School, South Wales, New York.

[a combination cookbook and family memoir.] Trisha Yearwood, *Georgia Cooking in an Oklahoma Kitchen* (New York: Clarkson Potter, 2008).

["Brooks gave country music the ambition and presence to strive for universality,"] Author conversation with Edward Morris, 2008.

[Hank Williams was competitive] Observations on Hank Williams's personality are taken from an author conversation with Faron Young, 1986.